A Home by the Hooghly

By the same author
THE HOUSE BY THE DVINA

A HOME BY THE HOOGHLY

◇ ◇ ◇ ◇ ◇

◆

A JUTE WALLAH'S WIFE

◆

EUGENIE FRASER

◆

MAINSTREAM PUBLISHING

To My Long-suffering Husband

© Eugenie Fraser 1989

Reprinted 1989 (twice)

First published in Great Britain 1989 by
MAINSTREAM PUBLISHING COMPANY (EDINBURGH) LTD
7 Albany Street
Edinburgh EH1 3UG

British Library Cataloguing in Publication Data

Fraser, Eugenie
  A Home by the Hooghly.
  1. India. Social life, ca 1947–1964—Biographies
  I. Title
  954.04′2092′4

  ISBN 1-85158-268-1

The publisher acknowledges the financial assistance of the
Scottish Arts Council in the production of this volume.

Typeset in 10/12pt Palacio by
Blackpool Typesetting Services Ltd., Blackpool, UK.
Printed and bound in Great Britain by
Billing & Sons Ltd., Worcester, UK.

Contents

1   *Last Years of the Raj*   7

2   *Wartime Calcutta*   79

3   *Scottish Interlude*   131

4   *Old Hands in New India*   147

  Epilogue—Thailand and Scotland   213

We represent the burra sahibs who live in west Bengal
And frankly we're not liking now the look of things at all
In fact we find it difficult to summon strength to call
Bearer! Chota peg lao! (Bring a small whisky!)

Ditty as presented by Pat Kay
and Betty Ankers, cabaret artistes
in the Grand Hotel, Calcutta, 1950s

1
LAST YEARS OF THE RAJ

'So this is the Hooghly,' I said, looking down on to the murky swell beating against the ship. The *Mulbera*, after her long journey, had halted at the mouth of the river to await the arrival of the pilot. 'Why is the water so dirty?' I turned to the young purser, standing beside me. 'Is the anchor stirring up the mire?'

'No,' he laughed, 'the anchor has nothing to do with it. It is the silt that's carried from the hills and the Ganges down to the Hooghly. It always looks the same – mud-coloured.'

I was disenchanted. Who would wish to swim in this, I thought, remembering the crystal waters of the northern Dvina in Russia where I spent my childhood and the silver-dappled Tay of my youth in Scotland. Yet, on the following morning when the ship resumed her journey I realised I had been wrong. Bengal *is* green. The Hooghly, with her coffee-coloured waters seen against the lush emerald banks, spangled here and there with crimson blossoms, has a beauty of her own.

The *Mulbera* was now zigzagging up the river on her last lap to Calcutta. It was there that my husband, Ronald, would be awaiting my arrival. It had been a long time – almost two years – since his last leave in Scotland, when we had decided that the child we were expecting would be born in Scotland and that later the babe and I would embark for India. Such were our plans. All went well, but when our son was six months old and I, with cheerful optimism, began to prepare for our departure – fate stepped in. Our child was struck down by a serious and prolonged illness at the end of which he died. Ronald never saw his son.

Six months later, in August 1937, I packed my bags and set off for India. My mother, who a year earlier had seen my brother leaving for Venezuela to join the British Controlled Oil Company, decided to accompany me to the ship. We travelled together from Dundee to

London where we spent two nights, attended the theatre, saw the sights and eventually, after some exciting moments when our taxi became wedged in the traffic, boarded the boat train.

Aboard the ship some friends joined us for lunch. It was a cheerful gathering soon to be interrupted by the call of, 'All friends ashore!' I have a memory of my mother, a forlorn figure dressed in brown, standing a little apart from the others, calling out in a bantering tone, which I knew was only to hide her sense of loss, 'Try to control your passion for cream and chocolates – don't eat so much – you must keep slim!' I laughed and waved my hand. All around me people were hanging over the side, calling out their last farewells. Gradually the figure of my mother grew smaller, soon to vanish out of sight.

The cabin, shared with a pleasant lady from Cornwall, was spacious and comfortable. I soon became acquainted with the wives of two tea planters and a lady from our own parts who was the wife of a jute mill manager and returning to India from a visit to her own people in Scotland. Having spent a few years in India she was very knowledgeable and free with her advice and instructions to such a greenhorn as myself. The journey as a whole was uneventful. The ship halted briefly off-shore from Tangier. There, for the first time, I caught a faint smell of the East. On the distant horizon a string of camels were seen wending their way. Later, in Malta, we were allowed to go ashore. The day was hot and sultry. We strolled around, admired the Cathedral and bought some hand-made lace from ladies dressed in black. In passing, a large white hat caught my attention. I bought it and wore it on the launch returning to the ship. A playful gust of wind suddenly carried it away. There was nothing I could do but watch my precious hat slowly vanishing beneath the waves of Valletta harbour.

Prior to my departure for India I received a letter with instructions from Ronald. 'When you arrive in Port Said,' he wrote, 'you must go to Simon Artz and buy yourself a topi. It is very important that you should wear one. The sun can be very dangerous in the tropics and a topi will protect your head.' When we arrived in Port Said I duly went to Simon Artz, the departmental store which seemed to sell everything and can perhaps be remembered still by those who travelled east in those far-off days. There I saw a topi and also an attractive ring with a semi-precious stone. I put aside the topi and chose the ring. Perhaps, unconsciously, I was ahead of my time. When I left India twenty-six years later very few people wore topis.

Back on the ship we were off again and sailing past the monument to the creator of the Suez Canal, Ferdinand de Lesseps, whose extended arm is seen pointing to the East.

In the years to come I was fated to travel several times through the Suez Canal. On each occasion I experienced a sense of wonder at the magnificent achievement of the French engineer who cut a passage of a hundred miles through the dusty desert and shortened the journey to the East by many weeks. How good, how peaceful, it was to relax on the deck of a ship gliding serenely between the banks. How strange to watch a modern car speeding along the smooth highway on one side and on the other the desert, sand and camels.

After the Canal there was a short halt at Suez and then on to the Red Sea. The hot, hot Red Sea. I have heard friends say that they had sailed through the Red Sea when it was cool and pleasant. Such luck didn't come my way. Memory has only retained four stifling days and sleepless nights. Yet it was here during this torrid spell that a strange coincidence took place, a coincidence which suddenly transported me to a distant Arctic land of dark winter days and white nights of summer.

One evening, as I was changing for dinner and struggling with the fastening of my dress, I heard the sound of someone singing in the saloon. There was something familiar in that song, something that I seemed to have heard a long time ago. I realised that this was a song popular in the north of Russia and whoever was singing was singing in Russian. How could this be? I asked myself. I must be dreaming. I am back again, a little girl in another world far away – standing in the garden on a warm summer's day, listening to our cook Dunya singing in the kitchen beside the open window where she is washing the dishes. Her voice, rich and strong, is resounding throughout the garden. It is all about poor Marusya who had been betrayed by her lover and had taken poison. The words are silly, yet the melody is haunting. But now the mysterious voice is singing a joyful song and still in Russian. This is unbearable. I had to find the owner of this voice. Hurriedly dressing I rushed upstairs. In the saloon sitting beside the piano was a well-built, fair-haired woman. She had stopped singing as I entered and was now softly strumming some melody. I sat down a few paces away from her.

'Excuse me, please,' I addressed her, a little timidly. 'I have been listening to your singing – are you by any chance Russian?'

She turned and smiled in a friendly way. 'No,' she rejoined, 'I am Norwegian, but my father was the Norwegian Consul in Archangel, in the north of Russia, where he spent many years. My sister and I grew up there. My name is Falsen – Lulu Falsen.'

'I am also from Archangel,' I said.

She rose and sat down beside me. 'What an amazing coincidence,' she exclaimed. 'Here we are, out of all these passengers only two people from Russia and not just Russia but from the same town. Where did you live in Archangel?'

'In Olonetskaya Ulitza.'

'Our doctor lived there – an extraordinary, big, dignified man.'

'Yes,' I agreed, 'he was my step-grandfather.'

She laughed. 'Another coincidence. I remember one day when I developed a painful throat and imagined that this was serious and that I would probably die. When your grandfather came into my room I threw myself on his broad chest crying, ''Dear doctor, please save me. I am too young to die.'' He patted my head and told me that I wouldn't die and that I would be better in three days. He was right, I soon recovered.' Our conversation continued. 'Wasn't there a rather pretty Englishwoman married to one of the sons?'

'She is a Scot,' I corrected her. 'My mother.'

We went on talking, the words tripping over each other, until the bell rang for dinner.

Later, during the journey, we used to meet and hold long conversations about the people we both knew in Archangel and all the events that happened during the tumultuous days of the first and second Revolutions.

After a brief halt in Aden we sailed into the cooler winds of the Arabian Sea. With the exhausting heat of the Red Sea behind us it was pleasant to relax and watch flying fish and dolphins dancing along the side of the ship.

Three days were spent in Colombo. There was more sightseeing and a trip to Mount Lavinia. I would have loved to have spent more than just a day in that tropical paradise of waving palms and a blue sea lapping the sandy shores, where in the nearby hotel we were served with a memorable lunch of cold lobster accompanied by many exotic trimmings.

After Colombo there was Madras, where more passengers disembarked. It was the last port of call before Calcutta. The journey of almost five weeks was becoming tedious and the nearer we drew to our final destination the more impatient I became. But now at long last I was sailing up the Hooghly.

There is no recollection of any outstanding features as the ship continued moving up the river, excepting the low-lying shores of the jungle, some huts and brickfields and a mass of little fishing boats following in the wake of the *Mulbera*. It seemed as if this meandering around each bend would go on for ever, when, suddenly, my attention was caught by the appearance of the first compound of a jute mill lying on the right bank. From that moment I stood watching, with mounting elation, as one small craft after another came sailing towards us from both sides of the river. Lying close to the shores could be seen well-laid-out gardens, smooth lawns, flowerbeds, bushes and stately trees. Behind the gardens stood stolid light-coloured buildings and still further back could be glimpsed the chimneys of the mills where, in the sweltering heat, laboured the Europeans and thousands of Indian workers. As I stood absorbing this unfamiliar landscape my eyes were drawn to a compound that seemed to stand out from all the others. Above a two-storeyed, cream-coloured building was the name LAWRENCE in gold letters. 'Lawrence,' I repeated to myself, hardly believing what I saw. This is the place of which I had heard so much, the place that was to be my home, the place where I would start again my interrupted married life. Someone was waving from the garden as it was gliding out of sight to be replaced by other scenes.

Some minutes later the *Mulbera* halted. A launch carrying the harbour-master drew alongside. Some men were standing behind him and in their midst I recognised, with joyful astonishment, the familiar figure of Ronald. He climbed aboard. After a long absence we were reunited.

Calcutta, that great metropolis of the East, was not altogether alien to me. From my early childhood, living in the north of Russia, I used to hear many tales about the mysterious land of India from my mother, whose brother, Uncle Henry, had left Scotland for India about the same time as she embarked with my Russian father for Archangel. Being close to each other, mother and Uncle Henry kept up a steady correspondence, mostly by postcards, showing in turn many aspects of life in India and Russia. After my mother's death all these postcards fell into my hands.

One of the most memorable events during my childhood occurred in the hot summer of 1913 when my Uncle Henry Cameron decided to visit us. The Cameron family were all adventurous. Six out of the nine children of my grandparents left their home in Broughty Ferry to settle in various corners of the world. In the same spirit of adventure Uncle Henry decided to spend part of his leave in Russia. Leaving Calcutta, where he was employed by a firm of brokers, he boarded a ship which took him to Vladivostok. From there he travelled by the famous Trans-Siberian Railway and eventually arrived in St Petersburg.

Meanwhile in Scotland, his mother, my Granny Cameron, likewise decided to embark for Russia. She crossed the sea to Finland where she was met by my father's sister, Aunt Olga, whose home was in Helsinki, who put her aboard a train to St Petersburg. Mother and son

11

were reunited in one of the well-known hotels. After spending a few days in this glamorous city, they went on to Archangel, a journey of two days and nights, and duly arrived to an ecstatic welcome.

Uncle Henry, in his immaculate tropical suits, young, handsome and with a pleasing manner brought a captivating aura of the magic East. He charmed everyone and was warmly entertained by all our relatives and friends. My young brother and I, like two faithful puppies, followed him wherever he went. His arrival also enhanced my own ego.

'My uncle,' I told my playmates, 'has arrived from a far, far away place called "Kalkutta" (Russian version) where the sun shines all the time, the river never freezes and there is never, never any snow. In his garden there are lots of monkeys and parrots, in the house many servants. He never has to dress himself – all he has to do is to stick his foot out and the servant will rush to put his sock on. He likes to go shooting tigers. Tigers are more dangerous than wolves, but my Uncle is very brave. Here we sit on sledges and droshkies, but when my Uncle goes to town he always rides on an elephant!'

My *babushka* (granny) decided to mark the occasion of Uncle Henry's visit by having a photograph taken of a family group in the garden. Here it is lying before my eyes, this scene caught on a hot summer's day, when the world was young. They are all there. I am sitting on the grass at my uncle's feet, unaware that I would one day follow in his footsteps – a quarter of a century later, when only his grave could be found in a Calcutta cemetery.

During the First World War Uncle Henry had been an officer in what was known as the Calcutta Scottish Regiment. While on manoeuvres up-country he contracted a serious illness and died a few months later.

My cousin Mae, the daughter of my mother's brother, Andrew, had also gone to join her husband in Calcutta some years before my arrival. She wrote descriptive letters of her life there and my husband, too, in his correspondence with me used to portray a very clear picture of Calcutta and the mofussil.*

Now, driving in one of the American saloons which served as taxis in the mofussil, with Ron pointing out the various landmarks, the racecourse, the Cathedral, the Victoria memorial on the maidan,[†] I had the feeling that although everything was new and exciting it was also not wholly strange to me.

Earlier, when we left the ship, Ron had suggested that we should stop at Firpo's for some refreshment. Firpo's, the meeting place for

---

* Mofussil: In India, all outside the capital or large towns, i.e. provincial, rural.
† Maidan: A wide open expanse of grass and trees in front of Chowringhee Road.

jute wallahs, tea planters, burra sahibs and even at times Maharajas, was renowned throughout the East for its perfect cuisine and service. Inside the restaurant the Edwardian decor, crystal chandeliers, snow-white tablecloths and orchestra, presented an atmosphere of gracious living. In the adjoining veranda we found a corner overlooking the maidan. There, on a wide open parkland in the fading twilight, were seen groups of people walking about or standing talking together. The bearer served us with tea, sandwiches and delightful waffles with maple syrup. We would have liked to linger for a while, but before us there was a journey of twenty miles. Already the short twilight had vanished, Calcutta's sultry night was closing in.

Back on the road we passed Belvedere, the imposing residence of the Viceroy when visiting Calcutta, during which time could be seen handsome Bengal Lancers on horseback guarding the gates. Then we carried on through the fashionable suburb of Alipore, home of many affluent Indian and European members of society. Soon we were on the Budge-Budge Road – a country road flanked by fields, strips of jungle, and villages with groups of men sitting in the tea-houses. At times, caught in the beam of the headlights, a shadowy white figure would dart across the road and vanish into the jungle.

Some three miles beyond the Oil Depot of Budge-Budge lay the Albion jute mill in the compound of which lived my cousin Mae. It was too late for visiting. The launch to carry us across the Hooghly lay at the Albion jetty. The *serang* (boatman), a dignified man, helped us into the launch.

I remember well that first crossing. The stillness of the night, the starlit sky, the wide expanse of the dark river, lights twinkling on the opposite shore. No one said very much, but when we were almost half-way across there came drifting over the water the sound of male voices singing, 'Far frae my hame I wander, but still my heart returns'. 'That,' Ron explained, 'is a party the bachelors and grass-widowers are holding.' The singing continued to accompany our crossing, but gradually died away as the launch approached Lawrence. It was a low tide. The jetty stood high above the water. With some trepidation I climbed onto the pontoon and up the sloping gangway to the main jetty.

'So this is it,' I said to myself, as we left the jetty. 'A mere few hours ago I was sailing past this place and now here I am walking on the lawn in front of the married quarters.' On the top veranda of one of the flats a small group sat talking in quiet voices. A few yards ahead was our bungalow. This bungalow had always been occupied by two *keranis* (mill clerks), but to provide us with accommodation the junior kerani

(Derek) moved into one of the adjoining married quarters. A few steps led to a wide veranda. The bungalow, surprisingly spacious, consisted of two large public rooms, three bedrooms and a pantry, known as the *bottle khana*, off the dining room. Each bedroom had a bathroom attached with a three-piece suite and hot and cold running water. All beds were fitted with a framework, resembling old four-posters, to support the mosquito netting which covered the frame and was securely tucked under the mattress early every evening.

All furniture was of solid teak, made in the mill. At one time it was dyed a mahogany shade but through the years of many layers of varnish it had become black and taken on a heavy funereal appearance. Later it was fashionable to strip the dark layers and bring back the natural shade of teak which was more pleasing to the eye. The dining room, in spite of the dark appearance, was well furnished with table, sideboard, chairs and extra serving tables. The bedrooms, likewise, had wardrobes, chests of drawers, chairs and dressing-tables. The lounge, however, with its large shabby sofa, the springs of which were broken, and a few equally shabby basket chairs, presented a dismal picture. I could not hide my disappointment, but before I could express it, Ron assured me that the head office had given permission for us to acquire, at their expense, a new suite, carpet and curtains. That considerably raised my spirit. I looked forward eagerly to buying items and planning my own colour-scheme.

What struck me as very strange was the sight of an enormous black display cabinet standing on high, thin, spindly legs. It was similar to those seen in certain museums and large enough to hold a big stuffed bear or some creature like it. It was completely empty, but on closer scrutiny I found a tiny egg on one of the glass shelves. It transpired it had been laid by a lizard. In passing I may add that I became almost fond of lizards and liked to watch them dashing around the walls catching flies, mosquitoes and moths bigger than themselves. They used to make clear ticking sounds, quite loud in comparison with their size. These little creatures were considered to be lucky. Throughout my years in India I never harmed or killed a single lizard and was grateful that they had this ability to move like lightning when attacking unpleasant insects.

Meanwhile the monstrosity, which I referred to as 'my black joy', was soon banished to a small room adjoining the bottle khana where it provided a certain usefulness.

To the left of our bungalow was a hedge dividing the manager's and salesman's garden from the rest of the compound. In the garden was a large semi-detached house shared by the manager and the salesman.

In the grounds grew many stately trees, bushes and flower-beds. Along from our bungalow, to our right, was a two-storeyed building divided into four spacious married quarters. Each one contained two public rooms and two bedrooms with bathrooms attached. Between the married quarters and the *mess khootie* were three tennis courts. In the mess khootie lived the single men and men whose wives were in Scotland. Each man had a lounge and bedroom with bathroom attached. The whole compound, including gardens, tennis courts and the swimming pool, beside the back door of our bungalow, was looked after by an army of gardeners and workers under the supervision of the engineer. All the cookhouses and the servants' quarters were situated behind the houses. Similar compounds were scattered up and down the river but not all had the spaciousness of Lawrence.

Behind the residential quarters lay the mill buildings and warehouses enclosed by fencing and guarded by watchmen. Outside the gates were the well-laid-out coolie lines where many of the workers lived. The local workers preferred to live in their own homes in the surrounding jungle.

Such then was the scene where I began my life in India.

On that late evening of my arrival to the compound the bearer and the cook were standing on the veranda waiting to welcome me. Both men salaamed me. The bearer, speaking in Hindustani, informed Ron that our dinner was ready. After refreshing ourselves we went through to the dining room and sat down at a table that was meant for a dozen people. The bearer served us dinner. I have no recollection of that meal except that tinned peaches figured prominently.

During the night I was awakened suddenly by the sound of a terrible storm, a howling wind, torrential rain and of something crashing. I sat up in alarm. Beside me, sleeping soundly, Ron didn't even stir. Comforting myself with the thought that perhaps this storm was not so unusual in India I turned on my side and soon fell sound asleep.

The following morning was Sunday. I awoke rather late.

Ron was wandering about the house. 'Do you know,' he said, 'there's been a hurricane, two of the barges laden with jute have sunk beside the jetty and further down in a neighbouring mill a jetty's been smashed to pieces. Have a look at this,' he added, pointing to the garden in front of the veranda. There, a few inches from the bungalow, lay an enormous tree. It had been uprooted in the manager's garden and, smashing through the hedge and narrowly missing our bungalow, had landed on the lawn. We were very lucky.

After breakfast, the manager's bearer called. 'The burra-sahib', he said, 'sends his salaams.'

'That is an invitation for drinks,' Ronald explained.

We duly arrived there. I found the manager a courteous, pleasant man. Also present were two ladies and their husbands, who were mechanics in the mill. Lily and Alice were both attractive and friendly. We were joined by Tom, the salesman, holding on for the one at present on leave. The junior kerani, Derek, was also present. The conversation centred on the hurricane and the havoc it had created. They were all amused that I should have imagined that a storm such as this was nothing unusual in India. Both women described how terrified they had been. 'I thought the roof would come down any minute,' remarked Alice. 'Were you not afraid at all?' she asked.

'No,' I replied truthfully. 'When I saw Ronald sleeping so soundly I felt there was no reason to be alarmed. This was India.' We spent a pleasant morning. I was glad to have met these two women who would share a part of my life in the compound.

Ron and I returned for lunch and later retired for the customary lie-back. Not being used to sleeping in the afternoon, I got up and wandered about the house from room to room scrutinising everything that may have escaped my notice. Some voices outside our back entrance attracted my attention.

On going out I was presented by an astonishing spectacle. It transpired that Derek was having a rather wild party. There were a few men of different ages from the mess khootie as well as the manager and Tom the salesman. Some of the men wore bathing trunks and were diving in and out of the pool. Derek, in bathing trunks, was prancing around the edge of the pool while holding an umbrella over his head and emulating a tightrope dancer. There were also two young ladies in swimming suits, who had arrived with some men-friends from Calcutta. One of the girls was swimming about while her friend, who had long tresses down to her waist, was dancing on the edge and, at the same time, coyly professing a certain fear of the water. In the middle of the pool one of our stalwart men from Angus, fully dressed in white drill trousers and jacket, was standing up to his waist in the water and calling out encouragement to the girl: 'Jump, lassie, jump. Dinna be faird – I'll kape you – you'll no fa' on yer airse . . . '

Later when describing to Ron the fun at the pool and suggesting that perhaps we also could join the party, I was reminded that this was a bachelors' party to which none of the married couples was invited.

In the evening we crossed the river again to Albion to visit my cousin Mae and her husband, Jim Dakers, who was a salesman with Andrew Yule & Company. Both Mae and I, having no sisters, had always been close from the time when I arrived in Scotland from Russia as a young girl. It was a strange and happy coincidence that I should have landed in a compound directly opposite her own. We were overjoyed to meet each other after an absence of almost two years when she was on leave in Scotland and when, prior to her return to India, she had had to leave behind her little daughter, Patricia, to be educated in Scotland.

Mae was suffering from insomnia. Although she kept assuring me that she was well and happy I realised that deep down she was missing her daughter and suffering the same grief and anxiety that is the lot of all the mothers who have to part with their child when it reaches school age and has to leave India to receive an education in Britain. Mae was eager to hear the latest detailed news from Scotland. Monday was a working day. It wasn't usual for people to stay up late. At five o'clock in the morning, the bearer knocked on our bedroom door. Soon after, Ron left for the office. There he continued working with breaks for meals and a lie-back. At seven in the evening the working day was over. All the sahibs were to be seen, tired, hot and often drenched in sweat, wending their way back to their respective homes.

Ronald was a kerani. The kerani is the man in charge of the mill office and all the clerical staff. He was responsible for the safe, all the large sums of money delivered every week for the wages of the workers and the salaries of the European and Indian staff. The keranis of all the mills, up and down the river, were young men recruited from Dundee and its district. Most of them had a grammar school background and had served their apprenticeship in the offices of jute mills and brokers. They also had attended the Dundee Technical College and were, in short, qualified to embark for India. Usually after a certain time working as keranis in the mill offices they were promoted as salesmen in the various head offices, situated mostly in that promised land of Clive Street, Calcutta. The other men, the overseers, in different departments in the mill had held similar positions in the mills in Angus and also attended the Technical College. In addition there were engineers with sea-going experience, prior to taking up a post in India.

In Lawrence there were in all some twelve Europeans, including the manager and the salesman who travelled every day to the head office in Calcutta. Some five thousand workers were employed inside and outside the mill. Each mill had a dispensary with a qualified Indian doctor in charge.

Indians usually referred to the European staff, not by their surnames, such as Smith sahib, but according to their position in the mill. To the married woman was added the title of memsahib. I, for instance, was referred to as the kerani memsahib. The manager was the burra sahib; his wife, the burra memsahib. The mechanic was the mistri sahib; his wife, the mistri memsahib; and so on. Talking among ourselves we naturally referred to each other by our own names, but when talking to the Indians, such as the bearers and other servants, we used their style of naming us. 'Take this note to the mistri mem-sahib,' I would say to the bearer. He would know exactly whom I meant.

During my first week in India, Alice and Lily called. They were accompanied by a third lady – Jean Hebenton, a small woman whose sweet face reflected a warm and generous personality. In time, as I got to know her well, we became good friends. They gave me some good advice regarding all the matters with which I had to cope – such as the food the cook brought daily from Calcutta. 'You must handle well the meat and mutton before cooking,' they told me. 'In this way you will have it all to yourself. The Muhammadan servants consider us, Euro-pean women, unclean. They will not cook it for themselves after you have handled it.'

I did not follow that particular advice. There was a lot that was strange and puzzling, but gradually I began to understand the way of life in a compound. My difficulty with the language was, at first, a problem. From Ronald, who spoke fluently in Urdu, having passed the lower and higher exams, I picked up a few phrases, which I fondly imagined were understood by the servants. Occasionally a look of amazed horror would cross my husband's face on hearing my 'jungli' conversation with the servants, where for some reason the word 'chota' (little) figured prominently in spite of having no connection whatsoever with what I was trying to convey.

Hindustani, perhaps, is not such a difficult language. An effort on my part might have produced some fluency, but arising from indo-lence combined with the feeling that sooner or later it would not be required when we retired, I never learned anything more than what could be described as 'Kitchen Hindustani', similar to the way many of my lady friends spoke.

We had three servants. Two we employed ourselves; the third, a sweeper, was supplied by the company. The days when people employed numerous servants — even as late as during the time of the First World War – were over.

Our bearer Sofi Khan – the head servant – and I got along together quite well, once there was an acceptance on my part that Sofi Khan's priority at all times was his sahib. It had always been so and if now there was an interloper in the shape of a memsahib he saw no reason to change his ways. He was a good man, faithful and honest. We trusted him completely as we did the man who followed him some years later.

It was the custom of many memsahibs to carry the keys of their store cupboard and presses in their pockets or tied to handkerchiefs. I once tried to emulate them for a matter of a few weeks, but invariably the keys got lost. During a frantic search that followed, the bearer would quietly produce the keys saying, 'Memsahib, the keys were in the pocket of your other dress.' I never carried any keys again.

I have to admit that Sofi Khan was a bit indolent, as were most of the house servants, when compared with the workers inside the mills. His duties consisted of making the beds, setting and serving at the table, helping the cook dry the dishes, doing a little light dusting – never above his head or below his knees (that was the sweeper's task), taking meticulous care of all his sahib's clothing, keeping in perfect order inside the wardrobe shelves of socks, shirts, underwear and, most important of all, providing the tired sahib at the end of a day's work with a chota peg of whisky and soda.

I could never remember the name of my first cook in Lawrence. He was quite a good cook but it was always difficult to keep a cook for any lengthy period on account of there being no roads to the mill on our side of the river.

Every evening all the cooks in the compound would set off to walk a mile and more over a rough road to the station. There they would board a train and duly arrive at Howrah station in Calcutta. A bus took them to the New Market in the centre of Calcutta. Where and how they spent their nights I have never discovered but suspect that like many of their brethren they would sleep curled up in some corner near the market. Early in the morning, their shopping completed, they would embark on the return journey.

They never carried their baskets from the station to the mill but engaged coolies to do so. My task was to examine the food laid out on the table of the bottle Khana and later mark down in a bazaar book the prices dictated by the cook. It was always a source of amazement to me as to how he was able to account for every anna and bring back the correct change. He just stood there beside me, rattling off all the items with never any bits of paper to jolt his memory. There was no hesitation – no mistakes. Of course, he had to have his perks. Who could blame him as long as he didn't overdo it? I argued at times over his prices and the quality of the fish he called *bhekti*. It is a name that was familiar to every memsahib up and down the river. The flesh of this popular fish was something between cod and halibut. There were three qualities of the same fish. The one caught in the sea was the best, the second came from the river and the last from some of the local tanks, which had a nasty taste of stagnant water. It was difficult to argue over the quality of meat, mutton or chicken. They were all poor and the chickens, especially, stringy.

The reason for the cook having to bring the food daily was that there was no refrigerator until some two years after my arrival. Everyone had ice-boxes. Ice was delivered to us daily from Ludlow jute mills down the river where it was manufactured. It would have been comparatively simple for the launch to pick up the ice after a short journey of barely a mile, but the launch was not allowed to be used for that purpose. Instead two or three coolies set off every day on a dinghy to collect the ice, at times rowing laboriously against the tide. The dinghy loaded with ice had even a harder journey back to Lawrence where the ice was divided according to the various positions held by the sahibs. The largest portions were given to the burra sahib and the salesman, less for the kerani and still less further down the line. By night the ice melted away. At times, sitting at peace, suddenly we would hear a loud crash and wonder what had happened only to discover it was the ice melting and breaking inside the ice-box.

I still remember the great joy of seeing my first fridge. I kept patting the smooth surface and could have kissed it. It made such a difference to our lives.

Because we lived not far from the sea the water was hard and slightly salty. It was used only for baths and domestic chores and came from the tube wells in the compound. This water was also supplied to all the workers' quarters. The water for drinking and cooking was brought daily from the Budge-Budge depot on the other side of the river where there was a tank supplied with water from Calcutta.

Every day the coolies from the mill would set off in a dinghy and return with containers, resembling milk churns, filled with Calcutta water. The containers were distributed to all cookhouses. The drinking water was boiled, put through a filter in each house, then poured into empty whisky bottles and kept in the ice-box and, later, in the fridge.

As it was impossible to wash one's hair in the bath water, something that I discovered to my cost, all married quarters were supplied with condensate from the boiler house in the mill. A bucket or two was brought and emptied into a container in the bathroom. This water, as soft as silk, was used for washing our hair and articles of clothing which otherwise would have been ruined by the hard water. The *dhobi* (laundry man) had no option but to use the available water. In those days there were no soapless detergents with the result that gradually all our towels took on a dull grey tinge.

In spite of many problems the way of life in the compound, with the help of many hands, ran like clockwork. In our house it was the sweeper who brought each day the condensate from the mill and who polished the tiled floors daily, cleaned the bathroom, the bottle khana and emptied the refuse bucket.

As the bungalow for many years had been occupied only by bachelors I took into my head, one day, that many unseen corners may have been neglected and suggested to Sofi Khan that he should extend his dusting to the top of the wardrobe in addition to the dressing table. This simple request was met with horrified amazement. He left the room and returned with the sweeper carrying a step-ladder. There standing on the top step, surrounded by a cloud of dust, the sweeper with great energy attacked the layers of grime accumulated on top of the wardrobe throughout the years. I realised then that such an undignified assignment was never meant for Sofi but only for the sweeper for whom no task was ever too lowly, too dirty or too unpleasant. He was the untouchable, a member of a class of people whose presence and even shadows are offensive to the higher castes.

I am reminded of an incident that took place years later which had aroused my indignation. I was very friendly with a charming Indian lady, who was gentle, kind and very likeable. She was also well educated, spoke perfect English and enjoyed reading all the English classics. One day as she was setting off in her car, the sweeper, anxious to please, was polishing the door handle. She stopped and, glancing coldly in his direction, remarked, 'How can I possibly touch that handle after your hands have been in contact with it?'

The untouchables have been untouchable for generations and remain so at present. At times I ask myself why is it in this great land of India, where there can be found so many enlightened and educated men, that this obscenity, degrading the human spirit to the lowest possible level, should have been allowed to continue for centuries and will, short of a miracle, persist in the future?

We Europeans were inclined to accept the status quo; we had no choice. After all, were we not simply birds of passage?

In late September, when I arrived, the rainy season was drawing to a close. With the humidity so high, it is a sticky unpleasant time. From the rain-drenched earth, now drying out, steam rises, the air is heavy. All creatures that creep, crawl, sting and bite appear from nowhere. There is also the ever-present menace of mosquitoes.

I had been bitten before in the Arctic regions of Russia, where I was brought up, and likewise attacked by clouds of midges in the Highlands of Scotland, but never had I known such ferocity with which I was devoured by the mosquitoes of Bengal. 'You'll be all right in time,' the ladies tried to console me. 'It happened to us all when we came out at first. The mosquitoes love new blood.' They certainly relished mine!

Worst of all was when one of these winged marauders succeeded in getting inside the mosquito netting. I remember how on one such occasion I had tried in vain to catch it. How I had crawled, clapped my hands and leapt from one side of the bed to the other until a plaintive voice reminded me, 'Don't you know I have to work tomorrow?' There was no option but to fall back on my pillow and eventually drop off to sleep to the torturous buzzing of that pest hovering above me. But in the morning there it was, clinging to the netting, satiated, blown up, unable to escape. How sweet was my revenge when at last I caught this odious tormentor and squeezed it hard against the net. Everything passes. In time I did acquire some immunity but not before every bit of my exposed skin on legs and arms was completely covered by bleeding sores and scratches.

There were compensations such as the day when Ron and I set off together on a shopping spree. We crossed the river, hired a taxi for the day and duly arrived in Calcutta. Inside Hall & Anderson, a shop renowned throughout the East, we chose a three-piece suite in a pleasant shade of beige, an almond-green carpet and curtain material to match. We bought some other bits and pieces including a few *dekshis* (cooking pots) requested by the cook.

Gradually the lounge took shape. My boxes had arrived safely with nothing damaged or broken. A new attractive fitment, made in the mill from natural teak, now held all our books including Russian classics, treasured since my childhood. Some ornaments, an etching or two, a mirror and table lamps were arranged on walls and tables. The old shabby sofa and chairs were thrown out. Gone was the dreary bareness of the room. Instead there were now comfortable chairs, soft lamplight, coloured cushions and curtains. We had a home by the Hooghly.

Early one morning in late October, while standing on the veranda idly watching the *malis* (gardeners) planting out the seedlings, I became aware of a change in the atmosphere. A pleasant little breeze was wafting over from the river, the air seemed lighter, the garden fresh and bright. This was the start of the cold weather. The glorious cold weather – 'just like a perfect day in June', as Mae used to describe it. A new lease of life took over. Gone was the exhausting heat, the clammy sweat, the weariness.

By the middle of November the garden was transformed by a riot of colour. The homely annuals – cornflowers, phlox, zinnias, large-headed dahlias – all blossomed at the same time as the autumn flowers of Scotland, such as asters and chrysanthemums. Large flowerpots, brimming over with blossoms, decorated the steps of the veranda.

It was the season of tennis parties, of entertaining, of weekend visits to and from friends living up and down the river. A tennis party could be arranged well in advance in the secure knowledge that the weather was not likely to let you down. Distance did not mean very much. People travelled up and down the river just for the pleasure of spending a few hours or a weekend with friends. It was a pleasant change to get away for a little while from the enclosed life in a compound.

I can still remember how we spent my first weekend away from Lawrence. We left on Saturday morning and, after hiring a taxi, arrived in Calcutta. In Firpo's we were met by Jimmy Stewart, one of Ron's oldest friends, who lived in Kinnison jute mill, near Barrackpore, a further eighteen miles up the river from Calcutta. Two other friends joined us for lunch: George Stevenson, who was a close friend of Ron's since early childhood, and Lyn Foulis, a man blessed with an unusual wit and a sense of humour which kept us laughing throughout the lunch.

Firpo's food stood up to its reputation. Especially delicious was the renowned prawn cocktail, the like of which I have never found elsewhere, nor solved the secret of the ingredients when attempting to emulate a cocktail with the same elusive flavour.

Lunch over, we all set off to the New Empire Theatre to watch a film in which Greta Garbo was performing in her usual languid style. Later it was back to Firpo's where, following a lengthy session on the veranda, we adjourned for dinner. By now most of the tables were occupied. The bearers, immaculate in long white coats and turbans, hovered around carrying trays loaded with food and glasses. Perhaps because there seemed to be so many people who knew each other and who, moving from table to table, would stop to talk and laugh with some acquaintance, including us, prior to joining friends in their own group, there was this free and easy atmosphere rarely seen in any other restaurant.

The evening wore on. It was quite late when we finally left for the Barrackpore Road, eventually arriving in Kinnison at midnight.

Jimmy was the junior salesman in the head office. He lived in a pleasant house facing the river. A man with a congenial personality, perhaps a little on the stout side, he was an excellent host, who enjoyed entertaining his friends. He was one of our close circle of friends into which on my arrival I was accepted, perhaps on account of sharing the same kind of humour and being a kindred spirit. Time

23

has sadly removed him from our scene, but I can still see his face, the eyes reflecting a warmth and a sense of fun, still hear his laughter.

That evening on arriving so late we were too jaded to linger and after a drink or two gratefully retreated to our respective bedrooms.

In the morning, after breakfast, it was decided that we should go to the Barrackpore Golf Club. There I was introduced to two married couples, friends of Jimmy and Ron. Soon the men went off for their game of golf while I remained with the ladies.

The Barrackpore park is a beautiful part of the district which lies close to the grounds and country residence of the Governor of Bengal. I remember someone telling me once that in the distant past the wife of a Governor, perhaps longing for her home and wishing for the park to remind her of England, had expressed a desire that only a variety of stately trees should be planted, excluding all palms.

I do not know how authentic that story is, but the layout of the lofty trees did resemble that of a park in Europe. I certainly have no recollection of ever seeing a single palm growing there. At a certain corner of the park, close to the river, was a place known as 'Scandal Point' where people liked to meet and exchange the latest gossip. The park was also popular with the *ayahs* (nursemaids) and their little charges.

Inside Barrackpore were the barracks housing the regiment stationed there at the time. The whole area was known as the cantonment. It was here in Barrackpore in 1857 that the first rumblings of the Indian Mutiny began, but fortunately the surrounding European population was spared the horrors of what took place in northern India.

The whole of that district with the old style of bungalows, trees and gardens had a certain charm and reminded one of bygone days.

When the golfers returned to the Clubhouse, tea, sandwiches and cakes were served. We sat talking for a little while with golf being the main subject. Having no aptitude for golf, or any other ball games for that matter, I tried to display some interest in the conversation but was secretly relieved when Jimmy suggested we return to Kinnison.

Refreshed by a hot bath and change of clothing we settled down for the evening and at this point were joined by Jimmy's neighbours, Robert Campbell, who was the assistant manager in Kinnison, and his wife Phil. Phil was blessed with a lively sense of humour and a quick wit often exercised at the expense of some other body, but funny just the same.

We were to meet again under different circumstances, but meanwhile we sat down to dinner accompanied by a lively conversation, jokes and laughter. It was all most enjoyable and we would have liked to stay on, but with a long journey ahead we had no option but to take leave of the congenial company and set off for home. The drive of some two hours in the cool of the night was pleasant and uneventful. Back to Albion Jetty once more we found the faithful serang waiting in the launch to take us across the river. It was good to be back in our house, to crawl under the netting, to fall back on the pillow, to fall asleep.

Tomorrow was another working day.

One of the most popular events in Calcutta, during the cold season, was the celebration of St Andrew's Day when the Caledonian Society presented a concert in the New Empire Theatre. The Scots community flocked to it. We also would set off on the long journey, dressed in full evening dress, to join our group of friends in Firpo's. There to the background music of the orchestra and lively hum of voices we would sit down to dinner and go on to the theatre. Among our friends were Max Kidd and his wife Mary, who had been friends of Ron from the day of his arrival in India. Mary had a wonderful voice and usually took part in the concert. There was a fair amount of talent in Calcutta and the singing of the Scottish airs brought back a bit of Scotland with a certain nostalgia. At the end of the concert the performers and the audience stood up and joined in singing 'Auld Lang Syne'.

This was followed by a return to Firpo's for some refreshments, a little more talk, reminiscences and finally the journey home.

Christmas was heralded by the arrival of the Viceroy. Guarding the gates of Belvedere were seen once more the picturesque figures on horseback of the Bengal Lancers.

Christmas in Bengal was something very special, and something in the air brought a feeling of expectation, of change into our everyday existence.

Often during this time my thoughts would travel far back to the Arctic land of snows and frosts, to those distant years of my childhood. I would see again a troika rushing through the gates, hear the jingling of bells, sit once more at a table surrounded by the faces of those so dear and long since vanished, stand again beside a Christmas tree that reached up to the ceiling and which I imagined was a part of heaven to where little children sometimes went.

How unpredictable was fate! Little did I dream then that I would one day see a Christmas so diverse – a garden blooming in the warmth of a tropical sun, stately palms, trees spangled with exotic blossoms, a swift-flowing river not fettered by frosts and snows.

Yet the spirit of Christmas was very much alive not only among the Europeans but the Indians as well. I recall how the other memsahibs and I would share a taxi and set off to Calcutta for our Christmas shopping. On arrival in Lindsay Street we would scatter on our errands inside the famous 'New Market' (Sir Stuart Hogg Market). What an amazing place that was with all the sections, each one offering their own particular line of goods. There was the 'Curio Shop' where one could find a great variety of oriental treasures, the shoemakers, silversmiths, toyshops, bookshops, grocers, fruiterers and, in the far background, the stalls of butchers and fishmongers, live chickens, guinea-fowls and pigeons in cages – a part I avoided.

Very tempting were the shops displaying dress materials. The shopkeepers standing beside the entrance would call out to the passing memsahib, 'Come inside, memsahib, come inside. I have something very good – just out from home. You don't have to pay today. Please come to look.' Sometimes you were tempted, went inside and sometimes you paid later. The shopkeepers knew us and knew we could be trusted.

As Christmas drew nearer a frenzied activity started. There could be seen the Indian businessmen buying gifts for their clients ranging from simple baskets of fruit and nuts to silver and jewellery, the European memsahib hurrying from one alley to another with the patient coolie following from shop to shop carrying the purchases in his basket. Everybody rushing somewhere, something in the atmosphere, the smell of the sweet Darjeeling oranges and spices all combining to symbolise the enchantment of Christmas.

With the exhausting shopping in the market over, there was a pleasant break for lunch in Firpo's, followed by more shopping in Whiteway & Laidlaw or Hall & Anderson in Park Street, and finally a visit to Flury & Trinka, likewise in Park Street, for a cup of tea and cakes prior to embarking on the long journey home.

I still remember with pleasure our Christmas expeditions into town and the drive back in the soft darkness through the country road and the bazaars, the twinkling lights, the smell of smoke, the crossing of the river, the cool wind blowing in our faces.

As Christmas drew nearer there was the *baksheesh*. During the festive season baksheesh was a recognised institution. The Indian is a giving man and in most cases the baksheesh was offered as a friendly gesture. They were offered in various degrees according to the position, but everyone received them, no one was excluded as far as I believe. The arrival of the *dolly* (basket) containing fruit and other gifts was a welcome feature of the festive season. The Christmas post from home – cards, letters and gifts – was a great joy. I remember receiving from my mother an enormous Christmas pudding which I later produced as a great treat at a dinner party. Christmas Day, being a working day, was spent quietly. In the evening we invited the married couples for drinks and short eats, but there were no special celebrations. So passed my first Christmas of 1937.

The New Year celebrations were always more important than Christmas to the Scots and although all the mills were working on New Year's Day, the assistants were not compelled to turn out and the Indian workers ensured there was no loss of production, as they were all in favour of the sahibs celebrating their annual holiday.

On Old Year's Night we were again in Firpo's, along with George and Jimmy, to join two married couples for a dinner party. There was a third bachelor in our group – Jimmy Mechan, a young man who, like Ron, was a kerani sahib in our firm. Firpo's wore a festive air with every table booked ahead. That evening Mr Firpo excelled himself by presenting every lady with a large, beautiful doll. My doll wore a handsome gown of silk and lace in Louis XIV style. One of the ladies informed me that these dolls were often used as a decorative finish on a bed. I was delighted with my gift. An aura of gaiety pervaded the restaurant which increased as the night wore on. The dance floor was crowded with couples dancing to the music of an orchestra playing the latest as well as old-fashioned tunes.

I remember waltzing with Jimmy Mechan. Our steps seemed to complement each other. We danced with ease and pleasure to the haunting strains of a Viennese waltz, but as we continued dancing, spellbound by the magic of the melody, the music suddenly ceased. It was midnight and the start of another year.

At the end of the celebrations while on our way home we called on some friends in Calcutta. We had been travelling in George's car and on returning to it found, to our dismay, it had been broken into. My lovely doll as well as all George's belongings were stolen. Nothing was ever found.

Soon after the start of 1938 George departed for his home leave in Scotland. Before he left he spent the weekend with us and brought his Scotch terrier, Pik, to be kept by us for the duration of his leave. Throughout my life I have been fond of all animals, especially dogs. A dog's intelligence, complete honesty and selfless devotion places him above all the others – even the horse – in the animal kingdom. The dog will never betray you, but you can betray it if circumstances force you to do so and later feel the bitter taste of guilt. I was happy to have Pik, especially so as he brought back memories of another Scotch terrier, once brought to Archangel by my father from Scotland. Scottie, renamed Scotka, which came easier to the Russian tongue, became a loved member of the family and a treasured part of my childhood.

Unusually intelligent he was also unique, being the only Scotch terrier in town. In the years to come, however, and even after his death his progeny were seen running around in our district – little, bushy-tailed, husky mongrels with the distinctive features of a Scotch terrier.

Now here was Pik. George prior to leaving for home didn't have time to have Pik inoculated against the deadly rabies. This had to be done and particularly so as around Lawrence, rather isolated and so near the jungle, rabid jackals were known to prowl at times close to the compound. Everyone still remembered the terrible experience they had had to undergo some eighteen months previously.

It so happened that some time, prior to his leave for home, Ron and the junior kerani, George Adams, who shared the bungalow with him, invited all the married couples and some of the assistants for short eats and drinks. It was as usual an enjoyable party with Ron's pet mongrel, Billy, a great favourite in the compound, running out of and back into the bungalow and being petted by everyone. Billy was fond of chasing frogs. The frog is known to spit back when defending itself, so that when Billy appeared with a little foam on his whiskers no one thought anything about it. The next morning, however, Billy became ill. Ron sent for the local veterinary surgeon, who assured him that Billy was suffering only from a sore throat and prescribed a medication to be applied to Billy's throat which Ron did as directed. The following day – Sunday – Ron set off for a round of golf across the river, where he succeeded in bursting a blister in his hand while playing. On returning to the bungalow he found that Billy was rather restless and tied to the leg of the table in the bottle khana. Ron, after applying the prescribed treatment by holding Billy's jaws apart with his injured hand, went to have his bath. When he came out the bearer, Sofi Khan, informed him anxiously, 'Sahib, Billy is mad.' Billy was mad and exhibited all the deadly symptoms of rabies.

It was imperative that the dog be taken immediately to Calcutta. There followed a frightening struggle with the dog being dragged by Ron and George over the lawns, into the launch and across the river, where a taxi awaited them. Ron and George got in beside the driver and Billy was tied firmly to the footrest in the back. At all times contact with him had to be avoided. The nightmare journey of some twenty miles continued until they reached the vet in Park Street. It was impossible to get Billy out of the taxi. Held down by tongs he received the lethal injection while still in the car.

At the Pasteur Institute they were informed that Ron and the sweeper, who used to groom Billy, were the two most open to danger and had to have the full treatment of twenty-eight injections – fourteen on each side of the stomach. All the others who attended the party had to have fourteen injections. There were also further instructions: no alcohol, no tennis, or any form of vigorous exercise for a month.

The injections administered into the stomach are very painful, but everyone took the treatment in good part. The ladies decided that they would lie down together on a double bed in one of the married quarters and steel themselves to face up to their ordeal. The resident doctor, Dr Dutta, arrived to apply the treatment. The poor man was terribly embarrassed by being confronted with a row of exposed stomachs waiting to be jabbed, but the ladies with their inherent Scots humour took it all in their stride and were later heard joking about the rows of blue buttons on their tummies. As for Ron, he said his looked like Dinnet Moor with the purple heather in full bloom.

A few weeks later, after the way of life in the compound returned to normal, Ronald developed a high temperature which steadily rose higher until it was decided that he had to be rushed to hospital in Calcutta. I remember Jean telling me later, when I came out to India, how everyone in the compound became alarmed not knowing what the cause might be, but all the various tests proved negative and in the end the doctors came to the conclusion that Ron's appendix might be at the root of all the trouble. No one was actually quite certain what was the real reason for this high temperature – was it the aftermath of the anti-rabies injections or perhaps some other mysterious source? An operation took place, the appendix was removed and on recovery Ron sailed for his leave to Scotland. Shortly after his arrival we were married.

With the recollection of Billy's illness and its consequences still fresh in our minds it was clear that Pik had to be treated without delay. The local veterinary surgeon arrived to administer the necessary injections, but in the face of Pik's open hostility the man became terrified and handed the needle over to Ron who carried out the operation as directed. Although furious at such perfidy Pik suffered the injections but later refused to have anything to do with Ron. All friendly overtures were treated with lofty contempt. There was no warm welcome for Ron when he returned from the office and no more sitting at his feet. All affection was transferred to me instead. Gradually the old loyalty returned. Pik began to follow Ron to the office and settle down once more beside him in the evening.

As the compound offered little scope for adventure, we decided, one Sunday afternoon, to take Pik for a walk in the surrounding jungle. The jungle was not a wild jungle of leopards or tigers and not one where it was possible to get lost, but it was still a jungle, alive with snakes, jackals, a few civet cats and monkeys.

The day was cool and pleasant when we set off on a narrow path through the thick undergrowth, passing now and again little clearances, mud cottages with thatched roofs and astonished children running behind us, pointing to Pik and saying, 'Bhalu ka bacha hai' (it's a bear cub!). As we continued walking we met coming towards us a colourful wedding procession. The little bridegroom, perhaps as young as ten years old, all dressed up with an ornamental cap on his head and looking very pleased with himself, was being carried shoulder high on a litter. He was on his way back to his own house, where he would remain until such time as he and his young bride were old enough to consummate their marriage.

We went on following the footpath until we reached a bamboo bridge thrown across a small stream. The crossing was tricky as we could move only sideways with Ron carrying Pik in his arms. In a little while we arrived in the bazaar adjoining the Bowreah cotton mill. Close to this bazaar lay a small neglected cemetery.

Sometime during the last century when the cotton mill was started a group of Lancashire mill girls were brought out from home to instruct the local workers in the various techniques required to run a cotton mill. It was the era of long journeys on sailing ships, a time when there were no injections against cholera or typhoid. The girls did not live very long and judging by the barely discernible names on the tombstones some had married Muhammadans.

I paused for a few moments. On one side of the road was the teeming life of an Indian bazaar, tea-shops, bare-footed children, pi-dogs ambling around, and on the other, the neglected cemetery, broken tombstones with the English names of girls, laid to rest in alien graves so far removed from the homely scenes of their native land.

The short Indian twilight was over when we were back in Lawrence to a hot bath and dinner and Pik, well pleased with his adventure, sleeping at our feet.

I may add I never saw any snakes or civet cats and throughout all the years in India have no recollection of any confrontation with snakes, a statement that seems to astonish my husband who, by contrast, had had several encounters with them.

I may have been lucky for soon after our trek through the jungle, Jean, my neighbour, had a frightening experience. She awoke in the morning after John had left for work and lay in bed casually scanning the bedroom. Her eyes fell on the dressing table where she noticed what she imagined was John's tie hanging over the mirror. She wondered idly what possessed John to throw his tie in such a manner when to her horror she saw the 'tie' move and realised it was a snake. Leaping out of her bed she rushed for the servants. The snake turned out to be the deadly cobra which was soon dispatched by the servants. The Indian knows more about snakes than the average European and in this case the servants believed that another one was probably near by. They turned out to be right, for after searching around they found the second cobra under Jean's bedroom window and gave it the same treatment.

Slowly, imperceptibly, with each passing day the hot season moved nearer. A mere few weeks ago the golden disc of the sun shone with a benign brightness, but now it seemed to draw closer with a fiery heat. The harsh glare on the river became unbearable, and it was not long before *jilmils** had to be closed and the *chicks*† lowered over the veranda.

The flowers that grew in such profusion now slowly withered away, but were soon replaced by trees and bushes flourishing in the heat. Nature was kind. On the table appeared mangoes, a delicious fruit I had not seen or tasted before. There were also the round sweet litchis with the faint flavour of roses and, as always, the health-giving papayas.

The hot weather is not the best time to start up a family, but such surprises are not uncommon and are usually accepted with good grace as was our case.

Earlier we had other ideas. Ronald's leave was due in a year's time. We planned to sail from Calcutta to Hamburg where we hoped to buy a cheap car, see something of Germany, Switzerland, France and go on to cross the Channel and tour through England to Scotland. One should never make plans too far ahead, never be certain, for there is always that little fairy with the evil eyes listening and saying, 'I'll show you!' – and it did.

We faced up to our problems most of which were financial. The Managing Agents who employed Ronald held certain rules. All keranis had to pay for their return fare to Scotland but at the same time received full salary during their leave. The assistants, on the other hand, had their return fare paid, but received only £15 per month during their leave. A mere ten years later every man, his wife and children had their passages paid with full pay at home. The original system can be described only as iniquitous. The times, however, were

* *Jilmils:* Slatted shutters.
† *Chicks:* Hanging sun-blinds of laced bamboo strips.

31

such that there was no option but to accept the rules in force. During the hungry Thirties, whether in India or in Britain, men were only too glad to hang on to their jobs.

As well as having to pay for the two passages we were now confronted with the fee for the doctor and charges on the nursing home. The expenses for having a child at home were considerably less than those in Calcutta. I remember the total of our expenses for our first baby was in the region of £25, which included not only the doctor's fee but the stay in one of the best nursing homes in Dundee. A modest sum such as this is beyond belief nowadays. We knew it would be a different story in Calcutta.

I had to go to Calcutta for a consultation with Colonel Gow, the renowned gynaecologist, who is still perhaps remembered by the women of my generation who lived in Calcutta and district and even in the tea plantations. A forthright Scotsman from Dundee he was often described as friend and mentor to all females young or old, all of whom he addressed as 'child'. A shrewd man, he had a very good idea of the salaries paid to Europeans in Calcutta and based his charges accordingly.

'Well, child,' he announced, after our little talk together, 'you will have a fine Christmas present for your husband. It will arrive in early December. Come back and see me again in two months time.' After some tentative inquiries as to his fee he told me the price would be Rs 400 – or £30 – which was better than I expected.

For the next two months of the oppressive heat I rarely went up to Calcutta. Here in Lawrence, although isolated, the air was fresher with an occasional cool breeze to uplift the spirit. It was a better place to live in.

Calcutta has been described as the worst city in India. I am not in a position to make any comparisons as, with the exception of a few days in Bombay, I had never known any other city. My first impression of Calcutta with the wide streets, the open green expanse of the maidan and fine buildings, was favourable, but soon confronted by the spectacle of dire poverty, dirt and squalor, I was forced to change my mind. Worst of all was the sight of limbless beggars, the lepers, the blind, the woman hanging outside the market with a helpless infant in her arms which she deliberately nipped as she approached you, so that the pitiful wailing would arouse compassion. Whole families lived, ate and slept under the overhanging verandas of the wealthy owners living in some of the main streets.

How was it possible, I used to ask myself, that such horrors were allowed to go on in this day and age. 'Could not something be done to alleviate such wretchedness' I would inquire anxiously, only to hear the same reply: 'Nothing at all.' In time, perhaps realising that it was outwith the power of the ordinary European to abolish the shocking exploitation of human misery, the mind became blunted and accepted the status quo.

At the same time it has to be said that there were many Indian businessmen who fed daily, at their own expense, large numbers of the poor.

In May the temperature in Bengal rises to the point where it becomes difficult to bear such heat. Our bungalow, being single-storeyed and facing south, received the full blast of the sun's searing rays. I remember writing to my mother and saying, 'I am sitting in the lounge and slowly cooking to a turn.' My kind neighbour, Jean, often invited me to come along to her house, which, being the lower flat of the married quarters, was very much cooler than our house. A respite of a few hours was always welcome.

Between our bungalow and the married quarters grew two handsome nim trees. During the hot weather these trees were covered by small star-shaped cream blossoms. The scent of these flowers is much favoured by Indians and the twigs are often used in the cleaning of teeth. I found the sickly sweet scent of these flowers revolting. The trees attracted clouds of black flies and the heavy smell pervading the house was nauseating.

Feeling I could not bear it any longer I appealed to Ron to request the manager to have these smelly trees cut down. My husband was appalled by such a proposition. 'Do you really think for one minute', he rejoined, 'that I would ask the manager to remove those trees because my wife dislikes the smell?'

Everything passes. Gradually, to my relief, the blossoms faded away and the tormenting smell vanished with them.

One morning our cook, with whom I got along quite well, left for what I suspected was a better proposition across the river.

Our bearer, Sofi Khan, set off for Calcutta to buy fresh food and if possible to bring back a new cook. I decided to open a tin of corned beef and add some boiled eggs. On finding that the stove in our cookhouse had not been lit, I went along to ask Jean's permission to boil my eggs in her cookhouse. Her cook happened to be in her house and took away the pot with the eggs. We remained chatting for some time and then having decided that the eggs must be ready went down to the cookhouse.

Jean's dinner was cooking away on the stove, but there was no sign of my eggs. Some kind of intuition made Jean lift the lid of her soup pot and there bubbling merrily in the lentil soup were my eggs! She calmly removed the eggs and taking the pot outside emptied the contents on to the ground. Jean's husband, John, was deprived of his favourite soup that night.

In the evening Sofi Khan returned and introduced the new cook who produced a glowing reference from someone with whom he was supposed to have worked previously. Feeling a little uncertain I thought I would try him out and ordered a simple roasted chicken for our dinner the following evening. The bird was duly brought to the table. In the background the cook was watching eagerly. The moment of truth had arrived. I plunged the fork and fell back in horror having pulled out a part of the chicken's intestines. The man had removed only the feathers and roasted the bird complete with all the innards, legs and claws. He had never been a cook and never worked for any one as such. It was all too much! Ron rose from the table and the last I saw of my new cook was him sprinting along the path with Ron hot on his trail. He beat Ron to it at the gate and vanished never to be seen again.

That night there were more tins to be opened, more eggs to be boiled.

I promised myself there and then that come what may I had to have a small electric cooker before the arrival of our child so as to be completely independent of any cook if an emergency should arise. Luck favoured me. A few weeks later a cooker was provided and served me well for many years ahead.

Meanwhile I crossed over to Albion to see Mae in the hope that she might be able to solve my problem. I remembered how earlier she had mentioned that her own cook's brother was looking for a job as his present employer was leaving for home. To my joy and relief the young man turned up and in the early evening crossed over with me to Lawrence.

Mae had ordered lunch to be served and there, by coincidence, another strange thing happened. After the first course was served a roast chicken was due to appear, but somehow, although we waited and waited, nothing happened. A lot of anxious talking was heard coming from the bottle khana until Mae, losing her patience, left the table. She returned with an angry glint in her eyes. It transpired that the bearer carrying the chicken from the cookhouse omitted to place the usual cover over it. A kite suddenly swooped down from the skies and carried the chicken away.

My new cook, Abdul, although very young, turned out to be the best I ever had. He belonged to that breed of men to whom the recipes were handed down from father to son for many generations. Every dish he presented bore the hallmark of a first-class cook, and that in spite of primitive conditions in the cookhouse. He never overdressed anything as some cooks were given to doing, catering for the eye rather than the palate, as on one such occasion when invited to dinner the potatoes appeared in the shape of small birds with wings, tail and beak all fashioned out of toast and cloves for their eyes. I had sat looking down at my plate wondering just how much patting, smoothing and hand-work had gone into this sickly creation and had longed for a plain, wholesome potato.

At first Abdul chose to ignore my electric cooker, but on discovering what a boon it could be he never looked back and rarely used the stove in the cookhouse.

The Indian usually has his own way of doing things. For anyone to try and impose other ideas is a futile exercise. I learned the hard way to leave them alone even if the methods they used were contrary to my own. For instance, there was the business with the dhobi. I had no idea that the method of washing sheets, towels, etc., was not by scrubbing and rubbing in the European style, but simply by battering them against a stone surface. My fine linen sheets, brought out from home, were reduced to bundles of rags in a matter of weeks. Fine linen was not meant for India – cotton stood up best to the harsh treatment. On the other hand dresses, shirts and light clothing for men were usually beautifully presented.

One day, in good faith, I handed over a fine silk suit to be done up. It had been bought at home and at the time my extravagance worried me a little, but not enough to stop me from buying it. I treasured this suit and wore it only on special occasions. In due course the dhobi delivered the jacket in perfect condition – as good as new. The skirt, however, he explained was to be brought later. A week went by, but there was still no skirt. On the following Saturday we were invited to a luncheon party in Calcutta. Determined to wear my suit, Sofi was instructed to deliver a curt message to the dhobi to that effect.

On the Saturday, to my relief, the skirt arrived but for some reason was well wrapped up in paper. On undoing the wrapping I found, to my horror, a cotton patch some ten inches square neatly placed over my bottom! At this moment Ron appeared on the scene. The dhobi took the top step of the veranda and the path below in one leap. I did not see him again for several weeks. The laundry was delivered by one of his assistants. Eventually, secure in the belief that my wrath had subsided, he appeared, smiling broadly, as if nothing had happened. He was mistaken. I gave him the best of my Hindustani. What infuriated me was not so much the loss of my suit, but that he should have imagined I would be content to walk about with this large patch – not even matching – covering my bottom.

In the end a philosophical attitude was adopted. There was no other option.

Changes were taking place in the compound. Our senior salesman, Ernest, and his wife, Gwen, returned from their leave in Scotland and Tom was posted elsewhere.

Gwen was English. She had met and married Ernest who was an officer during the First World War. At first Gwen seemed to be a bit aloof, but once I got to know her I realised she was a kind and generous woman. I, for one, had reasons to be grateful in the months to come. On account of perhaps feeling lonely, with Ernest being away all day in the Calcutta office and also missing her little daughter who had been left behind for her education in Scotland, Gwen often called on me during the mornings. We would sit chatting together over a refreshing drink of lemon juice. Occasionally there was a diversion when the box wallah or Chikan wallah would appear on the scene. The Chikan wallah sold hand-embroidered tea-cloths, napkins, pillow slips and other items. He would spread his work on the floor of the veranda for our inspection. The work was done usually by the women of his household who in this way tried to augment their income. Some of the embroidery, especially on white lawn, was beautiful and exceedingly fine.

It was the custom to bargain in the belief that the Indian might be trying to do you down or simply just for the fun of it. Now, when at times I pause to admire the delicate stitching on a tea-cloth, used for many years and still as good as new, there is a feeling of regret that we should have bargained at all. This exquisite embroidery which must have strained the eyes of these poor women and taken many weeks to accomplish cost the princely sum of Rs 20.

'John Chinaman' would also come along with his huge bundle and offer embroidered linen, handsome dressing gowns and underwear in silk. We never attempted to bargain with this Chinaman. If you said to him, 'John, this is too dear – I'll give you five rupees less,' he would simply put the article back, roll up his bundle and walk away. Bargaining was beneath the dignity of this proud gentleman.

There was also the *darzi* (dressmaker). What would we memsahibs have done without our friend the darzi? That little man who travelled up and down the river, measuring, fitting and in the end delivering a pleasing garment. Not all darzis were perfect. Some would turn out exactly what you ordered, or copy an expensive model brought from home with amazing accuracy, but on the other hand there were occasions when the finished article arrived the complete opposite of what you had hoped to see. The fault was often due to the fact that he simply didn't get the message. Our Hindustani was not so good, his English not much better. Memory recalls a small fat man with a little round hat on his head. It was my firm belief that his diet consisted of pure garlic and nothing else. Holding my breath I would stand while he measured me and long after the aura of his presence would still hang around the house. His work, however, was excellent.

Nowadays as I run around the shops, so often in vain, trying to find something that would fit and please me, there comes a cry from the heart: 'Darzi, dear darzi, where are you? How gladly I would suffer your garlic breath if only you were here turning out such lovely dresses as in the past.'

There seemed to be no end to the hot weather. Each oppressive day followed another with no sign of a breakthrough in the cloudless sky. During these sweltering days a great source of relief was the swimming pool behind our bungalow. It was a simple matter to don my swimming suit, step out of the house and dive into the cool waters of the pool. I was often joined in this ploy by the other memsahibs. We would spend the morning swimming and splashing until such time as when our sahibs arrived for their lunch.

With lunch and the short respite of a lie-back over, Ron returned to work, the servants to their quarters and I to my bedroom with the closed shutters and whirling punkah. A deep silence took over at times broken by the peculiar calling of the 'fever bird' from the burra sahib's garden. It would begin on a low note, but then, as if propelled by some urgency, the call rose higher and higher until it suddenly stopped – only to start all over again. Occasionally while listening to this monotonous dirge I would doze off for a short while, but one day, after a sleepless night, it lulled me into a deep and strange dream vividly etched in my memory and never forgotten.

I dreamt I was back in Archangel running along a path flanked by birches. Through the leafy branches of the trees I saw quite clearly the river, flowing below me, shimmering in the sunlight. On my right were the gardens and houses, beyond them the familiar church and further along our cream-coloured house.

My father is standing on the balcony. He looks young and fit. Beside him, both dressed in white, are my young Aunt Marga and cousin Marina. They are all laughing and beckoning. I am overwhelmed by the joy of seeing them and a happy belief that at long last this is not a dream but reality. There were dreams before and disappointments on awakening, but now it is different. Everything is just the same as it used to be, and all that was sad was only imagined and never took place.

I long to be with them and hurry to the gate, but for some odd reason the handle will not turn. I know that in the house they are all waiting for me. The gate has to open, but all my frenzied attempts continue to be in vain. Dreams are held by a slender thread and cannot hold such despair.

The sudden awakening is puzzling at first. What is the object whirling over my head? Why am I here in this darkened room?

It was only a dream, like all the others. There is no gate, no house and no one is waiting for me. My father has long since gone.

The reality is the punkah, the room, the bird still calling in the garden. The reality is here in India.

I do not know why this dream keeps recurring. Is it that deep down there is a feeling of remorse? My mother, my brother and I escaped from Russia during the terrible aftermath of the Revolution. My father, seriously ill, was unable to accompany us and in any case would never have been granted permission to leave. It was hard to go, but judging by the events that followed, had we stayed we would have seen the gradual disintegration of our way of life.

Meanwhile the days slipped by, following a pattern similar to that in the hundred jute mills scattered up and down on the banks of the Hooghly. The location, however, did affect the quality of life such as in Lawrence, lying so far down the river, but although this isolation did at times create a feeling of restriction, we tried to make the best of what was available. The launch at our disposal allowed us to cross the river to the Golf Club where we met other people and enjoyed the tea parties there. It was possible to have contacts with our friends and on occasions attend a dance held in the Budge-Budge Club.

During the usual run of the day it was the custom, in the late afternoon, for the ladies to meet in the garden. The jetty, jutting out over the river, was a favourite place to stroll up and down and enjoy the cool breezes. In the corner of the lawn grew a magnificent Gul Mohur tree, bedecked in scarlet blossoms. There was a seat beside it where we often sat talking of many things and especially about what was nearest to our hearts – of home, friends, relatives, children, left behind in Scotland.

Now when I look back over the long decades it seems strange to me, that no one, including myself, was perturbed by or even referred to that dark shadow spreading over Europe. We were not alone in this.

Not many realised that the whole world was on the brink of a terrible catastrophe.

Best of all I liked the quiet evenings when I sat with Ronald on the veranda, at peace with the world, watching the river and all the little boats, of every description, darting across a moonlit path and disappearing into inky darkness. Occasionally a British India (BI) ship, ablaze with lights, would sail past down to the sea on her way to Britain.

The stars in the Indian skies are very bright – and the nights silent. At times drifting over the dark waters, there would come the wailing sound from some lonely boatman singing away to himself in tones that are alien to European ears, but merge so well with the Indian scene.

Early one morning, during a solitary swim in the pool, there came a sudden gust of wind followed by a deluge, the like of which I had never seen before. The long-awaited monsoon had arrived. I scrambled on to the ledge and lifting my face up to the sky allowed this heavy torrent to pour all over me. It was glorious, glorious!

At first the rainy season had been welcomed and the cooling rains were a boon, especially to those who suffered from the prickly heat, but as the weeks of heavy showers, dull skies and sticky atmosphere continued, the monsoons became wearisome. Steam rose from the ground accompanied by all kinds of strange insects such as the multitude of winged ants appearing out of the earth and setting off like minute planes on some assignment, only to be drawn by the lights of the veranda where they cast their wings and vanished. The heaps of all these tiny wings, which had to be swept away, never failed to amaze me.

Other events happened. There was the day of the flood, when the waters of the Hooghly poured through the hedge and continued rising until they reached the top step of our veranda. I had visions of all our precious belongings being ruined for good – but no, happily the flood subsided. All was well once more.

There was also the bore that came at certain times, the tidal flood which rushed up the river with great violence sweeping everything before it. Warning signals were hoisted at Budge-Budge, thus allowing all little boats such as our launch to proceed to places of safety. It was an awesome sight when suddenly this high wall of solid water came into view, heralding its approach with a thunderous roar and, leaping over our jetty, continued travelling with tremendous speed on to Calcutta and beyond. I once witnessed a small fishing boat with three occupants caught up by the bore, thrown up and disappear from sight. Poor souls, I thought, all will be drowned. But soon, to my amazement, three heads appeared bobbing on the surface – the men swimming strongly to the shore.

During the monsoons, Derek, the junior kerani, was posted to another mill. The double workload landed on Ronald's shoulders. There was no more sitting at peace on the veranda. Ron continued working in the house well into the night. My instructions were to nudge him when, overcome by exhaustion, he dropped off to sleep.

The relieving kerani who was at home on leave was not due to arrive for another two months.

Meanwhile the empty married quarters were being redecorated. During the course of these preparations a gossap was found cowering inside one of the rooms. It is a creature similar to a lizard but much larger. From what I have heard I understand it is carnivorous, but harmless to human beings. The sweepers caught it and ate it.

I am reminded of a strange incident which took place many years later in the early 1950s, when we were living in another compound of a mill where Ron, by now, was manager.

In one of the married quarters lived a young couple, Bill and Peggy, with their small child. Like most couples, when relaxing in the evening, they were in the habit of enjoying a drink or two while sitting talking together. One evening, Peggy, preparing for bed, went into the bathroom, but immediately came running out, terrified out of her wits. She had seen, she explained, the frightened head of an animal inside the toilet. Bill, on examining the toilet, found no such creature. 'This thing', he told her, 'is only in your head,' and dropped the matter. The following evening, however, Peggy came rushing out again and this time in a fit of hysterics kept repeating that the creature was trying to reach up and bite her. Bill went back once more and still found nothing at all. He became rather worried. Peggy was a calm woman not given to such strange behaviour. 'You'll have to get off that bottle,' he warned her. An alter- cation followed, a situation often found between the best of couples, of bitter exchanges and hot tears – but Peggy proved to be right, for the following morning Bill likewise discovered the creature peeping up at him from the pot. An army of coolies and sweepers arrived. The drains were disconnected. A poor large gossap was found trapped inside. He was also killed and eaten.

In late September, when already there was a faint promise in the air of cooler days to come, I set off for Calcutta for the usual appointment with Colonel Gow.

The session was brief, but as I was leaving he told me to come back in a fortnight. I left with some misgivings, wondering why it was necessary to return so quickly when the child was not due to arrive before 10 December.

On my way home I called on the nursing home in Elgin Road to arrange a booking for early December.

During the course of our conversation the matron asked me whether I hoped for a boy or a girl. 'I don't care,' I said, 'as long as the child is healthy,' but added, 'I've always been fond of little boys.'

'You'll get your boy,' she answered. 'We've had nothing but boys for the last few months. It's a sign of an approaching war and, frankly, I don't like it.'

It seemed a strange thing to say, but I thought no more about it.

A fortnight later I went back to Calcutta. This time the Colonel spent some time sounding me with his stethoscope and appeared to be listening for something. He was joined by his nurse, who likewise, moving her stethoscope over my body, kept listening anxiously. In the end, she shrugged her shoulders and left the room, followed by the Colonel. He returned shortly afterwards. 'Child,' he said, 'I will not pretend – there is something bothering me.'

Some intuition made me say, in desperation, 'Colonel, could it not be twins? They run in both sides of my family.'

'This is just what I was hoping for,' he rejoined, 'but the nurse and I can hear only one heart beating. We do not think it could be twins. However, I have made an appointment with Colonel Shorten to have you X-rayed this afternoon. Twins won't be a problem, but if there is some other factor I may have to operate. Do not worry, I will save the baby, but I must have a clear picture of the situation. Come back after the X-ray and we will have another talk.'

With those unhappy words ringing in my ears I left for Firpo's. On my way there I halted to buy a pair of shoes. Ron, travelling past the shop, saw me sitting there. He stopped the taxi, walked into the shop and sat down beside me.

I immediately broke down and wept. 'It's twins or something serious requiring an operation,' I tried to explain through my tears, quite oblivious of the young man who, while fitting my shoes, was exhibiting a lively interest and joining in with some comforting words in our conversation.

After saying goodbye to our solicitous friend we went on to Firpo's and from there for my appointment with Colonel Shorten. The Colonel, immaculately dressed and complete with monocle, was a debonair figure. He was also kind. His nurse escorted me into a changing room where I undressed and changed into a gown that was meant for a dainty little woman, never for one larger than life and taller than the average female.

'Oh, to be invisible,' I said to myself, as I was being taken standing for my first X-ray. When completed the nurse removed the plate and vanished into another room. I was now directed to a couch where I tried to arrange myself for the next position. At this point the nurse returned and after speaking to Colonel Shorten in an urgent manner left him.

The Colonel walked over to the couch. 'Are you worried, Mrs Fraser?' he asked, looking down at me with compassion. I nodded, on the verge of tears. 'I'm not supposed to tell you this,' he went on, 'but feel that perhaps you'll be relieved to know you have no cause for anxiety. You are definitely going to have twins. It is not necessary to take further X-rays.'

How joyful was the relief to hear those lovely words. I dressed hurriedly and rushed into the waiting room. Regardless of all the patients sitting there I called over to Ron, 'Everything is all right, nothing to worry about – we're going to have twins!' This glad announcement evoked an enthusiastic response from all those present.

Colonel Gow had already received the good news by the time we arrived for my further consultation. He was obviously relieved, but at the same time pointed out that I had to be extremely careful. 'You have quite a bit to go yet,' he warned me, 'every day will count from now on.'

A long time after, Ron told me that on the following morning Colonel Gow phoned privately to warn him that it was possible for the twins to arrive before their time. He repeated the importance of taking great care.

Meanwhile, full of optimism, we returned to Lawrence.

During the following week, our friend, George, arrived from his leave in Scotland and stayed the weekend with us. We spent an interesting evening hearing all the latest gossip and news from home. George, an eligible bachelor, had enjoyed his leave to the full but returned still unfettered by any romantic notions.

Pik, immediately recognising George, moved over to his side, never letting him out of his sight and sleeping in his bedroom. They left on the Sunday. The last we saw of Pik was him joyfully leaping into the launch without even a farewell wag of his tail. For a few days something seemed to be missing in the house, but soon other events took up my attention when the other kerani, James, and his bride, Helen, arrived and moved into the married quarters. We now had another kerani memsahib. Helen was a pleasant friendly woman, who like myself soon settled down to the way of life in a compound.

Actually, they were lucky to have the married quarters, as this had always been a problem for the keranis who were not encouraged to be married until they held a position in the head office. Eventually this restriction was abolished but did nothing to relieve the shortage until further building took place. The lifting of this ban was marred by a terrible tragedy. The first kerani to benefit joyfully set off to meet his bride arriving in Bombay, but during his journey on the train was murdered by an Anglo-Indian with whom he had struck up a passing acquaintance. The motive was robbery. The news had to be broken to the poor girl who was left with no other option but to return to Scotland.

We were now approaching the *Diwali* (Festival of Light), when in every Hindu house were seen lights, burning in small saucers, placed on windows, balconies, walls, everywhere. The magic of these twinkling little flames, glowing against the soft darkness of a tropical night, always evoked a memory of a similar scene in my childhood, where, following the Easter service, on every street of our Arctic city, men, women and children were seen, all carrying lighted candles. I still remember that great mass of lights moving between the snowdrifts and hear the church bells ringing out their glad message.

People were stopping to exchange their Easter greetings even with complete strangers. A young boy came up to me saying, 'Little girl, my light has gone out,' I lit his candle. 'Christ has risen,' he said.

'Truly He has risen,' I replied. We kissed and continued on our way.

Easter always brought a happy feeling. The dark winter days were drawing to a close; spring was just around the corner. At home a festive table waited. Friends and relatives gathered round, all full of goodwill to each other.

With the discovery that twins were due to arrive, a problem arose with Lawrence being so isolated in the event of an emergency. This, however, was solved when friends, residing in Calcutta, kindly invited me to stay with them towards the end of November.

On the last Sunday in October, I took into my head that more garments were required for the layette and spent the day standing over a table cutting out small nightgowns, after which, content with my efforts, I said to myself, 'Tomorrow I shall run them up.' The twins had other ideas.

We went to bed as usual, but early in the morning I was suddenly jolted out of my dreams by something untoward happening and realised at once that the twins were on their way.

Ron immediately leapt out of bed and rushed for our resident doctor. The bearer was sent for Jean, who arrived, wringing her hands, anxiously explaining that, not having had any babies, she could not advise me what to do and added, 'I think you ought to send for Gwen.' Gwen arrived, cool and collected.

Ron returned with Dr Dutta, who brought his little bag but then promptly panicked. 'You will have to send her off immediately to Calcutta,' he advised. 'It is impossible for me to help her in any way. I have never experienced delivering a child from a European woman and would not like to start now.'

When Ron, dismayed by such an answer, suggested that Dr Dutta at least should accompany us on the launch he still refused, using the same pretext.

Jean and Gwen assisted me to dress and packed my bags. A small procession was formed with Dr Dutta, still carrying his little bag, walking beside us. We crossed the lawn on to the jetty, down the gangway on to the pontoon and from there into the launch with Ron and Gwen supporting me. We waved to Jean and Dr Dutta.

At this point I should explain that Dr Dutta was the exception to the rule and in fairness to him should add that, faced with twins in the offing and by no means a straightforward case, he simply lost his nerve and panicked.

The serang of the launch was wonderful. Earlier, when Ron explained to him that he might be required urgently, this good man immediately volunteered to sleep on the launch. When we arrived he was already there waiting. Likewise the taxi owners, on the other side, offered to have a man on call daily for twenty-four hours until the emergency was over. All this was done for no other reason but out of the goodness of their hearts. After we reached the other side, I once more had to undergo the arduous climb from the launch to the pontoon and walk up the gangway. The waiting taxi was a welcome sight.

It is my belief that women, faced with the travail of childbirth, are granted an inner strength to accept whatever the outcome may be.

I remember feeling strangely calm, content to sit and watch the passing scenes that seemed to stand out very clearly in the brightness of that morning: the awakening of life in the bazaars; an old man carrying a load on top of his head; a dog suddenly dashing across our path; the crossing of the Majerhat bridge; a group of policemen, in khaki shorts and scarlet turbans, being directed to the various beats; a stout Indian lady in a rickshaw with a basket at her feet, probably on her way to the market.

We passed on through Alipore and turned into Elgin Road. The matron, although warned, did not expect me to arrive so soon. My bedroom was not ready. I was directed meanwhile into a small cubicle.

Colonel Gow arrived. 'There you are,' he said, 'rather early I'm afraid.'

'Will they live?' I asked him anxiously.

'I will be honest with you,' he rejoined. 'You are here forty days before your time. The babies are in the wrong position.'

'Colonel Gow,' I interrupted him, 'you are a clever man, please, please turn them.'

'Turn them?' he echoed. 'Turn twins? Do you think, child, you have an inside like Hyde Park? I promise you that as soon as I see the first child I will tell you if it will live.' He turned to Ron. 'I advise you, my boy,' I heard him say, 'to go back to Lawrence – nothing will happen before four o'clock.'

After the Colonel left and Ron and Gwen were alone with me, I begged them not to return to Lawrence, but go for breakfast in Firpo's and come back to the nursing home. They went away, leaving me with my own dark thoughts. It was now eight o'clock and to wait until four seemed an agonisingly long time. The twins, however, once again decided otherwise.

What followed took on a dream-like quality. The nurse rushing in and out followed by the matron in a state of frenzied hysteria directing servants to carry me in a chair to the now prepared bedroom; the terrible procession there, with the matron terrified out of her wits calling out, 'Hold your breath – I cannot possibly deliver twins'; and the blessed appearance of Colonel Gow, seeing him removing collar and tie, rolling up his sleeves, washing his hands and donning a rubber apron. Then came the relief of oblivion followed by an awakening to the protesting cry of a child.

I heard the Colonel say, 'You've got a fine, strong John Willy.'

'Will he live?' I muttered.

'With lungs like these – of course he'll live, but now we must see what the other one will be.' A further oblivion and an awakening to the weaker cry of my second son. 'You have got another John Willy,' proclaimed the Colonel, who always referred to baby boys in this way. 'Do you know, child,' he continued, proudly,' I brought them safely home – both came backsides first. An ordinary practitioner would have been panic-stricken.'

No one realised that better than I. Colonel Gow was a man of great experience who on that same day delivered another set of twins and a single child in the military hospital.

Meanwhile far back in Albion my cousin Mae was informed by the *durwan* (watchman) that her *didi* (sister) was on her way to Calcutta. She immediately got into her car and in due course arrived at the nursing home. The door leading into my bedroom was ajar. I caught a glimpse of Mae and heard the matron telling her that Mrs Fraser was too exhausted by her labours to see anyone at all.

'I'm not too weak,' I called out. 'She is my sister, please let her see me.'

Mae was allowed to come in. 'I have just seen your twins – they are strong and healthy.' She gave me a quick kiss and left me.

As she was leaving the nursing home in her car, she saw Ron and Gwen driving in.

'Nothing can happen before four o'clock,' Ron had called over.

'You are mistaken,' Mae replied, 'you have two lovely sons.'

After seeing the twins, Ron and Gwen were allowed to spend a few minutes with me. Ron, much relieved, kept assuring me the twins were well and strong.

We were joined by the matron. 'You see,' she said, 'I've kept my promise – you have got your boys. There are now five of them in the nursery and only one girl.'

Ron and Gwen went off for lunch and to buy a pair of small eiderdowns which the matron maintained were necessary for the twins with the cold weather now approaching.

While they were away the nurse brought in the twins, giving me a first glimpse of my sons.

In the adjoining rooms were four mothers, three of whom were the wives of tea-planters from Assam. Further along was a young mother, still only in her teens, from Gujerat. It was considered to be rather unusual for a Gujerati mother to have her child born in a European nursing home and engage a European specialist to attend to her. It so happened that the baby was the only male child to be born in the family, all the others being girls, who, sadly, were never so welcome as boys. Every night the happy father, uncles and grandfather, stood waiting to express their gratitude and respect to Colonel Gow making his rounds. The child, unfortunately, was rather difficult and cried a lot. The nurse, who looked after me and the Gujerati mother, explained that this was owing to the young mother not wanting to be bothered nursing the baby for any length of time. The food also, on account of her caste, had to be brought from outside and being highly spiced disagreed with the baby.

Meanwhile there were two problems for me which had to be resolved; the first being that an ayah had to be found and brought to the nursing home. The idea behind this was to train her to deal with the twins, but in reality to spare the nurses some of their chores. It was difficult to find an ayah who would be prepared to live so far from Calcutta and have the double task of caring for two babies. Ron, in the end, did succeed in engaging one and presented her to me. Jetty Ayah, as she was called, was a Gurkha of uncertain age, rather plain and wearing a nose ring. She was, however, of a cheerful, willing disposition. With complete confidence she took over the tasks concerning the twins and me, but at the same time dealt very firmly with anyone misguided enough to attempt foisting on her chores which she considered were meant for the nursing home staff.

The other problem concerned the nursing of the twins, something that proved to be very difficult. The twins, although healthy, were not strong enough to deal with me and usually after a prolonged struggle fell asleep which left them hungry and didn't relieve my own suffering. This kind of misery reminded me of how, during the time of the Russian Revolution, cows, lowing pitifully, with their udders swollen to bursting point, were found in the deserted village. I now knew how the poor beasts felt.

One evening when Colonel Gow was paying his usual visit, the matron brought my problem to his notice. After studying me for a few moments he turned to the matron. 'What she needs', he said, 'is a strong hungry child to start her off.'

'Well,' the matron hesitated, 'there is the hungry little Gujerati.' She glanced at me uncertainly.

'Bring him to me, bring him,' I interrupted. The Gujerati baby was duly brought to me. He was dressed in a bright, emerald-green knitted waistcoat with tiny boots to match. His small features were finely etched, the eyes like black cherries, the hair on his little round head dark and as soft as silk. He attacked me with the strength and vigour of a tiger cub. The relief was wonderful beyond all words and with the twins following him everything worked smoothly. The nurses were especially delighted. 'Bless you,' they said, 'there is peace now in the nursery.'

The little Gujerati was brought to me twice daily, the twins five, but the young mother also had to have her baby for a short while which worked out very nicely.

One day the nurse, after taking the baby to his mother, returned saying that she had found the young mother rather puzzled. 'Why he sleep?' she had inquired. 'Before he cry, cry – now he sleep.' 'I could have told her,' the nurse concluded, 'little do you know he's got a drop of Scotch in him.'

The whole exercise had to be kept secret. There would have been a great furore if the Gujerati family had discovered that a European woman had wet-nursed their child.

Another day Mae called. I was sitting up, cradling my little Gujerati. 'My God,' Mae exclaimed, 'if only your mother could see you – what would she think?'

I was indignant. 'It would not bother me in the slightest. He is sweet and I shall miss him sorely when he goes away.' And miss him I did when he left a few days later for the fertile plains of Gujerat.

Nowadays when I look back on those distant scenes I ask myself, where is my little Gujerati with his black cherry eyes and hungry mouth? The years have passed so swiftly, he'll be a man, a father, perhaps a grandfather, but whatever he is and wheresoever he might be I trust that Lakshmi – the goddess of prosperity – will always stay beside him.

I spent an extra week in the nursing home, following the advice of Colonel Gow who believed that a little more time would allow the twins to gain more strength. If anything untoward should happen, he pointed out, Lawrence was too far away for him to spare the time to go there.

The additional expense did not worry us unduly, but what gave me some anxiety was the thought that the Colonel might double his fee because there were twins. One day, unable to contain myself, I asked him if this would be the case, a question that seemed to amuse him. 'Consider yourself lucky, child,' he laughed,' you've got a bargain – two for the price of one.'

Our friends, Mary and Max Kidd, who lived in Calcutta, invited us to have dinner with them on the last night of my sojourn in the nursing home. I looked forward to that dinner with eager anticipation, for it has to be said that, although the accommodation and attention received from the nurses was satisfactory, the cuisine left a great deal to be desired. Only the gnawing pangs of hunger forced me to swallow the food which in normal times I would have described as repugnant.

I have heard of loving husbands bringing bouquets to their wives, but in my case I asked Ron to bring me only sausage rolls from Firpo's. Every night, to appease my hunger, he would arrive with rolls, sandwiches, pies and cakes which not only pleased me, but delighted the nurses who were likewise badly fed. 'What has he brought you tonight?' they eagerly inquired, in the firm belief that I would share the goodies with them – which, of course, I did.

On my last evening in the nursing home Ron picked me up and we set off for our friends' house where we received a warm welcome along with a delightful dinner, much enjoyed by me after three weeks of semi-starvation. As we had not seen each other for some time a great deal of talking had to be done with the hours passing all too quickly. It was approaching midnight when Ron dropped me with the final instructions to have everything packed and ready for my departure the following morning.

The night nurse was sitting at her desk as I passed along the corridor and went on to the nursery to find the twins sleeping peacefully under their eiderdowns.

At this point I have to say that out of all the staff the night nurse was the only one with whom I was never at ease. There was something sly and furtive in her manner which repelled me.

After reaching my bedroom I undressed and crept under the netting into bed. Perhaps on account of having been out, and the exciting thought that the next day there would be the journey back to our home, sleep eluded me. I lay, wide awake, staring into darkness. From the corridor, through the half-open door of my bedroom, a shaft of light lay across the floor. Suddenly a white figure appeared in it and stood still. Although startled I realised that this was the night nurse. Moving slowly on her tiptoes she came up to my bed. Thinking that she might want to converse with me, I closed my eyes pretending I was asleep. She drew closer and bending down peered at me through the netting for a few moments and then moved over to my bedside table where she appeared to be searching for something. Through half-closed eyes I saw her run lightly across the room to the dressing table, lift some object and hurry out – only to return immediately and replace it. She once again tiptoed up to my bed and after silently watching me for a moment or two finally left the room. I realised at once that she had been looking for my handbag which I remembered leaving on the dressing table prior to getting ready for bed.

With this unnerving, strange experience all hope of falling asleep left me. When, at last, daylight broke, I slipped out of my bed to find my handbag lying where I had left it on the dressing table. The money, however, was gone. For a mere Rs100 this nurse had put me through a frightening ordeal!

Sometime later I was asked why I did not challenge the nurse. The answer is simple. I was afraid. We were on the top floor where there were only a few patients and helpless babies in the nursery. It is impossible to know how she would have reacted if I had tried to confront her. She might have turned on me or hurt the children. A cornered thief is capable of anything. I simply could not risk it.

In the morning when the usual routine took over and the nurse brought me my breakfast I described to her my experience, but at the same time asked her to keep it to herself. I was leaving in a few hours and had no wish to be involved in any unpleasant scenes. She, however, pointed out that recently sums of money large or small were being stolen from the patients. No one knew who the thief was. Any one of the nurses could have been suspected.

After breakfast, as I, assisted by Jetty Ayah, was preparing for our departure the matron called.

'My dear,' she began in honeyed tones, 'I was so sorry to hear about your nasty experience. The hundred rupees, of course, will be deducted from your bill and the sweeper dismissed.'

'The sweeper?' I echoed in astonishment. 'There was no sweeper there at all – it was the night nurse and nobody else.'

'You are mistaken,' she contradicted. 'You only thought it was the night nurse while actually it was the sweeper. My nurses',' she added in a voice that brooked no opposition, 'would *never* steal.'

So that was the crux of the matter, the reason for lying, I said to myself. The sweeper could be blamed, but a nurse never – the reputation of nursing had to be upheld. Against such odds one could not argue. I returned to my packing.

Two weeks later I had occasion to call on the nursing home to visit a friend who was a patient there. In the hall I met one of the nurses who had attended me. During our conversation I casually inquired how the night nurse was getting along.

'Oh, that one,' the young nurse rejoined. 'She's not here any longer – she was dismissed the day after you left.'

We were all set and ready to go when Ron arrived to collect us. After expressing my thanks to the nurses who came out to see us off, we piled all the bits and pieces, the twins and Ayah into the car and cheerfully set off for Lawrence. I have a happy memory of that morning, the pleasant drive, the sunshine, the enchantment of the cold weather, the overflowing joy of going home.

Our faithful serang, smiling broadly, welcomed us at the jetty. The twins, lulled by the movement of the car, had slept soundly in our arms throughout the journey and didn't open their eyes until we reached the other side and scrambled up on to the jetty where some members of the staff surrounded us. One of them, a rather wild lad, whom one would never have suspected of being religious, came up to the twins and after whispering a little prayer made the sign of the cross over them, a gesture I found very touching.

One by one the ladies called to welcome us. On the table, to my surprise and delight, I found the little nightgowns I had cut out, but left unfinished when forced to depart for Calcutta in such a hurry, were now completed with touches of embroidery by Gwen. Knowing how time-consuming such work could be I was very grateful and especially so as she had never mentioned that she had done this for me.

We settled down to a new way of life – at times enlivened by various problems. The twins, bottle-fed at regular intervals – the last one being ten o'clock – awoke with the exactitude of a clock four hours later to begin their demands for another feed. Night was turned into day, a peaceful sleep a thing of the past.

During the Thirties there was a book on baby care, widely read and faithfully followed by many parents. According to the gospel of the author, the baby was not to be fed throughout the night and all demands were to be pacified by giving it a little water with the addition perhaps of some orange juice. It proved to be a futile exercise. The little darlings refused to be duped by this blatant trickery. Their shrill protests continued with a tenacity astonishing in such small creatures.

Not being naturally inclined to pay much attention to any instructions verbal or written, I was all for producing another bottle, but met with strong opposition. My husband, refusing to give in, spent hours circling the bedposts to the accompaniment of lullabies with little or no result. The struggle continued until there came a morning when, utterly exhausted by his efforts, he crawled into bed and fell into a deep sleep, during which he suddenly sat up and, gently patting his shoulder, began to sing a lullaby to himself. I realised at once, enough was enough, something had to be done. 'Ron,' I pleaded, 'please phone Colonel Gow and tell him that you have a foolish wife who does not listen to words of wisdom and is determined to feed the twins in the middle of the night. I promise you that I shall abide by his decision.'

Ron phoned and the message he brought back was clear and simple: 'Don't you know, my boy, the mother always knows best.' I didn't flaunt my triumph being only too relieved to have some peace at long last.

Our other problem concerned the pram. My mother had sent the pram, originally used by the child we had lost. She never dreamt that on the scene would arrive two babies. It duly arrived and although it was possible to use it for a short period a larger one had to be found which we intended to take home when we went on leave in April.

One morning I set off for Calcutta to purchase a double pram, but after spending the whole day searching in all the shops I realised that there was not such a thing to be found anywhere. However, in one of the shops a helpful assistant informed me that he knew of a place where a second-hand large pram was going for sale at a reasonable price. He kindly offered to take me there if I should wish to see it for myself. My hopes rose. 'This pram', he continued, 'has belonged to a Maharaja and is manufactured from the best possible materials with silver fittings and was once especially ordered for four babies.'

'Four babies?' I cried in amazement. 'How could that be?'

'Madam,' the assistant informed me, 'the Maharaja is a very wealthy gentleman, one who could afford to keep several wives – and so it was natural for all the children to be born about the same time. It is also possible that some of the babies belonged to his brother. This is not such an unusual situation in India,' he concluded.

For one moment I saw myself pushing this enormous vehicle along the streets in Broughty Ferry, with the twins, no doubt having high jinks inside such spaciousness – and then I said to myself, this is not for me, no not for me.

I thanked the kind assistant for his offer and returned home empty-handed. There was no other option but to utilise the existing pram until our departure for Scotland where we hoped to buy one immediately on our arrival there.

Meanwhile Jetty Ayah managed quite well to deal with this problem. On arriving, usually, at six o'clock in the morning she would proceed to change and feed the twins, squeeze them comfortably into the pram and set off for a walk around the compound. She formed a certain routine and turned out to be very efficient, having obviously had previous experience. I knew nothing about her background except that she came from Darjeeling where she had a husband and three children to whom she faithfully sent her earnings every month.

It was always a source of wonder to me how she could deftly turn over with one hand each child to bathe him and massage a little oil into his small body which she considered to be very beneficial.

Gradually the twins got to know and recognise her. In spite of her unprepossessing appearance it was Jetty Ayah who got the first smile, the first happy gurgle as, bending over them, she would talk in her own style and sing the well-known little lullaby which still comes back to me over these long years: 'Nini baba nini. Roti, makon, chini. Roti makon hogaya, chota baba sogaya.' (Sleep, baby, sleep. Bread, butter, sugar. When bread and butter is finished, little baby will be sleeping.)

Like all Gurkha ayahs she wore the usual skirt and blouse with shawl over her head and shoulders, all of which were rather shabby, soon replaced by me. As her woollen shawl was worn and dirty, I, in a moment of what Ron described as a mental aberration, presented her with a beautiful Cameron tartan shawl in fine wool, given to me by my mother who in turn had been presented with it by an old aunt. Jetty Ayah accepted it in her usual enigmatic style without any sign of gratitude. She wore it during the cold weather at times using it as a handkerchief as well, a sight which rather startled me and aroused pangs of regret over my impulsive gesture.

There was, in the background, a certain rivalry between Sofi Khan and the ayah. Sofi, who had served faithfully long before there was any memsahib and babies appearing on the scene, resented this interloper trying to assert herself above him through the importance of her work with the babies. Sofi on one or two occasions warned Ron that the ayah was not to be trusted, a warning we chose to ignore being aware of the state of war between him and the ayah.

There was, however, a strange incident that took place one day. During the cold weather it was Ron's custom in the early morning to wear a small Fraser tartan scarf as a cravat. On this particular morning, as he prepared to leave for the office, the scarf could not be found. Ron, determined to find it, searched, together with Sofi, through every drawer and press including the laundry basket, where every article was taken out, shaken and placed back again, but there was no trace of the scarf.

Later during breakfast, while Sofi was serving and the ayah hovering around, Ron, referring to the loss of the scarf and speaking in Urdu to Sofi Khan, said, 'Only members of the Fraser Clan wear the scarf and should any thief try to wear it, the scarf will tighten round his throat and strangle him.'

Shortly afterwards, prior to Ron leaving for the office, Jetty Ayah appeared, triumphantly waving the scarf saying that she had found it in the laundry basket. Jetty Ayah did not know that the basket had already been searched. Ron thanked her and said no more. She was a good ayah and good ayahs were difficult to find.

In conclusion I have to add that this story to Western ears may sound improbable, but in India superstition is rampant and many strange things have been known to happen.

Christmas that year was very happy, enlivened by the arrival of many varied gifts, in duplicate, from friends and relatives in Scotland and from people whom we didn't even know, such as one of my brother's Texan drillers in far-off Venezuela who was so taken after hearing about the twins that he decided to express his delight by sending them a present. The parcel duly arrived. Inside I found two frilly pink dresses with sun bonnets to match enhanced by flowers and ribbons. I was taken aback and stared in silence. It was impossible to visualise our sons dressed up in such ridiculous finery looking like little girls.

Later it transpired that the Texan had instructed his sister in the United States to choose a suitable gift, but somewhere along the line the message went off-key and what was chosen was meant for twin girls, not boys. I wrote to our Texan friend, omitting all reference to the mistake and expressing my thanks for his wonderful gesture, far greater than the gift which some time later I gave away to a worthy cause. Our friends, George and Lyn, came to stay with us over the Christmas weekend. There was tennis, tea on the veranda and in the evening a lively dinner party where our young cook, Abdul, as usual, excelled himself. During their visit a short film was taken of us all including the twins. Nowadays, on rare occasions, we run the film through to see ourselves again on that bright Christmas morning. George and Lyn, our debonair bachelors, are seen strolling across the lawn. Their smiling faces tell me that they are sharing a joke together. Ronald is on the veranda holding in his arms two small white bundles and I appear to be engaged in some ploy. It is a little moving to see us all so young, as if we are transported back in time, across the half-century to relive again a small part of our lives – lives that are no longer shared by many friends. George and Lyn have long since left the scene, the small white bundles are now middle-aged men, and we ourselves are old, quite old.

That year all the married couples along with some of the bachelors decided to cross the river and join in the Hogmanay festivities held in the Budge-Budge Club. As we all knew each other well, it turned out to be a very free and jovial party. We arrived in time to join in the Eightsome Reel, followed by Strip the Willow, Gay Gordons, Lambeth Walk, and in the end waltzed our way into the New Year of 1939 – never dreaming what that fatal year would bring to us and the whole world.

The party finished in the early hours of the morning when already the stars were fading and a pale golden haze was spreading from the east. A cold wind was blowing across the river as, in the same happy mood – some happier than others – we boarded the launch and sat there huddled together under coats and shawls with the Hooghly resounding to our laughter and singing.

With Christmas and New Year behind us preparations began for our leave in April. We had the choice of two methods of travelling home. The first being to sail on a BI ship, leaving conveniently from Calcutta on the leisurely round trip of some four weeks, in the same way as when I first arrived in India. The other was to cut across India by rail to Bombay, involving a journey of thirty-six hours, to board one of the P&O ships which would take us to Britain in a matter of eighteen days. We decided on the latter course. These large ships offered two classes: first and tourist. There was also the ruling that children under three travelled free – a great boon to many parents.

One morning Ron set off for Calcutta to arrange our booking, but on returning I noticed he was upset. It transpired that the free ticket for children under three applied only to one child, not for twins, and in our case, although they were only five months old, we had to pay a quarter fare for one of them.

It was not so much the extra expense that was upsetting, but that we considered the ruling to be unjust. Ron, discussing the matter in the booking office, inquired what would happen if by chance we decided to travel separately, each with one child. The answer was, 'The child would travel free.' On pointing out that such a rule seemed rather illogical, Ron received the reply, 'That is our system – take it or leave it.'

That evening as we sat discussing our plans there suddenly came a thought. But do we have to go to Scotland? After all we were paying for our tickets and could go where we pleased.

'How would you like to go to Kashmir and live in a comfortable houseboat on a beautiful lake?' asked Ron.

'Kashmir, glorious Kashmir,' I echoed in disbelief – suddenly transported to my starry-eyed youth when enraptured I listened to 'The Indian Love Lyrics' – conjuring up entrancing love scenes beside the Shalimar, a place mysterious, enchantingly romantic.

The more I thought, the more enticing was the vision of our sailing around on a peaceful lake with the backdrop of magnificent scenery, with our ayah taking care of our clamouring twins and the bearer and cook attending to our wants. What woman could ask for more?

Certainly it was sad that we would not see Scotland, our relatives and friends, but that would surely come again. Meanwhile, the chance to see Kashmir, especially for Ron, who, in spite of many years of service in Calcutta, had not seen much of India, was an opportunity which might never come again.

The following morning, Ron, after informing Ernest, our head office representative, of our decision to go to Kashmir, went off to the travel agents in Calcutta to arrange a booking. I waited anxiously all day, but on his return saw once more that something had gone awry. It transpired that on Ron's arrival at the booking office, there was a message awaiting him to get in touch with his head office. He did so and when Ernest came on the phone his first words were, 'Hold your horses, Ronald – head office has decided to pay the keranis' return passages to Scotland.'

The question of finance intervened again. We knew that the free passage applied only for the trip home and not for Kashmir. With mixed feelings we reverted to our original plan and in the end never did see Kashmir.

On the day when we were leaving for Bombay, our good friends, Max and Mary Kidd, suggested that instead of travelling from Lawrence direct to the station we could come to their house for a light meal and a short rest prior to leaving for the evening train – an offer we gratefully accepted.

It was the start of the hot weather. The preparations for the journey were endless and exhausting as apart from all the articles required for the journey, our personal belongings in the house – china, books, ornaments, lamps – had to be packed and the boxes sent for storage. The servants also had to be remembered. Sofi Khan, Jetty Ayah and the cook all received their six months' salary in advance. Ron firmly believed that they also deserved their holiday even if it was by no means certain that they would all be there when we returned. (They were.)

After a pleasant break with Max and Mary in Calcutta we were driven to the station and were met by friends who came to see us off – Jean and John from Lawrence, Jimmy, George, and others whose faces I have since forgotten.

The Howrah station, not a place where one would wish to linger, was hot and sultry, overlaid by the heavy smell of humanity. Around us was the usual motley gathering. Many were patiently waiting for trains. A sprinkling of Europeans accompanied by their friends, the familiar scene of the homeless poor, sitting curled up or stretched out sleeping, heads covered by their dhotis or saris – the everlasting vendors selling sweetmeats or calling out 'Pan-biri' (Pan leaf and cigarettes). No one enjoys prolonged farewells especially with little children. It was with some relief we saw Anwar, our contractor from Lawrence, coming over to tell us that all the luggage was safely in our compartment.

Jetty Ayah, who remained with us to the last moment, arranged the twins in their baskets, placed on the lower berth. The twins, wide-eyed, remained peaceful – perhaps wondering what all this was about. There were the usual last words – final goodbyes – the banging of doors and the train began to pull out of the station.

Our two-berth compartment seemed smaller than I imagined – what between our numerous bits and pieces, the twins' baskets and the large block of ice in an open tin box, occupying most of the floor space. Thus began a journey of more than 1200 miles, which, I heard later, our friend Jimmy described as his idea of a hell on wheels. I cannot imagine a more apt description.

It was decided that I would sleep on the top berth the first night and Ron the second, but as I kept jumping up and down to assist Ron with the twins, by now restless and fretting, we closed up the top berth and sat beside the baskets, sleeping the best way we could, for the rest of the journey.

We were travelling during the height of the hot season. By morning the ice block had melted away leaving the water in the container swishing up and down with an irritating monotony until we arrived at the first station when a fresh block was carried in. This was repeated at every stop.

It was the second day of our journey that still stands out – a day of terrible heat, discomfort and sheer misery. It began with the rising sun, growing fiercer with each passing hour. On either side lay the vastness of India – a great empty, dun-coloured expanse stretching away to the distant horizon, where for some reason, memory had retained the brief vision of a solitary woman walking along a dusty path, while balancing a large earthenware jar on top of her head. There is no recollection of seeing any greenery, fields or even activity with the exception of the stations, where as usual there was the noisy crowd of white-clad figures rushing up and down with their bundles pushing and scrambling to board the train, and others sitting passively watching. As in Calcutta there were vendors calling out their wares, the beggars stretching out their arms in supplication.

The triple windows offered a choice of glass, netting or jilmils. We kept the jilmils down as they provided air and shade from the blinding glare, but through them came the dust of the desert and settled on all our belongings, ourselves and the twins, turning their little faces black. All attempts to sponge and clean proved futile. The various tasks, however, kept us occupied. Water for the twins' bottles had to be boiled on a small spirit stove inside the lavatory, a performance far from simple against the erratic rolling of the train. The food and fruit, brought with us to avoid having to go to the dining carriage, provided diversion. The problem of the twins' nappies was solved, as, prior to our leaving, old linen sheets and fine lawn dresses offered by the ladies in the compound were cut in squares and after use were simply thrown out the windows. The road to Bombay was strewn with discarded nappies, underclothing, shirts and dresses.

By the afternoon the heat reached such a pitch that even the walls of the compartment were hot to touch. Ron, after years in India, was standing up to the heat far better than I was. Perhaps on account of having been born and brought up in Arctic conditions I found the extreme heat caused a kind of claustrophobia – something I could not escape from and therefore difficult to bear. The poor babies were likewise suffering. They were missing their ayah, the walks in the compound, the leafy trees, blue skies. They could not understand why they were suddenly transported in these uncomfortable baskets to a strange place that was so hot, and wept pitifully, helplessly. We tried to comfort them, by lifting them out of their baskets, talking and singing all the lullabies we knew in Scots, Hindustani and Russian. We also promised ourselves there and then that we would cancel the return tickets to Bombay and transfer to the BI round trip to Calcutta, thus avoiding another terrible journey. Well, little did we know what lay in store for us.

Meanwhile, the crimson disk of the sun vanished below the horizon. Another tortuous night lay ahead tempered by the realisation that the train thundering along was eating up the miles and drawing closer to Bombay.

In the morning we rose and opened the windows. A wonderful sight met our eyes. Against the pale rose-lilac sky was a string of hills stretching away to the right. Ron became quite excited. 'Look,' he said, waxing lyrical, 'this is just like Scotland.' I wasn't very sure if it was, but thought how good it was to know that the journey was almost over. We began to put ourselves in order, by changing and throwing all our dirty clothes out the window. We then tidied the twins, arranged the luggage and waited.

In Bombay our agent was at the station. 'Mr Fraser,' he said, 'the ship is not due to sail until the afternoon, but you can board it now if you wish.'

We had no intention of boarding any ship so early – our dream was to go to the Taj Mahal Hotel, where we could have a bath and breakfast. A taxi was ordered and we duly arrived there, to be shown into a spacious bedroom complete with bathroom attached. The journey had been a hell on wheels, but now we entered Paradise with willing angels ministering to all wants.

Our grimy, quite exhausted twins, when plunged into a bath, immediately blossomed out to kick and splash in blissful joy. After they were dressed and fed we laid them down on top of the bed where soon they fell into a deep sleep. For us as well it was a great relief to have a bath in turn and wash the desert dirt out of our hair. It boosted the morale and brought a glorious sense of well-being as we sat down to a sumptuous breakfast, served in the bedroom in the best tradition of the Taj Mahal and enjoyed to the full.

An hour or two passed, sitting relaxed beside the window looking over the Arabian Sea and the renowned 'Gateway to India', pride of Bombay, which appeared to attract a constant flow of people, standing or strolling up and down.

All too soon the respite was over. A taxi took us to the landing stage where the *Strathaird*, one of the giants of the P&O line, was waiting. Each holding a child, I with my hair still hanging wet, climbed the gangway. Our accommodation was in a passage of four cabins. The task of arranging our luggage in the cabin was left to the agent, but as we settled down we found to our horror that the basket containing all the twins' clothing was missing. It had been tied to one of the trunks but someone had removed the ropes. Ron immediately rushed up on deck, only to discover that the agent had vanished. By now the ship was moving. The fact that the man had never come forward to claim his fee was ominous. Ron, however, as anxious as myself, said he was prepared to search the whole ship if need be. With these words he hurried away. I remained holding one of the twins with the other at my side. The position was serious as every item of clothing for the children was in that basket. Nothing remained except the little vests and nappies they were wearing. Overwhelmed by such a disaster I could only weep.

In the open doorway of our cabin suddenly a woman appeared, smiling in a friendly manner. 'Cheer up, my love,' she called out in a strong cockney accent, 'it could be worse, you could have twins.'

'Twins,' I echoed, 'but I have twins.'

'Blimey,' she cried, 'what a coincidence, for so have I.' And indeed she had. Two strong boys, twice the size of mine. 'How heavy were yours when born?' she asked.

'Ten pounds in total,' I told her.

'Mine,' she rejoined proudly, 'were fifteen pounds between them – heavier than the Dionne's quins, but', she added ruefully, 'there were no roses for me!'

While this lively exchange was going on, which in some way eased my misery, Ron appeared on the scene. He had found the basket a few passages away, dropped perhaps by some coolie who had lost his way. The relief was tremendous. The mystery of why it was separated from the trunk, in the first place, was never solved.

In our gangway, in the cabin next to us, were the parents of the twins and a little girl six years of age. Opposite them were two ladies with a baby and across from us was a Forest Officer from India recovering after a nervous breakdown and travelling home with his wife, a very pleasant lady. They had spent four years in the depth of an Indian jungle far from all habitation. Quiet and friendly they never complained when at times the noisy chorus of all the twins with the single child joining in for good measure must have been rather hard to bear. The wife of the officer was actually quite sympathetic. I remember her recalling her own journey, when years earlier she had travelled all the way to Calcutta from England, with her small son. 'He was just a little devil', she said – 'and I was an old, old woman by the time we reached Calcutta.'

The father of the large twins was an army sergeant. He and his wife were easy-going. Throughout the journey we used to find them sitting on deck together with their twins and daughter cheerfully drinking beer, occasionally giving little sips to the twins to keep them happy. These babies, eight months old, were enormous with short red hair and bright china-blue eyes.

The passengers were a mixed bag. Missionaries, teachers, army officers, NCOs, tea planters, people like ourselves, including the wife of a jute mill manager who was travelling home to Dundee to be with her young daughter. Her name was Mrs Dott. Completely on her own she was pleased to join us, often helping with the twins. We also made the acquaintance of a lady who turned out to be Russian. Jenya Sherman was the wife of an Englishman in a shipping office in Calcutta and was on her way to some relatives in England. Jenya, like myself, had known the horrors of the Russian Revolution but in the end escaped with her family to China. With her relatives she had gone through a traumatic experience when they were caught up in a battle for the one particular town between the two opposing armies and were forced to hide in a cave where they remained for a week without food or water, being driven at times to eat the moss off the walls. They survived; but the suffering endured left Jenya with a psychological horror of starvation which led her to always keep some bread under the pillow no matter where she went, including aboard ship. We held long conversations in our own tongue and met again in Calcutta.

I know nothing of the luxurious first class, but have to say that for our money the food was quite good, the accommodation, although small, comfortable. The deck space, however, allotted for the tourists, was far too small in comparison with the numbers of the passengers. It was usually difficult to find a place to sit. The laundry facilities were likewise inadequate. I considered myself lucky when a kind-hearted member of the crew allowed me to hang my washing near the hold on condition that I removed it when in port.

The third berth for which we had to pay on account of having a second child was in a four-berth cabin near by, shared with two army officers. Ron placed our trunk on the berth and utilised one of the drawers. He also used the cabin for shaving and changing for dinner.

The ship halted at Aden. After it left Ron went to his cabin where he found a small, well-built man who introduced himself as the Post Master in the hinterland of Aden. Being rather puzzled as to why all four drawers were occupied and having been told by the officers that they had only one each, he asked Ron how many he had. Ron pointed out his drawer whereupon, with perfect sang-froid the new arrival removed one of the three remaining drawers and emptied the contents into the passage. The atmosphere between him and the officers was rather strained for the rest of the journey.

The journey continued through the hot Red Sea, the Suez Canal and stopped in Port Said. A few more passengers came aboard including a young woman who joined us at the dinner table in the evening and was placed beside me. She was an attractive girl but heavily made up, which was rather unusual for those times. My attempts to strike up conversation proved futile as she did not understand English. Pointing to herself she smiled, saying, 'Me – French-Italian.' When dinner was being served and the menu card, printed in French and English, presented to her she chose to ignore it and instead conveyed to the steward that she wanted the same dish as I was having. This was repeated with the second and third course. It was obvious she could not read. What was also noticed was that this smart and fashionably dressed young woman had not the slightest idea as to how to use a knife and fork, holding them tightly clutched in her fist as a child would, all of which was rather odd.

Sitting opposite, beside Mrs Dott, was a small woman with sharp features, hair rolled into a tight bun and wearing pince-nez. Speaking in perfect French she addressed herself to the girl, relieving me from further efforts to make some contact. It transpired that the lady was a teacher of languages in a school in Bombay. She continued talking to my neighbour throughout the dinner.

The following morning the young woman did not appear for breakfast.

'I see', I remarked to the teacher, 'your friend is not here this morning.'

'She is not my friend,' she replied with some asperity. 'Her kind never get up for breakfast,' and seeing I was taken aback, added, 'Did you not realise that she is a prostitute?' I shook my head. 'She is probably from a brothel in Port Said and going on to another in Marseilles. There are several classes of brothels. I rather think she belongs to the second class.' Our little teacher continued imparting her knowledge with the precision of one who had obviously made a close study of the subject – the last thing one could have suspected from a strait-laced spinster.

We did not see the girl again, but there was some speculation as to whether by some evil chance she may have been sold or stolen as a child, something, sad to say, by no means uncommon in the Middle East.

In Marseilles I went ashore with Ron to do some shopping and buy myself a hat. Mrs Dott, along with a tea planter from Aberdeen, a friendly man who was fond of children, offered to look after the twins. On our return to the ship we met the sergeant with his family happily strolling up and down the quay. They were carrying their twins who were all dressed up in white, starched dresses and wide-brimmed hats. They looked a cheerful contented lot.

On deck we found the tea planter and Mrs Dott likewise strolling side by side, with our twins, who didn't appear to miss us in the slightest. We much appreciated that little outing – the only one we had.

I cannot recall at what stage of the journey enteritis broke out amongst all the young children including the babies in our gangway. Our younger twin, not as sturdy as his brother, became very ill. We asked the ship's doctor to call but when the rather urbane gentleman arrived he merely gave the twins a cursory examination and told us it was nothing but a chill. The so-called 'chill' infected every child on the ship. All the mothers were convinced that the water was at the root of the trouble, an opinion shared by us. As if this trouble was not enough, on reaching the Straits of Gibraltar we were struck by an icy blast as cold as all the winds of Siberia. Our efforts to keep the twins and ourselves warm were of little avail.

Although it was never mentioned at the time, we later admitted that we seriously wondered if our children, and especially the younger twin, would survive the journey. Only the thought that a mere few days remained of the journey contained the despair we felt as we watched them growing weaker with every passing hour.

In the stormy waters of the Bay of Biscay, I, a hopeless sailor, became very seasick, leaving Ron to cope with the twins. Mrs Dott, not affected by the rolling of the ship, once more came to our rescue. Soon, thankfully, we entered the Channel where I recovered and on going up on deck saw with great relief the welcome shores of Britain drawing closer.

The docking of a ship is always exciting. We didn't expect anyone to meet us, but stood, holding the twins, watching the milling crowd on the landing stage exchanging greetings with their friends and relatives aboard the ship. Suddenly to our amazement we recognised Ron's mother and waved excitedly to draw her attention. Granny Fraser, who could not resist the temptation to be the first to see her grandchildren, had travelled down to London from Broughty Ferry. We were soon reunited and set off for the hotel at King's Cross where we spent the rest of the day and in the evening boarded the train for Scotland.

On arriving in Dundee we were met at the station by my mother, Ron's aunts and his father who had arrived with his car to take us to my mother's house. Thus began our leave. Unfortunately it was not an auspicious beginning as the twins were still unwell and I succeeded somewhere along the way in picking up a virus. The doctor was sent for who found the twins had enteritis and I the flu. However, within a few days after a good rest and home comforts, all recovered.

We were now in the summer month of May which turned out to be bitterly cold with a biting wind from the east, but as we urgently required a twin pram Ron and I set off on my first outing into town in search of one, leaving Mother along with a young woman she had engaged, called Lizzie, to deal with the twins. We returned, elated, having been fortunate to find a handsome, navy-blue twin pram, which on being delivered the following day allowed us to take the twins out for an airing.

That same week, remembering the frightful journey across India, Ron went to the travel agents to transfer our return tickets from P&O to a BI ship sailing all the way to Calcutta on 9 September. We had no idea at the time how fortunate we were to do so, as events proved later.

Meanwhile we tried to make the best of our leave in spite of all the endless chores involved with the twins.

Lizzie, whom Mother engaged as a house help on the recommendation of an agency as being reliable and hard-working, didn't live up to our expectations. She was cheerful with a pleasing appearance and rather large stomach. This, she explained, was a hernia which had occurred some time earlier when she had had the unfortunate experience of having to lift a heavy wardrobe. Further, she informed us, she was to be admitted to the Royal Infirmary in September to undergo an operation for the hernia. All this we listened to with sympathy, tinged with regret that it was not divulged earlier. Mother had engaged Lizzie for a matter of three months at the end of which we were due to spend the other half of our leave with Ron's parents. It would have been heartless to dismiss poor Lizzie now.

Lizzie never stood if she could sit. Her favourite occupation was to settle down in an armchair with the twins and sing to them. Lizzie had a wonderful repertoire. There was not a song that Lizzie didn't know, from 'Nelly Kelly' to 'Little Mickie had a stickie' or from the soulful 'I'll walk beside you', to the passionate 'Black Eyes', sung to Lizzie's own words, which she maintained were vastly superior to the original version in Russian. The twins listened peacefully. It was difficult to know if they were enchanted or mesmerised which was all to the good, as it kept them quiet and allowed us to get on with our work.

To be fair, Lizzie did condescend on occasions to dust the mantelpiece or peel a few potatoes for which mercies we were duly grateful. Our mornings usually began with Lizzie arriving to sing, Ron off to play golf, Mother to cooking and I to my chores. At times when Ron borrowed his father's car, the two grannies, the twins and I would pile in and set off for a run somewhere to have tea, with an ice-cream cone for the twins, for which they were developing a strong passion. The countryside was beautiful, a pleasant interlude for all.

Lizzie, being reliable, was left at home in the hope that she might do a little cleaning. Later I realised we should have taken Lizzie with us as in this way I might still have possessed some of the things I treasured.

After we returned to India I received a letter from Mother with some startling news. She was informed that Lizzie's trip to the Infirmary had not resulted in an operation for a hernia but in the gift of a bouncing baby boy! Mother was also very sorry to tell me that when she went to move a case in the wardrobe in which I had left some belongings she found it strangely light, and, on lifting the lid, discovered that all the first baby's fine clothes and two beautiful shawls knitted by Ron's aunt were missing. So much for our light-fingered songster. Ron's remark after reading Mother's letter was: 'See what you get for lifting heavy wardrobes!'

In early July we moved to Ron's parents' house in West Ferry. It was a spacious house with a pleasant garden conveniently situated near the church where the twins were christened some time later. It was in this same church of St Stephen's that Ron and I had married as had been my parents many years ago.

The two grandmothers, acting as godmothers, carried the twins to church. It was a joyful occasion, tinged perhaps for my mother with bitter-sweet memories of when, as a young bride after her wedding, she had travelled with my father to Russia from where a mere fifteen years later, with everything destroyed during the Revolution, she escaped with her children and eventually reached the house of her parents in West Ferry.

The twins, now eight months old, were able to sit up and take a lively interest in the proceedings. They were christened George and Michael – George, after my father-in-law, and Michael for no other reason except that we liked the name. After the service a luncheon party was held in the house, attended by a few relatives.

Towards the end of July, after Ron's mother and his sister Kate had offered to take care of the twins, Ron and I, delighted to have such a welcome break of a few days, set off in the car for a break. We first went to Edinburgh and spent the night there with my oldest friend, Maimie, who had been my bridesmaid and whom I had known since my first days in Scotland when we attended the same school. We went to the theatre together and spent the rest of the evening reminiscing about our early days. In the morning we left for Aberfoyle where we put up in a comfortable hotel and then we went on through the Trossachs to Loch Earn, Loch Tay, Aberfeldy, Perth and finally home. The weather was kind to us – warm and sunny. The Highlands were at their best. It was the time of the bell-heather, the first of the heathers to come into full bloom. Splashes of rich purple hues carpeted the brown mossy hills – a glorious sight. The beauty of the scenery, the peaceful relaxed atmosphere free from all chores made this short interlude the happiest part of our leave.

We were now into August. Although tension was mounting abroad no one in our immediate circle appeared to be aware of the advancing menace. Earlier, in July, there had been the reassurance to Poland of Britain's pledge but that event likewise did not seem to arouse undue concern. Life carried on as usual. People still went off for their vacations, the beaches of Broughty Ferry were packed with holidaymakers. Ron golfed with friends on leave from India and his father still enjoyed his off-day fishing in his favourite lochs. The housewives busied themselves with their daily tasks, made jam and talked about the quality of the berries. Every morning the twins, in their handsome pram, departed with Granny or sister Kate to the shops and favourite tea-room where they were shown off and much admired.

It was a warm pleasant spell that last summer of peace. It is my belief that the majority of people in Britain never expected a war and who could have blamed them? After all Mr Chamberlain and much of the Press had promised 'peace in our time'.

The first tremor of disquiet came with the startling news of the pact between Stalin and Hitler on 23 August – a strangely sinister alliance of two maniacs with opposing ideologies. On 1 September Hitler's armies invaded Poland. For Britain this meant the war was on her doorstep. Immediately there began a wholesale evacuation of children to the safer parts of the country. On the Saturday of 2 September, Ron's sister Kate, who taught at Albyn Girls School, Aberdeen, and who was still on holiday, received an urgent call from the headmistress to proceed to Aberdeen to assist in the evacuation of the boarders to Deeside. In this Kate was joined by another young teacher. The two girls, with Ron driving, set off for Aberdeen. The journey, normally of some three hours, was greatly extended as a result of dense fog. They eventually arrived in Aberdeen where Ron left his sister and friend to proceed with the painful task of the evacuation and turned for home. The mist, like a heavy white shroud, reduced his speed to a mere crawl. After a long and nerve-racking journey he reached Forfar. Leaving the town, Ron got out to check if he was on the right road to Dundee and finding that he was, turned back to the car. With that, out of the mist the dark shadow of a man loomed up and came towards him. 'Can you give me a lift to Dundee?' he asked. 'Get in,' Ron replied, only to be told, 'I have a bicycle with me.' Swallowing his displeasure at the needless delay, Ron lashed the bicycle to the luggage-carrier at the back of the car and the journey proceeded.

The man had a strange story to relate. It transpired that in the morning his little daughter had been evacuated with a group of children to Forfar to an unknown address. Immediately after the child left, his wife began to regret having allowed her to go and in the end demanded that he should get on his bike and bring her back. How he proposed to carry the child while riding a racing bicycle remained a mystery. The poor soul had searched throughout the town but was unable to find her. As he ruefully observed, 'Nae doot the wife will hae plenty to say when I return empty-handed.' During this enforced halt outside Forfar Ron had hoped that the cars following him would carry on, but instead they waited and allowed him to be their guiding light. It was a harrowing experience and a great relief to reach the suburbs of Dundee where he dropped his passenger and carried on to West Ferry.

It was well past midnight when Ron arrived at the house, white-faced and exhausted, to everybody's relief. He had never known or seen such a mist, he remarked when relating his experience. It was almost uncanny and made him wonder if the government had discovered a secret weapon to thwart the enemy!

During the forenoon of Sunday 3 September we gathered together in the lounge and stood listening to Mr Chamberlain's sombre announcement of the start of the war at eleven o'clock that morning. Memory has retained a lasting imprint of a solemn group of people – the grannies holding their grandchildren, my mother's resigned expression, the tear-stained face of Ron's aunt.

In the beginning of the week orders arrived from India for men on leave to return at once. All were collected, and, boarding one of the large P&O ships, set off for India. The wives meanwhile were left behind with the hope of joining later. This order was especially hard on those couples, who, like cousin Mae and Jim, had their leave cut a few weeks after their arrival.

We were singularly fortunate on account of having changed over to the round trip on the BI line, otherwise Ron would have had to join the other men on the P&O ship, involving a separation from his family for the duration of the war as I could not possibly have travelled with the twins being so young. As it was we were left alone to get on with our plans and in any case were due to leave on 9 September.

Only five days remained to the day of our departure; days of turmoil, anxiety and indecision as to whether I should travel with the children to India across submarine-infested waters or remain at home where there was no promise that it would be safer. In the end after a lot of heart-searching we decided that I should remain and be evacuated with the twins to some country place nearby.

We were acquainted with people who owned a cottage in one of the glens. On getting in touch with the owners Ron was informed the cottage was available and, if he cared to see it, there would be someone to show us round. We drove to the glen together with the twins and were duly met by an old man. The cottage was well furnished with bed-linen, china, cutlery, pots and pans. I did not notice, however, any taps in the kitchen and on inquiring was told, 'There are no taps in the house – you'll get the water from a pump outside.' Further inquiries revealed that there were no toilet facilities either. Thinking that perhaps there might be a discreet little hut that is often found close to a country cottage, I went outside. There was nothing to be seen.

'What do I do?' I asked him, with some apprehension.

'Ach, lassie,' he laughed, 'you just take a spade and dig a hole.'

'Dig a hole,' I echoed helplessly, by now quite shattered.

'It can be hard in the winter,' he admitted. 'We get snowed up at times for weeks on end. You have to keep a supply of food in case it does and a bucket or two of water if the pump freezes, but if the worst comes to the worst, you can get help from the hotel – it lies a field or two from here.' Sensing my dismay he added cheerfully, 'There's aye ways and means and it's real bonny here in the springtime wi' a' the wee lambs in the fields.'

Ron was most optimistic. ' I am sure you will manage, after all it would be safe here with the twins and you can always have your mother for company.'

I loved my mother, but at times she still imagined I was just a little girl, one to be instructed and corrected in the way I should go. Living together in such isolation was not conducive to the best of relationships. 'Why should my mother want to leave her flat and friends and have only me and some sheep for company?' I asked, by now in a black mood. There were more heated exchanges as we travelled back to West Ferry, but in the end I agreed there was nothing for it but to take the cottage and make the best of my stay here, in the hope that perhaps the war would soon be over.

As soon as we arrived at the house Ron phoned to inquire about the rent and finalise our agreement with the owners. I did not hear the full conversation but heard Ron's final answer: 'Thank you very much, but we do not think the cottage would be suitable after all.' An answer that made me almost leap for joy! It transpired that the previous modest rent had suddenly been increased tenfold, far beyond our pocket.

After further long discussions and with only three days left we decided that the twins and I would travel and we would face the future together and take what comes. During the last few days there was the usual organised chaos to have everything prepared in time. On a trip into town to confirm our booking and do some shopping, we met two memsahibs whose husbands were on their way to India. They were a bit put out on hearing that I was leaving with Ron and the twins, not realising that it was only by booking on the BI line that I was allowed to travel and thus happened to be the first woman to leave Dundee.

We left the ladies to collect our gas masks which we were told we had to take with us. Gas masks at the beginning of the war were issued only to adults. Ron, in case anything untoward happened, would allow the twins to be taken for only short walks in front of the house. The twins resented this short promenading, voicing their displeasure each time the pram turned at the end of the road. They missed their jaunt to the Ferry and the lick of ice-cream in their Granny's favourite tea-room.

A heavy curtain was hung over the door of the parlour with buckets of water placed beside it in case of fire. One day we heard the shrill wailing of the siren and rushed into the parlour expecting to hear the bombs dropping any minute. Nothing happened. It was only a practice.

On the eve of our departure I called on Mae. Her husband, Jim, prior to leaving so suddenly for India, spent some time instructing Mae how to drive a car, the idea being that Mae, in the event of any emergency, would get into the car and drive her daughter and mother-in-law to some safe haven. Where that might be was anyone's guess. As I was leaving she offered to drive me home saying that this would give her some practice. Although somewhat apprehensive I accepted her offer. Mae was a little woman who could hardly see over the steering wheel, but what she lacked in inches, she certainly made up for in confidence.

She began driving at a snail's pace which soon increased on a downhill road to the point where I was overcome by terror and wild excitement. She continued driving with the same panache through Broughty Ferry, with me by now resigned to my fate, until more by luck than good guidance we reached the house. 'That wasn't bad for my first solo drive,' she called over to me as she was leaving. Still trembling in every limb I watched her red head vanishing round the corner, driving with the same gay abandon, and prayed that she might arrive in one piece. She did.

The journey began in the late evening of 8 September. We drove through empty streets in pitch-darkness with not a chink of light in blacked-out windows or any brightness from the skies, as if the very moon and stars were hiding somewhere.

The station was likewise sunk in gloom. Only a handful of relatives arrived to see us off. My mother, her face white and drawn, came all by herself and stood a little apart, saying very little. Ron's father, who drove us to the station, was there as well as an aunt or two.

Sister Kate who had travelled from Aberdeen was later to recall the twins in their blue travelling bags and the feeling of sadness on seeing such young children embarking on a hazardous journey.

All doubts, endless discussions, were now behind us. We were reconciled to accepting whatever might lie ahead. At last the final goodbyes were over. The train began to move out of the station, soon to thunder over the Tay Bridge, on the first lap of our journey.

On arriving in London in the early morning a taxi took us to a small hotel where we booked in until it was time to leave for the boat-train. London was sweltering in a surprising heat-wave. The pavements were crowded with people going to work; girls in cotton dresses, men in short-sleeved shirts. As the room we booked, to be near the station, became uncomfortably hot, we undressed the twins and took them up to the flat roof of the hotel. Opposite were the windows of an office where a group of young people stood watching, waving and laughing, quite intrigued by the sight of us strolling up and down with the twins in our arms.

In the early afternoon we boarded the crowded boat-train and settled in corner seats, with a table between, on which the twins sat contentedly until we arrived at Tilbury.

The customs shed was packed with passengers, all waiting for the customs officer to examine their luggage. As the twins were due to be fed we wondered anxiously when our turn might come, but at this point heard the announcement that all those travelling with children were to be dealt with first. However, although waiting for some considerable time no one came near us, and by now, seeing all the passengers with children were out of the shed, Ron approached a customs officer and asked him if he would be so kind as to deal with us. The man appeared to take umbrage. He came over to the place where the porters had placed two heavy steel trunks one on top of the other. 'Take down that top trunk – I want to examine the one below,' he ordered in a dictatorial manner. Ron handed one of the twins over to me and proceeded to do as he was told.

As I stood holding the twins and watching Ron struggling with the trunk a very pleasant lady came up to me and in an attractive Italian accent said, 'Give me de baby.' Gratefully I passed over one of my heavy burdens. It turned out that this charming lady was the wife of Mr Falletti, the manager of the Taj Mahal Hotel in Bombay, who like ourselves were both returning to India.

The officer's unpleasant manner still continued. He demanded to examine every article in the lower trunk scattering all our carefully packed, harmless belongings. We could not understand this officiousness, described later by Ron as sheer bloody-mindedness. This little drama had been watched by an official from the Bank of England who was there to check the currency being taken out, and who came over to express his regret that he was not in a position to deal with such a display of malice, and added that had this officer been one of his staff he would have dismissed him on the spot.

We thanked Mrs Falletti, who had stood patiently holding our child for some considerable time and, with our luggage and pram all safely aboard the ship, we climbed up the gangway.

Our ship, the *Modasa*, was the sister ship of the *Mulbera* on which I had travelled two years earlier to India. We were fortunate to have a three-berth cabin with a window looking out on to the top deck. It was decided that I would use the bunk below the window, the twins the lower one opposite, with Ron on top.

Thankfully getting into the cabin we placed the twins on the top bunk and, as it was long past their feed time, hurriedly began to prepare their bottles but then to our horror, Michael, always the lively twin, took a dive off the bunk and landed on the floor before we could catch him. Fortunately, to our great relief, beyond a small lump on his forehead he was none the worse. Thus began our return journey to the East.

I have no recollection as to when exactly the ship sailed, but remember when I went out on deck the following morning being overwhelmed by the wondrous sight of the convoy – all the ships strung out in a long line with the Royal Navy like a faithful shepherd guarding his flock. We were crossing the Channel, the morning was bright with the foam-flecked waves sparkling in the sunshine. The grandeur of that scene, all these ships, proudly, serenely sailing in defiance of the unseen enemy and my own feeling of thankfulness that we were not alone, is still etched in my memory.

The *Modasa* was carrying a full complement of passengers. To accommodate late bookings in several cases husbands and wives had to travel in separate cabins. Many of the male passengers were asked to join in keeping a look-out for enemy submarines according to a roster compiled by the ship's captain. Ron was excused from this duty as it was considered he had enough to do looking after a wife and twins.

During the long journey we got to know many of the passengers, most of whom were from different parts of England. At our table, for six, was a young man going out to a tea plantation in Assam; a young woman with a small girl, on her way to join her husband in the civil service and a very pleasant lady called Ada with whom we became very friendly and who was travelling to Calcutta, where her husband was employed as an engineer. There was also a very elderly Anglo-Indian lady who rarely joined in any conversation. Sitting at the adjoining table was a very attractive young woman named Helen, of French extraction, engaged to be married to a judge in the ICS who was a Scot and, like Ron, educated at Dundee High School. Helen, along with Ada, formed our own special circle.

Our journey continued with nothing untoward happening, until one morning when I looked out on the great expanse of the Atlantic and saw to my dismay our escorts were no longer with us. We were abandoned – naked and alone. Later we were told that prior to leaving us the leader of the convoy transmitted a message to the captain which went as follows: 'If attacked don't give in, but turn tail and run!' According to my husband's estimation the speed of the *Modasa* could not have exceeded 10-12 knots flat out, therefore the chances of eluding a German submarine were slim. However, no one appeared to be unduly apprehensive. Soon we reached the safety of Gibraltar where another convoy was formed and we sailed for Malta.

In Malta we went ashore with the twins to purchase hats for them. The lady in the little hat shop was quite intrigued by the twins and their names of George and Michael. She informed us that there was an Order of St Michael and St George established in the beginning of the nineteenth century all of which was news to us.

After buying the hats we hired a Maltese picturesque carriage known as a 'carrozinni' and set off for the Governor's garden. There was a light breeze blowing which involved several stops to pick up the twins' hats, but eventually we arrived at the gates of the garden. We had fondly imagined that the little horse would take us through the garden and we would admire the trees and flowers from the comfort of the 'carrozinni', but it turned out that no carriages or horses were allowed inside. As we saw no joy in lugging around the twins it was decided to forego the pleasure of seeing the garden and to return the way we came. On the whole it was quite pleasant to have a tour through the old streets of Valletta. We admired the buildings, the fine churches and enjoyed the unusual sight of goats being milked on the pavement. It was a welcome break from the confinement of the ship. The following morning the *Modasa* left for Port Said.

It was the custom aboard the ship for the children's lunch to take place at midday. The twins were at that delightful stage when they opened their mouths wide, like hungry chicks in a nest, and allowed us to shuffle in great quantities of some revolting mixtures such as minced chicken mashed up with sauce and spinach. It was a sight that always delighted the head stewardess, a formidable lady, who disapproved of spoilt children screaming, 'Mummy, I don't like this – take it away,' and the despairing cry of the mother, 'Eat it or I shall beat you when I get you into the cabin.'

It was during one of these noisy interludes that, while seated beside the window, we observed one of the escorting ships throwing over from the stern strange objects followed by muffled sounds of explosions and great fountains leaping out of the sea. The stewards serving us panicked and, throwing their trays aside, rushed for the door. The head steward, a man who stood no nonsense, ran out of his adjoining cabin, where he was enjoying his lunch. Waving his napkin he lashed out at the men, barring their way and ordering them back to the dining saloon, an order they meekly obeyed. We were told that what we witnessed was only depth-charge practice – there were no submarines in the vicinity; a story that was contradicted later by one of the captains we met in Calcutta who had been on the ship and who assured us that the submarine was there and was dealt with by the destroyer.

A day or two later, while still in the Mediterranean, one of the male passengers, no doubt bored with the blackout aboard the ship, got gloriously drunk, switched on the light in his cabin and opened the porthole. Immediately a destroyer came rushing along, calling out, 'Put out that light, you bloody fool.'

With no more exciting episodes to enliven the monotony of the journey, we duly arrived in Port Said.

In Port Said the head stewardess kindly offered to take care of the twins while we went ashore one evening. She was, as I have already mentioned, a formidable lady who imposed strict discipline not only on her own staff but even on some of the female passengers when required. There was the instance when one night we were awakened by two little girls running up and down the passage, screaming for their mother who had left them for some amorous adventure. The stewardess soon winkled her out of her love nest and chased her back to the cabin, meanwhile expressing in no uncertain terms what she thought of the lady in question.

We were grateful for the chance to get off the hook for a little while. Prior to leaving we prepared the twins' bottles and showed the stewardess where she would find them should the children awake before our return. We left easy in our mind, knowing we were leaving our children in safe hands.

Our little group of Helen, Ada and some others departed for the Eastern Exchange Hotel where there would be music and dancing. Inside the hotel, ablaze with lights, the band was playing to a crowded floor. We succeeded in finding a table and settled down to watch the dancers and enjoy a few drinks. To our left sat a few attractive girls described as dancing partners. I was rather intrigued by the tactics of the hard-faced major-domo ordering the girls to approach various tables where they could entice some young men to dance with them and order up champagne. Beside us was a table where sat the solitary figure of a young man whose friends were on the dance floor. At this point one of the hostesses was ordered to come up to him. I watched with amazement the complete shamelessness of her approach, with one hand on her hip and beckoning with the other in a manner that left little for the imagination. The young man, bearded, with a saintly expression, who, from the red cross on his arms, I judged to be a hospital orderly, was acutely embarrassed by this public display of seduction. Suddenly he rose and for one moment I thought he was ensnared, but instead he came over to our table and asked if he could join us. With a disdainful toss of her head the enchantress retreated to her seat.

On returning to the ship and finding the twins still sound asleep, we decided to go up on deck for a little while. It was pleasant to relax. We sat at peace watching the mass of lights on the shore twinkling against the soft darkness of the night. After a few minutes, however, we felt we had to go down to the cabin to see if all was well.

A strange scene met our eyes. Our helpful friend, the stewardess, was standing swaying from side to side with a carafe in her hand. She was blind drunk, barely able to stand. 'I was just going to give them a little drink,' she began to explain in slurring tones as Ron removed the carafe before she had time to drop it on the sleeping twins. 'It was such a happy party – such a reunion,' she went on to tell us.

Out of her jumbled rambling we understood that the *Mulbera*, sister ship of the *Modasa*, had arrived in Port Said on her way to Britain. There had been a great reunion between some of the staff during which our friend got gloriously tight, but at the same time in her muddled head there was a vague thought that she had something to do, she wasn't quite sure what it was but decided that the twins might like a little drink of water. All our careful instructions were forgotten. We shuddered to think what might have happened if we had not arrived in time to snatch the carafe out of her hand.

With a gracious nod of her head our lady rolled out of the cabin. We didn't see her again until the following morning. She was her usual proud self. Not a word was said. It was as if the episode of the night before had never happened.

In fairness we had to admit that the stewardess, along with all the members of the crew from the Captain down, was suffering from an intolerable strain right from the moment we left London, for it has to be remembered that the *Modasa* was one of the ships that set off on a dangerous journey a mere nine days after war was declared.

We had one other outing prior to the ship leaving. The quarter-master, a friendly man from the Western Isles of Scotland, helped Ron to carry the pram on to the pontoon. With the twins wearing their little white hats from Malta we pushed them round the streets of Port Said, arousing curious glances from some of the passers-by.

It was a great relief to sail through the Suez Canal into the vastness of the Indian Ocean. We were alone, no longer in convoy, with only flying fish and dancing dolphins accompanying us. Rumours of lurking submarines abounded with the blackout continuing all the way to Calcutta.

By now most of the passengers were sick-tired of the voyage. Money was becoming scarce. We were solvent, but for some who spent a lot of time at the bar, never dreaming that the passage would drag on so long, there were problems. It was also noticed that certain people who were always seen together now tended to stay away from each other.

My special problem was the washing. The laundry man did up Ron's shirts and one or two of my dresses, but the nappy washing had to be done on the lower deck where the tubs were used by the Lascars for rinsing out their dishes. All traces of curry had to be removed before I could begin my task, an exercise that brought no joy to my heart.

Our endless chores kept us constantly occupied, but relief came from the adjoining cabin occupied by a tea planter and his wife. They had been at home on leave and had brought their ayah with them to take care of their little girl who was now left behind. The ayah returning with them was travelling as a lady of leisure. She was not exactly over-joyed when she was ordered by her employers to help us with the twins. We had her help for two hours daily and although the tea planter pointed out that the ayah was drawing her salary, the extra payment from us helped to smooth away any ill feeling she may have harboured. The respite of two hours was very welcome. We rested while the ayah strolled around with the pram. The twins had a naughty habit of throwing things out of the pram and watching their weak-minded parents picking them up. The ayah was made from sterner stuff. She merely ignored such capers and left Ron to gather all the toys, bunnies and teddies scattered over the deck.

There were the usual deck games which helped to pass the time. At night people gathered in the saloon where at times there was com-munity singing and on one occasion a Czechoslovakian gentleman, a Mr Pliva, the owner of a restaurant in Darjeeling, who, with his daughter, had escaped from Czechoslovakia, entertained us with very clever card tricks that kept us all guessing. Another day there was an able performance on deck by some talented passengers who sang and danced with great expertise all of which helped to break the monotony of a journey by now in the sixth week.

On arriving in lush Cochin a message awaited our friend Ada from her husband. Calcutta was rife with rumours of submarines prowling in the vicinity of India. He advised her to leave the ship and travel overland to Calcutta, advice she followed. There was a void in our small circle after her departure, but we didn't lose sight of Ada altogether as some weeks later we had a reunion in Calcutta.

There were other departures in Cochin. Our table emptied when the young tea planter and the silent Anglo-Indian lady left as well.

A few days later the *Modasa* was approaching Ceylon, now known as Sri Lanka. I stood watching the green shores drawing closer – my thoughts winging back to a school in a distant Arctic corner of the earth. I see myself again sitting beside my young classmates. It is a cold wintry day. A shaft of pale sunlight is filtering through the frosted panes. We are avidly listening to our talented teacher describing in glowing colours the island of Ceylon – a paradise of swaying palms, beautiful flowers, luscious fruits, rare birds, butterflies, exotic animals, where the sapphire seas are warm the whole year round. This paradise she tells us, pointing to the map, is curiously formed in the shape of a giant lemon.

Like my young friends I am enthralled by the vivid portrayal of this magic island, never dreaming that one day I would be there and tread those golden shores.

We spent three days in Colombo. Ron played golf and I in turn went ashore with Helen. We saw the wondrous Buddhist temple and later explored the shops. A shrewd-eyed gentleman tried to tempt us by a rich display of precious gems, but lacking the necessary knowledge and hard cash there was no option but to admire and walk on.

On the last evening, our group of friends decided to have a celebration in the Grand Oriental Hotel where we wined and dined in style. We talked of many things, our journey was drawing to a close. The following morning we bade farewell to Colombo, and set sail for Calcutta up the Bay of Bengal. We had been in transit for almost eight weeks, traversing dangerous waters, fraught with fear and anxiety, but at long last the end was in sight.

On 31 October 1939 – the day of our twins' first birthday – the *Modasa* sailed into the Hooghly. We saw once more the same familiar scenes. A fleet of crescent-styled fishing boats came sailing down on their way to the fishing grounds. We passed the Sundarbans, a tract of forest and swamps, the habitat of deadly snakes and tigers, and, further on, peaceful villages, mud huts and brickworks.

As we sailed on I was surprised to see a group of men in military uniforms, waving to us, and I recognised John Hebenton among them. Ron said they must be a detachment of the Bengal Artillery, the auxiliary force recruited from the men in the mills, to which he also belonged, taking part in coastal defence. It was an ominous reminder of how the war in Europe was affecting all parts of the Empire.

The first mill to appear on the right bank was Birla, then rounding the bend on the left bank was the county town of Ulubaria, followed by a succession of mills, and there it was. 'Ron,' I called, overcome by emotion, 'look, it's Lawrence – Lawrence at last.' I recognised the ladies in the compound waving over. The *Modasa*, by now, like a homing pigeon, was travelling full speed ahead. Mills, gardens, bazaars, bathing ghats appeared for a moment and vanished out of sight.

In Calcutta, Anwar, our agent, boarded the ship to deal with the luggage. He was a welcome sight but more welcome still was Jetty Ayah, standing behind him. Soon we were on the Budge-Budge Road passing the scenes we knew so well: the milling crowds in the bazaars; tea-houses; naked children; pi-dogs. The smells of India were back with us, some pleasant, some not so good. The serang met us with a welcoming smile – it was as if we had not been away. Another welcome was waiting at the jetty in Lawrence. There were warm embraces, kisses, the exchanging of news. Standing on the steps of the veranda was Sofi Khan, the cook and sweeper.

It was good to be back, but not everything was quite the same as it used to be. With India involved in the war there was a change in the air, which would increase as time went on. There would be a change also that would directly affect our lives. Meanwhile we unpacked our boxes and settled down to our old routine.

2
WARTIME CALCUTTA

We had arrived in time for the start of the cold weather, to the blossoming of the flowers in the garden, reunions with friends, trips to Calcutta. Christmas came followed by New Year and another gathering in Firpo's. There was dancing and singing of the current favourite song to the orchestra's accompaniment: 'We're gonna hang out the washing on the Siegfried Line, Have you any dirty washing mother dear?' Light-hearted optimism was in the air. Far away in Europe the phoney war continued. My mother wrote cheerful letters. 'The blackout is a nuisance, but my dear friend, Mrs Tullis, and I have decided to visit each other only when the moon is full.'

Meanwhile in Lawrence as the new year advanced Ron was faced with the problem of making a difficult decision. It concerned his position with the firm. Ron, who had worked for twelve years, was one of the senior keranis who came out in 1927. It was usual for a kerani after a period of a few years to be promoted to the head office, but now after some three terms, the door to the 'promised land' still remained closed. The reason for such a delay was simple. At the end of the First World War, the young men who joined the company as keranis, had had fairly rapid promotion to the head office and twenty years later were still a long way from retirement. That was understood and unavoidable, but recently there was a rumour, not without foundation, that the head office had decided that public schoolboys would be enrolled as keranis, given preference over the other keranis, such as Ron, and promoted to be head office assistant. This happened in some cases and proved to be a failure as the monotonous routine of jute mill life and long hours did not offer a very attractive mode of living and one in particular, who left to join the army after serving a short period as a junior salesman, made no attempt to return to India when the war was over.

One of Ron's friends had already been made an assistant manager, being the first kerani to be given such promotion, and Ron, though not the most senior kerani, was offered the chance to follow in his footsteps, as it was recognised that his fluency in Hindustani – he had passed the lower and higher exams in Urdu – enabled him to have good control and enjoy good relations with the workers in spite of a certain lack of practical experience in the mill. Faced with an unknown period of waiting to be promoted to the head office and with a wife and twin sons to keep on a meagre salary, Ron decided to change over to the production side and was duly promoted to be assistant manager in Kinnison jute mills.

In February 1940, at short notice to move to Kinnison, we hurriedly packed our boxes and took to the road. It was with some regret I said goodbye to the friends I had made in Lawrence during my first two years in India. Gwen and Jean came to the jetty to see us off as we boarded the launch for the opposite side where a taxi was waiting. The bearer and Jetty Ayah travelled with us, but the cook, with all his pots and pans, our heavy baggage and the twins' beds, came up the river.

After covering some forty miles we duly arrived in Kinnison and were directed to the married quarters – a tall, square building of four flats, similar to that of Lawrence. Our flat was on the upper floor. Below us lived two kerani sahibs and in the flat next to them resided the assistant manager, Bob Campbell, and his wife, Phil, whom I had met previously. The flat next to us was occupied by one of the two chief mill managers, Will Robertson, and his wife, Isa. Isa welcomed us warmly into her house where tea was served on the veranda. After a little while Ron went off with Sofi Khan to arrange some of our belongings leaving me to relax with Isa and the twins. As we sat talking the door leading on to the veranda opened and a young, attractive woman entered leading a flaxen-haired toddler. We were duly introduced to each other. Edie, as she was called, was the wife of Aikman Doig, the kerani in the adjoining Kelvin jute mill. The little boy, Alistair, was a few weeks older than the twins. During the days of their early childhood the three little boys used to play with each other until they had to leave India for their education in Scotland.

Kinnison, the largest mill in the group, appeared to have everything. Beside our married quarters to the left was a similar building housing four married couples. Further along was the mess khootie and facing it was a building, which on one side housed the offices of the chief mill managers, draughtsmen, chemist and cost accountants and on the other side of this building was the dispensary.

Between the mess khootie and the married quarters was a gate leading out into the main road, guarded by two durwans. From the gate was a road running the whole length of the compound on the right of which, overlooking the river, was a white semi-detached house named Rose Villa, where the senior salesman occupied the greater part and the junior salesman the smaller section.

On the left of the road, standing on an island, was an imposing two-storeyed house. The encircling water, resembling a moat, was crossed by two small road bridges and one footbridge. Known as the 'Jheel Khootie', or 'Island House', the surrounding gardens, complete with tennis courts, flanked by garages and servants' quarters, provided an attractive setting. The ground floor was the residence of the mill manager, Mr Lorimer, with his wife and daughter. On the floor above lived the other chief mill manager, Mr Peter Keddie, with his wife and two grown-up daughters.

There is a story that a visitor, leaving the island in an open two-seater car after a convivial evening, missed the bridge and landed in the water where he was thrown out over the windscreen and showered with all the loose tools as the boot opened behind him. He was none the worse, for as the old Scots saying goes, 'God looks after drunk men and bairns'.

At the end of the road was a gate with a durwan on guard. Behind this locked gate and high walls was a beautiful garden and a very unusual old circular house, aptly named the Beehive. Here lived Mr Montague Thomas, usually referred to as Monty, who was the head of the jute department. I very rarely saw Monty and even then could only catch a glimpse as he passed in his car *en route* to the Barrackpore Club. At times when strolling in the compound with the twins, the durwan would invite us in to see the little birds. I remember entering the forbidden garden and seeing, to my amazement, in front of the Beehive a marvellous aviary housing a great variety of birds. In this enormous cage, flitting about from perch to perch, were tiny birds like butterflies, parrots of every hue and size and many strange rare species, all happily congregated together, and all requiring their own special feeding. There was a young man engaged to take care of all the birds and the expense must have been prodigious, but this was Monty's great hobby, which as a wealthy bachelor no doubt he could afford.

On the day following our arrival Phil Campbell called and invited me to a tennis party. This gave me an opportunity of getting to know not only some of the ladies in the compound but also those from the surrounding district. Life took on a different style from what I had known before. There was always something going on – tennis parties, mahjong, trips into town and meeting other people.

Meanwhile, as we moved into the hot weather, the news from home caused grave anxiety. Holland and Belgium had fallen. What next, we wondered?

One afternoon in early June, Isa and I were on our way to Kelvin, where Edie was holding a mah-jong party, and as we passed the Campbells' door, Phil came out and in great distress told us that she had just heard the shattering news of the evacuation of the British Army from Dunkirk. France had fallen. The phoney war was over.

We continued on our way to Edie's house but none of us could concentrate on the game. Everybody had somebody back home and it was especially hard on those such as Phil and Isa whose young sons were left behind in the care of relatives. My cousin Mae was lucky. She had returned safely together with her daughter Pat. Unfortunately, now living forty miles apart we did not have the opportunity to meet as frequently as we did before our transfer.

As the days and months went by it became customary for Jetty Ayah to join the other ayahs to take the twins to the beautiful park in Barrackpore. Every afternoon a procession of ayahs and their charges could be seen wending their way through the adjoining bazaar. The older children walked, but the twins, being too little to toddle on the road, were pushed in the pram.

After some time, however, we noticed that Jetty appeared to prefer to remain inside the compound where she would stroll up and down the main road, or in front of the house, an exercise not favoured by the twins who by now enjoyed meeting other children. On being asked as to why this change was taking place, there were only a few evasive replies from Jetty.

At this point Sofi Khan, who still fought for supremacy in the household, was soon able to enlighten us. The reason was simple. Ayah was terrified to leave the compound as standing outside the gate, armed with his *kukri*, was her husband waiting to deal with her. On being questioned by Ron the man admitted that he was all set to cut off his wife's nose for her infidelity – a common punishment for erring wives. Ayah had a lover, but it wasn't her unfaithfulness that grieved her husband as much as the fact that she wasn't sending him any more money which meant hardship for him and the children. The money, he was certain, was being handed over to her lover. Who was the lover, we wondered? Sofi Khan provided further enlightenment. It was Abdul, our young cook; astonishing as this revelation was, Jetty being old enough to be Abdul's granny, I was reminded of the Russian saying, 'Age is no barrier to love' and was prepared to overlook her amorous nature, but the real and dangerous possibility of Jetty's infuriated husband attacking her in the presence of the twins could not be comtemplated.

This was not the end of the affair. Jetty, knowing who had exposed her, was determined on revenge. The bearer, she informed me, never boiled the drinking water, as was his duty, but merely filled the bottles straight from the tap. Ron, on hearing our voices, came out of the bedroom, where he was dressing a painful boil on his arm and had removed his shirt in the process. Ayah, full of triumphant glee, repeated her story. Poor, silly, Jetty did not realise this was her own undoing.

'And where was your conscience,' Ron exclaimed in anger, 'giving that water to the babas, knowing it wasn't boiled?'

Ayah was cornered. Like an infuriated wildcat she turned on Ron. 'A fine story I'll be telling in the bazaar about the naked chota burra sahib attacking a helpless woman.'

That was the end of Jetty Ayah, but not the final scene, for shortly after Abdul appeared and gave us notice.

'Why are you leaving, Abdul?' I pleaded.

'I love Jetty and cannot live without her,' was his reply.

I lost my good cook and never had another like him.

There was an ironic twist to this sorry tale. Lily, one of the ladies in Lawrence, had had a baby and was only too pleased to engage a competent ayah and an excellent cook.

My second ayah was a young Khasi girl from the Khasi hills in Assam. She wore a full snow-white skirt with a close-fitting blouse to match and frequently had flowers tucked into the heavy plait wound round her pretty head. Buxom and attractive, she was a jovial, friendly lass. I thought I was quite lucky to find such a treasure. Unfortunately, instead of living in the compound she always went at night back to Barrackpore where her mother lived and was usually late in arriving in the mornings. Also, on receiving her pay she was given to vanishing for a day or more which caused great inconvenience. There was a bold streak in her make-up which I did not find very endearing. On one occasion, when caught in torrential rain, she returned to the house and with her wet clothing clinging to her skin displaying every curve of her well-endowed, voluptuous figure, strutted in front of Ron in a rather fetching manner saying, 'Dekko, sahib, Dekko'. I said to myself, 'Enough is enough, the time has come for us to part!' Part we did and that was just as well for it transpired that her mother kept a brothel in Barrackpore ably assisted by her daughter.

My third and last ayah came from Calcutta. She was a young pleasant girl who settled in her quarters in the compound, but there again all was not well. I think she missed the bright lights of Calcutta, looking sad and constantly complaining of feeling ill, at times not turning up for work, forcing me to cancel some engagement. However, overall we got along quite well. She remained with us until the twins were older and a young boy was engaged who proved to be the best of the lot.

Like many another woman who sets foot in India for the first time I knew very little about the various aspects of life there nor of the deep divisions in the social structure of the resident Europeans. Enlightenment came later and with it the realisation that the whole system of governing that mighty land followed a certain pattern. I saw it like some high ladder stretching away to the skies at the top of which was the heaven-born ruling body of the ICS (Indian Civil Service), followed by the army – guardians of the realm. Far down this social ladder were the box wallahs, the businessmen, Indian and European, residing in Calcutta, that great metropolis and centre of trade and commerce.

Sometime, somewhere, I have read that the derogatory description of box wallahs began far back in the nineteenth century, when an enterprising lady in Calcutta created garments for women and children and then sent them off in boxes to the various out-stations to which the members of the ICS were posted.

Although not fully acquainted with the history of the British Raj I have several accounts of their lives and work in India by retired members of the ICS and the army. In some of the reminiscences there is a contemptuous attitude towards the box wallahs involved in trade and commerce, an attitude I could not understand as after all the first foothold in India began with the East India Company. It is my belief that great as were the achievements of the ICS and the army, trade and commerce also gave an equal measure of themselves to India and if it had not been for the box wallahs in Calcutta and the great industrial forces, from the men at the top to the most junior assistants sweating in the mills, the jewel in the crown would not have been so bright.

In Calcutta itself there were also divisions. Snobbery, precedence and protocol flourished. People with similar professions and backgrounds tended to stick together. The Indians also clung to their own kind. The Marwarris from Rajasthan, for instance, never mixed with the Bengalis. For some reason certain Europeans in Calcutta imagined that they resided on a higher plane that those who lived in the compounds at the mills, which was quite ridiculous as not many came out of the top drawer.

As for the Indians, I do not think we ever really got to know them. The caste system was quite complex and many of the deeply rooted customs were unknown to us. The greatest barrier to having a closer acquaintanceship was that the wives very rarely came along with their husbands to social meetings.

With the seasons of heat and rain over we were into sticky September, a time when out of the steaming earth surfaced all kinds of repellent creatures, large hard-backed cockroaches, thankfully rarer than the equally repulsive cockroaches seen scurrying across the floor of the bottle khana when the lights went on. There was also always the hidden menace of ants. The legs of all tables and furniture where food was kept had to be placed inside metal containers filled with phenyl and if allowed to dry up an army, a million strong, would arrive from nowhere to climb up and devour anything that might have been left on the table.

Meanwhile far back at home a battle was raging in the skies. People were glued to their radios anxiously listening, passing the latest news to each other. The whole world was holding its breath watching this life-and-death contest and to us, so far away, the announcement that the 'few' had in the end defeated the might of Goering's Luftwaffe and won the Battle of Britain brought pride and great rejoicing. Yet, we knew the price was high. 'The battle has been won,' wrote my mother, 'but my neighbours are desolate, their only son Jimmy is missing, pre-sumed to be lost.'

Life went on, and on 31 October the twins celebrated their second birthday. Some ten children arrived from neighbouring compounds, carrying gifts. From down the river arrived Mae with her young daughter to join in what turned out to be a lively party, much enjoyed by all, although the older boys in their excitement became mischievous and had to be contained. The ayahs likewise had a field day finishing off all the cakes and sweet dishes while Mae and I took care of the children.

With the arrival of the cold weather in November everything took on a new lease of life. Parties were being held up and down the river by groups of people entertaining their special friends. I also in my turn gave a party. It began in the early afternoon with tennis and tea served on the lawn. About a dozen friends arrived, including Edie and Aikman, our neighbours Phil and Bob, Isa and Will. There was also Edith Penny and her husband David. Edith I had known from the time of my early days in Scotland and we were now renewing our friendship.

In those days, friends living long distances away usually arrived for the weekend carrying tennis rackets, golf clubs and at times bringing their bearers as well, but on that occasion most of my friends came from neighbouring compounds with only Jimmy Mechan and George Stevenson travelling a good distance and spending the night with Jimmy Stewart, now living in Rose Villa in the compound. It was perfect weather with tennis continuing after tea until the short Indian twilight stopped play. Everybody left for their respective homes to have a bath, change and return later.

In the house preparations for the cold buffet got under way. At this point I was once more reminded of the loss of my treasured Abdul. With what ease he would have prepared a wonderful table and done me proud. My new cook, Akloo Khan, was a plain good cook, but lacking imagination and deadly slow. I suffered him for the whole of my sojourn in India. Hating to dismiss anyone, I would at times, exasperated beyond endurance, entreat him to find employment elsewhere, only to be asked at the end of my tirade, 'What does the memsahib desire for her khana (dinner) tonight?' He pleased Ron during my absence at home and that perhaps was more important than anything else.

The buffet that night, prepared under my supervision, as well as a lot of hard work and a dish or two from Firpo's, made a presentable appearance. The party was a success and lasted well into the small hours of the morning.

Soon Christmas came round with lots of presents for the twins and one or two 'dollies' for us. Because so many senior people lived in the compound there was a steady procession of cars bearing gifts, which I must admit aroused a little envy in our breasts. The gates of Monty's garden, however, were firmly closed with a durwan on guard. Christmas or not, no one bringing baksheesh was ever allowed to enter the holy precincts of the Beehive. Monty, a man of high principles, never accepted gifts.

I have found, like many others, that there are certain years associated with unusual events or scenes, for ever clearly etched in memory. Such was the year of 1941.

One Saturday in early January Ron and George went off to Barrackpore for a round of golf at the end of which it was decided that they would pick me up and we would drive to George's house in Kankanarrah where we would dine before returning home. On arriving we received the usual tremendous welcome from Pik who obviously had never forgotten his stay with us. The evening was spent quietly with Pik sitting on my lap, enjoying being petted and having his ears scratched. During the course of our conversation, George casually remarked that Pik had been off colour for a few days. To my anxious, 'I hope it's not rabies?' he hastily assured me that Pik had been examined by the vet who told him that beyond a slight chill there were no dangerous symptoms of anything else. We continued talking and in the late evening set off for home.

The following day, Sunday, was spent playing and strolling with the children. In the evening Jimmy Stewart called and after a peg or two returned to his house.

On Monday, during the forenoon, George phoned unexpectedly. He had an urgent message for us. Pik had developed rabies and was already put down, which meant that we had to leave immediately for the Pasteur Institute in Calcutta to receive the usual anti-rabic injection. On arriving at the Pasteur Institute and while talking to Major Nicols, in charge there, I tentatively inquired if it was really necessary for me to have these injections as I had only stroked the back of Pik's head and had not been in contact with his saliva. 'Give me your hand,' the Major asked and after a close examination pointed to a minute hang-nail on one of my fingers. 'That', he said, 'is quite sufficient to infect you with rabies.'

Ron, who had also been playing with Pik, was now forced for the second time in his life to undergo this painful treatment. Fortunately, it was only the half dose which consisted of seven injections. Our Dr Ghose in Kinnison administered the treatment by calling each morning at the house and giving the injection in the hip, which although painful was not as bad as Ron's previous experience when they were given in the stomach. We suffered no after-effects, but swore, there and then, that as long as the twins were in India we would never keep any dog.

Ever since the day when Stalin and Hitler signed their non-aggression pact, I had nursed the fear that Russia might join Germany in the war against Britain. At times, on hearing someone remark, 'On which side will the bear jump?' my fears would be confirmed, although I remained silent. There was also another reason for anxiety. After the death of my father and grandmother a desultory correspondence continued with the few remaining relatives. The last letter I received was in the spring of 1935. My uncle, five years my senior and more like an older brother, wrote asking me to send on some leaflets or a booklet regarding the breeding of silver foxes, with which he was concerned on behalf of the Soviet Government. He had also reminded me how in days gone by we used to travel together by horse and sledge to school and finished up by saying, 'I'm sure we'll meet again and when we do we'll celebrate and split a bottle of champagne!'

I sent some leaflets and a letter but received no answer. I wrote again and still there was this silence and from the other members of the family as well. In 1937 I left for India. In 1939 when home on leave some information might have been gleaned from Finland where some relatives lived, but Finland, being involved in the war with Russia, was also cut off.

We were now in late June 1941. One evening, full of dark thoughts and forebodings, I went out on to the veranda and leaning on the railing stood gazing across the compound. The monsoon had begun shrouding all the houses and garden in a heavy mist. There was no moon, not a gleam of a single star and not a sound to be heard – a silence suddenly broken by the arrival of the Campbells' car. Phil got out and having caught sight of me called out in great excitement, 'What do you know? Germany has invaded Russia!' So that was that – Russia was now our ally.

Perhaps I might be allowed to digress a little to repeat the words of an eyewitness of the invasion. My cousin, Olga, the youngest member of our family, after incredible adventures and hardships, had in the end succeeded in escaping from Russia and Germany to settle in the United States, from where she came to visit me in Scotland, sixty years after my own departure from Russia when she was just an infant.

'I was living in Ukraine,' she recalled, 'with my mother and young stepsister in the cottage of my stepgrandmother. My stepfather had been executed three years ealier. Life was hard, but we grew our own vegetables, potatoes, fruit, kept hens and somehow managed to exist.

'On that morning in late June we heard a great commotion and noticed soldiers rushing past the cottage. They were our soldiers, masses of them, hurrying and stumbling on the road. "Why are you running so?" my mother asked them. "Who are you running from?" "We are not running from anyone," a young soldier said. "We have to hurry to make room for our other regiment coming up behind us." My mother thought that was a strange thing to say, but, sure enough, soon the other soldiers appeared. They were also hurrying with tanks and guns, but they were dressed in green uniforms and spoke in German. My mother was terrified and put my little sister and me in the cellar below the floor. An officer came to our door and ordered mother to hand over our chickens. My stepgrandmother, who could speak in German, said to him, "Why are you doing this to us? We are poor and helpless women." He immediately became more polite and said, "Just give us what you can spare." We gave him a couple of hens. He thanked us and did not ask for more.

'My sister and I came up from the cellar and I sat down at the table. I felt very sad and could not speak. "Why are you crying, Fräulein?"

he asked me. I did not answer. I knew only that now there was more suffering for Russia.

'The following day that regiment left and other soldiers arrived. They rushed straight into our garden and removed all the hens, chickens, everything. "Your other soldiers treated us better," Granny told them. "But we are different," the soldiers replied, and continued robbing us. We lost everything and had a terrible time,' Olga concluded.

The old stepgrandmother died during the occupation and when the Germans in turn were retreating they took Olga, her sister and mother with them. Her mother and her sister were eventually sent back to Russia, but Olga miraculously succeeded in getting away, this time from the invading Russians, and after more hardships finally reached the United States.

Russia's entry into the war brought great relief all round. Britain was no longer alone standing up to the might of Hitler's army. It was also a boost to my morale as well, as shortly after our arrival back in India there was an order issued that all those of foreign origin and not our allies had to report to the authorities in Calcutta. This included me in spite of the fact that I had a Scots mother and was a British subject by marriage.

I found myself standing in a queue behind a lot of strange people from the Middle East, including an old sage from Baghdad who could not speak a word of English and very little Hindustani. Now with Russia on our side things became different for me.

A few days after this momentous turn of events, we had occasion to be in Firpo's where we were joined by George and a mutual acquaintance.

'So, Mrs Fraser,' he said to me, 'your country is in the war as well. It is a break for us, but I doubt if it will last very long. The Germans will go through Russia like a dose of salts and celebrate Christmas in Moscow.'

'Never,' I rejoined, with some asperity. 'Remember Napoleon; Russia will swallow Germany in the same way.'

After a further argument in the same vein we agreed to lay a bet on it. 'Anything you like,' I offered rather bravely.

'I'll be kind to you and make it ten rupees,' he said, and I agreed.

The incident was soon forgotten but a long time after we met again and he without referring to the matter placed Rs 10 on the table.

Meanwhile the daily routine of our life continued with occasional ups-and-downs.

Our ayah, tiring of life in the mofussil, left for Calcutta. To my rescue came an offer from one of the ladies in the adjoining compound. She warmly recommended a young boy who had been employed taking care of her son, but was not required any longer as her son was leaving for his education in Darjeeling. Pir Mahomed, a seventeen-year-old youth, turned out to be an excellent servant, tidy, honest and completely devoted to the twins. He was better than any ayah that I had had, for they were given to sitting around and keeping their charges close beside them. Pir Mahomed played with the boys and the favourite ploy was the game with kites. Indian boys are experts with kites. There were amazing and exciting battles between the kites flown from 'unseen' enemies in the bazaars or wherever, and our side, which were invariably won through the expertise of Pir Mahomed who knew how to rub the string of the opposing kite until it broke and the trophy would be seen tumbling down into the compound to the delight of the victors.

I never at any time had any reason to find fault with Pir Mahomed. He stayed with us for the next few years, until the sad and tearful day when the boys had to leave for their schooling in Scotland.

There was another break in the household. Sofi Khan, who was supposed to be on leave for a month, did not return when expected and at the end of a second month there was still no sign of him. The bearer engaged temporarily, Shamsher Ali Khan, was an energetic and a capable man. For some time Sofi Khan and I had not been on the best of terms. He was at all times a man's bearer who saw no reason why he should be burdened with other chores for the memsahib. When he eventually appeared some six weeks overdue I, in a moment of pique, dismissed him, and although Shamsher Ali Khan was an excellent bearer and remained with us for the rest of our time in India, there were moments when I felt a certain regret over my action. With hindsight, perhaps I did not have sufficient tolerance at that time to deal with Indian servants; this was gradually acquired as time went on.

Now that we did not have to cross the river we travelled more frequently to Calcutta and occasionally took the twins with us.

Calcutta has often been described in derogatory terms, not all of which are justified. At one time the capital of India, it was the capital of Bengal. There were many places of interest to see, old buildings with historical backgrounds, the Victoria Memorial which, although referred to as a white elephant, drew masses of people. A special attraction to Indians and Europeans alike were the Botanical Gardens, situated across the Hooghly at Sibpur and founded in 1786. Jim Dakers, Mae's husband, one day organised a trip on a launch which took us to the gardens. Our party consisted of Mae, Pat, the twins and

I. The trip itself was a lot of fun as we sailed between the banks of the Hooghly seeing all the sights and enjoying a picnic aboard the launch. The Botanical Gardens are very popular with Indians who are especially fond of trees. Crowds were strolling around admiring rare specimens of trees, plants and flowers. Of particular interest was the Great Banyan Tree, 220 years old, which stands 88 ft high and covers a circumference of 1,200 ft.

Another day there was a visit to the Calcutta zoo. As far as zoos go it cannot be compared with others in cooler climes. Tigers, leopards and other tropical animals thrived. The monkeys amused the twins but the white polar bears aroused compassion when watching them sitting around listlessly, languishing in the heat.

The calendar in India was punctuated by all the various festivals both Hindu and Muhammadan, but mostly Hindu. The Durga Puja held in September/October was especially popular in Bengal. On a stage set in the adjoining bazaar the goddess Durga – the universal mother – presided with her consort Shiva and son Ganesh, the boy with the elephant head who always held a fascination for us although Hinduism with all the accompanying legends, gods and goddesses was something very few Europeans knew anything about. Ron, as a gesture, occasionally attended the festivities in the bazaar. The ever-popular Diwali, Festival of Light, bringing joy and enchantment, usually arrived at the start of the cold weather.

It was shortly after the Diwali we received a cheerful letter from Ron's brother, who was an officer with the Royal Artillery in Singapore. George, a chartered accountant with the Anglo-Iranian Oil Company, at the outbreak of war had flown home to take up a commission with the Royal Artillery, having been an officer with the Garrison Artillery, in Broughty Ferry, prior to his departure for Iran. After the initial training his regiment was posted to Singapore.

In December just as the preparations for Christmas were under way, came the news of Japan's attack on the American Fleet in Pearl Harbor, followed by the tragic announcement of the sinking of HMS *Repulse* and *Prince of Wales* all of which cast a gloomy shadow over the festive season. With the start of the New Year word reached us of further disasters. The victorious Japanese marched through the whole of Malaysia and by 14 February 1942, Singapore fell as well. The war in the East was drawing closer to our own doorstep.

Immediately all kinds of activities sprang into life. One of the most important was the Lady Mary Herbert Fund named after the wife of the Governor of Bengal. Money was raised by various functions, dances, concerts, mah-jong drives, lotteries, sales and whatever.

In our district many of the women, including me, attended lectures organised by the St John's Ambulance Corps. Later we were examined by the Military Doctor. Like all those who passed I was very pleased to receive my certificate.

A Soldiers' Club was formed in one of the old houses in Barrackpore. Groups of some six and more ladies from the various compounds attended in turn each night for voluntary work there. Tea and cool lime drinks were provided free and for a few annas; sandwiches, cookies, fish and chips were offered to the men. It was quite hard work for us especially during the hot season, but much appreciated by the soldiers who flocked to the club in large numbers.

Earlier in the year, before the débâcle in Singapore, an English regiment arrived. The men were put up in tents on the Barrackpore Golf Course. The following day when walking past, Ron and I stopped to speak to two of the boys. They had almost been eaten alive by mosquitoes – their poor legs were inflamed and covered by blisters. We invited them to come along to our house, which they did and were exceedingly grateful for the hot bath, a good meal and having their legs dressed. We did not see them again as they had all left for what turned out to be Singapore where they arrived in time for the fall of the town and the humiliating surrender to the Japanese.

From that time on we made a point of inviting two soldiers every week for dinner. One of the boys came from Dundee and perhaps may still remember us. In the compound the ladies also got together and once a month invited a group of soldiers, who, after being shown round the mill, enjoyed a tea party accompanied by home-made scones and cakes.

Not the least important was the newly formed contingent of women willing to fight the enemy if need be. I do not know whose mighty brain produced this child and named it the Bengal Ladies' Artillery but a large number of women responded to the call with great enthusiasm – and I was one of them. We were measured for khaki trousers and shirts to match and ordered to wear topis which was not in accordance with the Military Doctor who in his lectures told us that topis were no longer necessary as there was no such thing as sunstroke, but heatstroke, a statement soon to be confirmed with the arrival of the American soldiers who wore no topis.

Twice-weekly transport was provided by the military to take us to and from the parade ground in Barrackpore. A young and rather bold sergeant-major taught us drill and wasn't sparing in his comments on our behaviour and deportment. We had to learn how to use a rifle. The Lewis gun also came into the picture and there it wasn't just sufficient to know the usage, but to be able to dismantle and reassemble it within a given time. Not being mechanically minded I was astonished at the ability so many of the girls possessed and with what amazing speed each piece was named as it was being placed in proper order. There was no hope for my competing with such efficiency, but I did redeem myself a little on the range where by some miracle I was lucky enough to score a higher count than most of them.

Meanwhile there was the tragic throng of refugees arriving in Calcutta. They had walked across the slippery roads and hills of Burma, stumbling, falling and dying on the way until they reached the safety of Assam where the tea planters welcomed and helped them in every possible way. In Calcutta there was not a day that we did not read in the *Statesman* the sad announcement of the death of some loved person – a child, a mother or a grandmother – who had died during that terrible trek which claimed the lives of hundreds of thousands of civilians.

In a lighter vein was the arrival of American troops who were now our allies. I was reminded of how twenty-four years earlier, when the Americans came to fight the Bolsheviks, I used to see them strolling on the streets of Archangel and how intrigued I was by the tabs on their shoulders depicting a polar bear or a white star and now here they were in tropical India – perhaps even some of them the sons of those who had fought in the Arctic regions of Russia. These American soldiers with their easy, unconventional ways gradually began to change the face of Calcutta. They were better equipped and higher paid than our soldiers. They called one evening at our Soldiers' Club. They were friendly and warmly welcomed but never came back. 'Uncle Sam' provided far better clubs and canteens.

There was also a small contingent of American girls, described as 'hostesses', whose duties consisted of writing letters on behalf of the boys and assisting them in many ways. The girls, pleasant and attractive, wore beautiful sky-blue uniforms arousing our admiration. Being in the officer class they were allowed to join the Calcutta Swimming Club where it was noticed that their ways were also a bit unconventional. At the back of the swimming pools, in the women's section, there was a long row of cubicles at the end of which was a large room containing wash-hand basins and several toilets. It was the custom for the ladies, when necessary, to attend the toilets and wash-hand basins prior to changing into a bathing suit in the privacy of the cubicle. The 'hostesses' reversed the process by undressing in the cubicle and walking completely in the nude to the toilets and then strolling casually back to slip on their bathing suit. This rather saucy practice, which my granny would have described as brazen, horrified the Indian women attendants who, like all their Indian sisters, were known to be very modest and even when bathing in the river never exposed their bodies. I was a bit surprised myself as were the twins who being young were allowed in the part reserved for ladies, but not too young as not to notice and express their astonishment at the 'shame, shame aunties'.

Many changes took place during that momentous year of 1942, and one of them took place in Kinnison as well. Monty Thomas decided to retire and went to live in Ootacamund. The aviary was dismantled and no one knew what happened to all these rare and beautiful birds. The Beehive was now taken over by the British anti-aircraft battery consisting of a few men and one or two officers.

Between all these various events the days seemed to slip by unnoticed. We were now in the midst of our third hot season. In normal circumstances we would have been planning for our home leave due to take place the following year. The war changed everything. No one went on leave, but a certain allowance was provided for those who wished to take a break of a few weeks in the hill stations of India.

I had often read about the annual migration to the hills of all the women and children at the start of the hot season, but that applied only to the families connected with the Civil Service and not to our community who remained on the torrid plains through all seasons until the long-awaited leave came round once more. I will not deny being somewhat envious as I read the passages describing the joyful exodus of these lucky people to the snow-capped mountains of such majestic places as Darjeeling, Naini Tal and Simla. Simla, especially, held some kind of magic for me and a longing to taste the delight of being there, if only once.

The war, however, gave us the opportunity of seeing a little bit of India. After a great deal of discussion we decided on Darjeeling as it was within easy reach of Calcutta. We planned to leave in early October and booked into Windermere Hotel for four weeks. In this we were joined by our friends, Edith and David Penny.

On the appointed evening we set off for Sealdah station and boarded the train for Darjeeling. The Pennys travelled in the adjoining compartment. The following morning after an uneventful journey we arrived in Siliguri. A delightful cool freshness welcomed us, as we stepped out of the train, a great relief from the steaming heat of Calcutta. After relaxing while having breakfast in the adjoining restaurant the journey continued with each party travelling by car.

Memory does not recall much of that drive, of an hour or more, except the constant zigzagging over a hazardous road, full of hairpin bends at times drawing close to the edge of a frightening void. From the car could be seen the toy train winding its way, clinging to the face of the mountain, at times vanishing out of sight, only to appear again – always climbing higher and higher.

In Darjeeling, a sturdy Nepalese woman removed our luggage and placing the heavy trunk on her back, supported by a leather strap across her forehead, proceeded to climb up the path leading to the hotel. Her husband, with an air of authority, led the way, carrying some of the lighter items of our baggage.

We were shown into a spacious, comfortable room. Our friends the Pennys were accommodated a few doors along from us. The whole of the running of the Windermere Hotel was in the capable hands of the owner – a lady, whose name after many decades, has escaped my memory. Everything was perfect – the food, the accommodation, and the situation of the hotel itself on the Observatory Hill. The hotel was filled with visitors like ourselves on holiday and also two or three women, the wives of the men employed by the Burmah Oil Company who had sent their wives and children to Darjeeling to be away from the danger of the Japanese invasion.

Our first objective was to find an ayah and we counted ourselves lucky when an elderly Nepalese woman brought in her young daughter. She turned out to be modest and efficient and also unusually attractive with her soft, long hair worn in a thick dark pleat, rosy cheeks and a dazzling smile. Her mother, however, kept a watchful eye on her daughter and appealed to Ron to escort her to and from the Gymkhana Club where we sometimes foregathered in the early evening. There were a lot of soldiers on holiday in Darjeeling who on meeting our pretty, eye-catching ayah gave the proverbial wolf whistle, but were not even rewarded with a smile. Both her parents, at the end of each day, never failed to call at the hotel to escort their daughter home.

A day or two after we settled in, Edie and Aikman also arrived in Darjeeling with Alistair. Every day, the three boys went out riding on their ponies with their respective ayahs walking beside them. We all used to meet in the Gymkhana Club where drinks were served and where we talked, laughed and danced to an orchestra playing the current favourites.

Darjeeling was lovely. The air was cool and crisp and there was this special atmosphere, difficult to define, but never forgotten. In the gardens of many fine houses, flowers grew in great profusion especially the large-headed, sky-blue hydrangeas, spilling over walls and never seen in the burning plains of India.

A path from the hotel led to the highest point of the Observatory Hill. Seen from there, across the wide sweep of the valleys, nestling houses, tea gardens, is the unrivalled splendour of the snow-capped Himalayas and in their midst the towering twin peaks of Kinchinjunga – majestic, awesome, giving rise to the thought that perhaps there is something in the belief that, in these shrouded heights, stands the throne of a powerful God, unseen by mortal eyes. Flanking the path were many rare and beautiful trees. Below one of them, perhaps a special pine, were found sweet-tasting kernels which I had not seen since childhood and which the twins and I gathered in handfuls.

On the Chaurastha, the main street of Darjeeling, there was a popular café owned by Mr Pliva – the gentleman who had travelled with us on the *Modasa* accompanied by his daughter. We often went there to enjoy a cup of coffee and his delicious cakes.

On the lower levels of Darjeeling were houses, shops and a busy bazaar which offered a great variety of goods. It was a very interesting and lively part of the town where we enjoyed wandering about.

At other times we used to sit outside the hotel drinking coffee, while the children in the hotel played together. The gardener, always working with his flowers, had a tray laid out beside us with the heads of the flowers drying in the sun. Amongst them, to my delight, were the large heads of sunflowers full of large juicy seeds. The poor man was not aware that sitting close by was someone who liked nothing better than to devour these seeds with the lightning speed of a parrot. Nibbling sunflower seeds is a favourite ploy with Russian peasants and I, although not encouraged by my elders, delighted in it during my childhood and many a time spent a single kopeck for a cupful of seeds which I would nibble in some quiet corner. Those that I found were polished off with the same old expertise to the astonishment of my friends, but the following day I found the same tray spirited away into a little sun porch with the door firmly locked.

What we enjoyed most of all was riding on the ponies. A group of Nepalis standing with their horses were always eager to let them out for hire. The twins and their ayah went out every day leisurely trotting in the vicinity, but we enjoyed riding further afield exploring the countryside.

Although during my childhood I was brought up with horses, I had not done any riding as in our parts horses were used for pulling sledges in the winter and carriages in the summer. We loved our horses and were heartbroken when two of them were taken away to the war and not seen again.

I enjoyed immensely riding in the beautiful surroundings of Darjeeling and imagined that I had some kind of affinity with horses. One day, however, through lack of knowledge, I suffered a frightening experience. On that day we had decided with the Pennys to ride out to Ghum, a village some five miles out of Darjeeling. I had been riding a horse which was not given to moving any faster than it wanted and I asked the Nepali owner to give me something a little livelier. He smiled and produced a horse named Flying Faun. It certainly was a beauty and decorated by a silver disc on its forehead. We all set off on the road to Ghum with Ron alongside riding on an easy-going pony called Slingsinghi. It was all very pleasant, until suddenly and for no reason my Flying Faun took off at tremendous speed, leaving the others far behind me. I could do nothing, the horse refused to obey me; there was no option but to hold on and hope for the best. Far below I could see a Tibetan cemetery and prayed that this was not an omen. Ahead were two young girls galloping at full speed. As I made up on them they called out, 'Please stop. Our horses think they are racing.' 'So does mine,' I called back in despair as I overtook them. We were now approaching Ghum. At this point, to my great relief, Flying Faun decided on a more leisurely style, probably because of the steep path leading to the village. In Ghum while waiting for the others I came off to have a closer inspection of the horse. 'What took you?' I asked, stroking it affectionately. I had the feeling that Flying Faun was laughing at me. My friends with Ron arrived on the scene. They had been terrified, expecting the worst, and were relieved to see that I was still in one piece. We rode slowly through the village, prior to turning into the lower road on our way back. For a mile or so all went fine, but then, perhaps impatient with the slow pace of the other horses, Flying Faun took off once more with the speed of an arrow from a bow. We all possess, if it comes to the bit, a reserve of strength and the will to survive. I was no exception. Some intuition warned me, when we drew too close to the railing, I had to lift my leg to avoid the stirrup catching and throwing me off into the gorge below, or to lower my head, close to the horse's neck from being dashed against the overhanging rock. We overtook everybody slow or fast. Far behind us Ron on his Slingsinghi was trying hard to make up, but it was hopeless. Slingsinghi was not given to exerting herself. Ron confined himself to anxious inquiries from riders coming towards him. 'Have you seen a lady in navy slacks riding to Darjeeling?' He halted a soldier on his horse. 'Yes sir, going like hell' was the answer. Another rider, whom he knew in Calcutta, was also stopped. 'Have you seen my wife, David?' 'Yes Ron – she'll be in Darjeeling by now.' And so I was. By the grace of God, who sometimes takes care of fools, I had survived. The Nepali had some questions to answer. 'Why did you give me such a horse?' I demanded. 'Because you asked for a faster horse,' was the cool explanation and pointing to the silver disk on the horse's forehead he added in his nonchalant manner, 'This is what Flying Faun received for winning the Cup in a race held the previous week on the Lebang race course!' Did I wish to have Flying Faun again, he inquired with a sly twinkle in his slanting eyes. It was a challenge. I agreed to pick up the horse the following day, but when I went along, it transpired that a young officer, holidaying in Darjeeling, had booked Flying Faun for the next three weeks and had removed it to his quarters. I had to be content with a more passive and obedient pony. 'Thank God for that,' was Ron's sole comment.

There was quite a lot to see around Darjeeling. We wanted very much to have a little trip on the toy train and one day set off on it to visit a pig farm in the vicinity of Ghum. The farm belonged to a firm known as Kaventers who supplied most of the dairy produce to Calcutta through their shop in Lindsay Street, where the best quality of milk, cream, sausages and fresh pork was sold.

The farm was kept in immaculate order. We, and especially the twins, were fascinated by the large healthy pigs which were all named after famous people. There was Greta Garbo, leisurely reclining while suckling her numerous rosy piglets; Winston Churchill, a large sturdy pig, importantly strutting around; Roosevelt; Joseph Stalin; Norma Shearer; Clark Gable – all soon to be seen as tempting joints and sausages in Calcutta.

The short return journey on the little train, twisting and turning on its way back to Darjeeling, was a delight in itself.

Some scenes, some people stand out in my memory. There was, for instance, the strange-looking man who used to sit on a form in the corner of the Chaurastha talking to a friend. He wore a slouch hat and a khaki-coloured mask with slits cut for his eyes and mouth. It was explained to me that the man was actually quite old, but when he was but a lad a bear attacked him, tearing his face and leaving him disfigured for life, unable to face the world without his mask. This account, truthful as it was, brought to mind something similar described by Rudyard Kipling in one of his numerous tales.

There is the ritual for most visitors to Darjeeling to go to Tiger Hill and watch from there the sun rise over Everest. We decided to go one day and arose early to set off on the long ride to Tiger Hill. The morning was fresh and cool with a faint mist rising. A group of little children had gathered in the valley and, as we passed, kept chanting, 'Salaam Sahib, Baksheesh – Salaam Sahib, Baksheesh.' On eventually reaching Tiger Hill we found to our disappointment that the mist had thickened and lay like a white pall over the whole of the distant vista. Everest was not to be seen, nor was there any chance of repeating the attempt as our lovely holiday was by now drawing to a close. The Pennys and the Doigs, however, were staying for another week and the Pennys did go back and did see the sun rise over Everest.

Prior to leaving I bought a few mementoes to remind me of the happy days spent in Darjeeling, the place where we had the holiday of a lifetime – the only one we ever had in India.

After sadly saying goodbye to Darjeeling we left by car for Siliguri. The car was shared by an acquaintance from Calcutta who had asked us if he could join us. Our friend had wined and dined well before he left. He was also a chain-smoker. Sitting in front of us beside the driver he never ceased smoking and the result for us, overcome by fumes of smoke combined with alcohol and the zigzagging of the car, was disastrous. With the exception of Ron, we all became very ill and with having to frequently stop the car we almost missed the train to Calcutta. It was a great relief to part with our fellow traveller and climb into our own compartment.

Back in Kinnison, the old routine took over. The servants, refreshed after their leave, resumed their tasks. The cook went off to market, Shamsher Ali Khan unpacked the boxes in which our personal effects – china, ornaments, glassware – had been stored during our absence and arranged them all in their proper places.

The twins and Pir Mahomed joined the other children, with their ayahs, on the daily trek to the Barrackpore Park. I was astonished many years later, when one of my sons, by now grown up, casually remarked how they all enjoyed being treated by Pir Mahomed and the ayahs to cups of tea when they halted in the bazaar on their way to the Park. 'They were brown earthenware little cups, which were later broken,' he added with some nostalgia. 'It's a good thing I did not know that earlier,' I replied. 'Pir Mahomed would have heard about it!' The bazaars were full of all kinds of germs and disease. Pir Mahomed and the ayahs had a build-up of resistance to infections which the children did not have.

In our company all members of the staff, their wives and children had to be inoculated every year, against typhoid and cholera as well as being vaccinated periodically against smallpox. Our Dr Ghose who came to the house to administer the injections was a gentle, likeable man. He was especially good with children. The twins responded to him by bravely stretching out their little arms to suffer the injection without creating any fuss. These injections were necessary. Before their introduction the death-toll was prodigious. The Calcutta cemeteries held countless graves of people who had died in the prime of their youth. Even in our time, in spite of inoculations, there could be an unexpected death lurking round the corner.

At the start of the war a bride came out and was married to one of our head office men. She was dead two years later having caught from some unknown source a virulent type of typhoid. Another day, when Ron and I were having lunch at the Swimming Club, word was sent round that one of our salesmen had died in the morning. Ron had to rush out to buy a black tie as the funeral was taking place in the afternoon. You could be talking to someone in the morning and see him being buried in the late afternoon. This was part of the Indian scene.

Meanwhile the whole of Bengal was in the grip of a devastating famine. People starving in the villages had rushed to Calcutta only to find the same shortage prevailing there. The pavements and stations were crowded with masses of dejected people, sitting, lying, helplessly resigned to their fate. The numbers of beggars increased tenfold.

One moving scene has remained in my memory of two small boys, maybe four and two years old, sitting close together on the edge of the pavement, the elder tenderly enbracing his little brother and trying to tell him something, perhaps a story. They were completely alone in a small world of their own. I placed some money on their laps and walked on. There was nothing I could do.

I am reminded as I write these lines of another more harrowing scene which I witnessed some time later. I had been purchasing wool in Dharamtala Street and was hurrying along the pavement, when my attention was drawn to a man sitting there with a small boy beside him. The child's head was resting on the man's lap. The man's face was evil itself. As I passed the boy raised his head and looked up to me. I had never before seen such grief and resignation in eyes so young and then to my horror I saw that both the boy's hands had been cut off at the wrists. The scarlet scars were still clearly visible. I was shaken to the core of my being. The first impulse was to snatch the child, hold him tight to my breast and run far from this obscene monster – run – but where? Overwhelmed by unbearable anguish I could only hurry past, crying out in hopeless despair, 'God, why do you allow this? Where was your mercy?' These grief-stricken eyes stayed with me for a long time and can still haunt me. Why is it, Mother India, that you –

benevolent and kind – are also so coldly indifferent to the cruel exploitation of your helpless little children?

The famine continued and reached its peak in 1943 to claim almost three million victims. It was widely supposed that the famine was caused by speculators buying up all the rice and hoarding it thus causing the price to rocket and ensuring them a handsome profit. Important names were mentioned in this connection but the truth never came out and no one was prosecuted as far as we knew.

Life on a compound in the mofussil tended to be quite apart from the bustle and politics of Calcutta. We had our own problems, our own way of life, close friends in whom we could confide our joys, our disappointments. Barrackpore was a lively district where there was always something going on – a dance, a party, people played golf, tennis, bridge, mah-jong and, of course, there were also the various activities organised for the war effort.

As the golf club in Barrackpore was taken over by the American Army, one of our friends suggested we join the main Barrackpore Club. We did so and found it very useful. It was a pleasant place, overlooking the river. It boasted an excellent library which was a great boon. There was also a fine swimming pool where we spent many happy hours with the twins. The park itself was an ideal place for an occasional picnic in which my cousin Mae and young Pat used to join us.

On the whole life was uneventful, but one afternoon when I was having my lie-back, the bearer knocked on the door. A sahib, he said, was standing on the verandah, waiting to see me. I hurried out and found a young man dressed in Airforce uniform. I recognised him at once. 'You are Roy Cameron,' I said. 'Helen's brother!' Roy was the youngest child of Uncle Stephen, my mother's brother. Years back when my mother became engaged to my Russian father, Uncle Stephen accompanied my father on a short trip to Russia. The idea behind this was my Scottish grandparents' wish to find out a little more about the country where their daughter was to spend her married life. Uncle Stephen was welcomed and widely entertained by the Russian family in Archangel, and on his return to Broughty Ferry assured his anxious parents by expressing his belief that all should go well for his sister Nelly and that the Russian side was eagerly awaiting to welcome the Scottish bride into their family. The wedding took place a few months later and after the reception my father took his bride back with him to Russia.

Uncle Stephen likewise married some three years later. During the early years of my childhood we spent many holidays with my grandparents in Scotland. I used to play with my cousin Helen, who was two years my junior, but with the advent of the First World War all our travelling ceased and we did not see Scotland again until eight years went by. During this time Uncle Stephen was an officer in the Royal Navy and took part in the Battle of Jutland. At the end of the war he decided to buy a coffee plantation in Kenya and settle there with his family. In the year 1919 when we arrived in Scotland after the Revolution, with Russia in the grip of a civil war, Uncle Stephen was already in Kenya and the family in the midst of preparations to join him. The five children with their mother were living in a house called Brightside. On account of being a lively lot and at times quite mischievous they were always referred to by our sedate grandparents as 'Brightsiders'. The youngest golden-haired child, Roy, was only a year old.

Meanwhile we, after a sojourn of eight weeks, returned to Russia in the false belief that the civil war was almost over and that our side was victorious. We were mistaken. After being trapped for a year we eventually escaped in 1920 and arrived once again on the doorstep of our grandparents' house in Broughty Ferry.

The 'Brightsiders' by now were all settled in Kenya. Now, standing on the veranda, bearing a strong resemblance to his sister Helen, was Roy Cameron. 'I remember you well,' I said to him. 'When my brother had a birthday party and we had all gathered round the table, you were standing on your own little chair refusing to sit down and continued standing throughout the party calmly accepting all the cookies and cakes being passed over, to our great amusement.'

With the outbreak of the Second World War Roy had volunteered for the Airforce and was now a sergeant fighter pilot in the Rhodesian Airforce. He had all the makings of a fighter pilot – young, debonair, brave. It was through my mother he got our address. He had been stationed at the Dum-Dum airport without our being aware of it. Mae also met him and for the rest of his time in Calcutta he used to spend his off-time with one or other of us. I remember how once during a session at the club someone asked him if it was true that some of the pilots were able to fly below the Howrah Bridge. 'Not true, quite impossible,' was the nonchalant reply. 'I have already tried it.' Another time to amuse the twins, in a true 'Brightside' manner, he flew low, past our house, more or less level with the veranda to their great delight, and, after a spectacular victory roll over the river, vanished into the clouds. Later the manager said to Ron, 'What the devil is your cousin playing at? He almost stopped the mill. The workers think the Japs have arrived.' The exhibition, although much appreciated by us, was not repeated.

102

It is my belief Roy enjoyed the little touch of home life Mae and I were able to give him. I remember how one morning, after spending the night with us, he sat relaxed on the veranda and talked to me about his future plans. The war, he thought, would be over within a year or two with the defeat of Germany and Japan. After being demobbed, he planned to buy a coffee plantation and settle down in Kenya. He loved Kenya, the free and open life there and did not wish to go anywhere else.

I have a deeply rooted fear of tempting providence. 'You are very sure,' I remember saying to him. He laughed. 'Do you think I'll not make it?' he asked. 'No, no,' I hastily assured him and spat a little to the left – the best known way of warding off the evil eye. Roy continued visiting us whenever he could. It was always a great joy to us and the twins to see the familiar figure arriving, but unfortunately with the Japanese menace now drawing nearer his visits were becoming rarer.

Meanwhile the daily routine continued as before. One evening during the cold weather we were entertaining two friends to dinner and had just finished the first course when the shrill warning of the siren cut short our meal. Hurriedly leaving the table we wakened the twins and rushed down to the air raid shelter. There was a standing order that in the event of an air raid all staff had to proceed to the mill office. The women and children were to be under the charge of the chief mill manager, Will Robertson. We were also told that if we should hear the sound of a rattle it was a warning of an approaching gas attack. As we were not provided with gas masks what purpose this warning would serve was open to conjecture. Ron and our friend's husband hurried off to the mill. Inside the crowded shelter it was hot and uncomfortable with the mosquitoes having a field day. One of our ladies, known as 'Spanish Mary' – not on account of being Spanish, but because she once had a holiday in Spain and never stopped talking about it – was regaling us with the delights of being in Australia where she had spent her last leave, and where, she added with a side glance at our senior lady, there was no jat and everyone was equal. This enlightening talk was suddenly interrupted by the dull thud of a bomb dropped somewhere in the distance followed by another. At this point, Will, who had been keeping watch outside, popped his head into the 'henhouse' and in a voice pregnant with foreboding announced, 'Ladies, I hear the rattle.' The effect was devastating. 'Do ye no mind', cried one lady in despair, 'how during the first war our soldiers peed on their socks and held them up to their noses. What can we do?' There were no suggestions. 'My bairn, my puir, wee bairn,' lamented another, clutching her child to her breast. She was joined by a wailing chorus from the children. It was all rather alarming. Just then the welcome 'All clear' sounded. Everybody joyfully scampered back to their houses.

Our dinner party continued. Nothing was ruined by the delay as I had fortunately arranged for cold dishes to be served.

The following morning we went off with the twins to Calcutta to see what damage was caused by the bombing. On our way we were met by the astonishing sight of a great exodus from Calcutta. Men, women and children, cars and lorries of all descriptions, donkeys, goats tethered to carts, parrots in cages on top of lorries, one solid mass of humanity were moving along the trunk road, all terrified out of their wits trying to reach a place of safety anywhere away from Calcutta. We continued on our way, but apart from a small hole in the road in front of the Great Eastern Hotel there was nothing much to see.

Through Christmas and New Year right on to March 1943 Roy kept in touch with us and then for some reason we did not see him again. In June, however, a letter arrived from Dinjan in Assam to which, Roy explained, he had been posted. 'I cannot tell you much about what we are doing here as the censor in any case would cut it out. At the present moment, as I'm writing, I'm sitting in a tent with the rain lashing down – the monsoon has arrived.' He apologised for not having been able to say goodbye to Mae and me, but hoped he might soon return to Calcutta. The letter was dated 22 May. We heard no more. In late July, Mae received a letter from Roy's mother. Aunt Jessie and Uncle Stephen had been informed that Roy was missing, presumed dead. No other information was given. They wondered if perhaps Mae or I living in India might have received some further news. Not being the next of kin we did not receive any official information, but one day by sheeer chance met an officer in the RAF who dealt with reports on missing pilots. He gave us all the information that was available. It transpired that on 24 May, Roy, along with another fighter pilot, was sent on a reconnaissance over Burma. Having completed their mission the two young men were talking to each other on the radio during the return flight when the surviving pilot lost contact with Roy. After circling around in a futile search for some sign and hearing no answer to his call and with his fuel running out he was forced to return to base.

The supposition was that both pilots were flying low up a valley and Roy was unlucky enough to strike the hillside. Somewhere on a hill in the wild jungle of Burma, Roy is still lying. Neither he nor his plane were ever found.

Prior to the events I have described, there had been other changes. Our friend George Stevenson decided to join the army. He went through the whole war, moving from front to front and at the end of hostilities found himself in Italy. Lucky enough to escape unscathed he returned to India after a short leave in Scotland.

Many of the boys in the Bengal Artillery were likewise released and went off to the war. Most of them were absorbed into the 14th Army and fought at Imphal and Kohima, others were sent to different fronts. All gave good accounts of themselves and many received quick promotion. One of our stalwart lads from Lawrence mill, placed in charge of transport in Bombay, was promoted to Lieutenant-Colonel. He called in at our head office on being demobbed where he was greeted with 'Hah, it's you, Middleton!' by the head of the department.

'Lieutenant-Colonel Middleton to you,' was the curt answer.

Meanwhile in Barrackpore the Bengal Ladies' Artillery was moving from strength to strength. We were also looking forward with eager anticipation to an important event when Sir Thomas Lamb, the Colonel of the Bengal Artillery, was coming to inspect the ladies' section. On that great day, having missed a few rehearsals, I arrived on the parade ground with certain misgivings. We were divided into three groups. I took my place in the last group. At the other end of the field Sir Thomas Lamb and other officers stood waiting. The march started. It was at this moment, overcome by wild excitement, that I suddenly decided that I was in the wrong group and scampered ahead to join the one in front, but there I received an indignant 'Get back!' and rushed to my old place where, judging by the black looks in my direction, I was far from welcome. Fortunately no one in front appeared to notice this lapse. Shoulders thrown back and tummies held tight, the march continued. 'Eyes right!' as we came up to Sir Thomas. 'Eyes front!' after we had passed him. Thankfully, my ordeal was over. Later we were highly commended on our performance and went home well pleased with ourselves.

In the evening I thought deeply about my future in the Bengal Ladies' Artillery. Somehow I just could not see myself with a rifle or Lewis gun defending India. What could the Bengal Ladies' Artillery do, I wondered, remembering the débâcle in Singapore? In the end I came to the conclusion that I was not created for any military service and would be better employed directing my energies into something which would give me more satisfaction. I decided to call it a day.

On the main road to Barrackpore lay a small building known as Dr Bose's Hospital. It catered for Indian patients in the mills and surrounding districts and especially for those requiring surgery. The man in charge was a brilliant surgeon who had gained his experience during the First World War and would have gone far if it had not been for his unfortunate weakness for Scotch whisky.

Equipped with my certificates for first aid and home nursing I joined a group of five ladies who gave voluntary service in the hospital. One of the ladies, an experienced nurse, was our leader. As her name eludes me now I shall refer to her as Mary. The rest of us, Nan, Lexy, Mae, Nancy and I followed Mary's directions implicitly. The hospital, although supported by the mills, was poor, but kept comparatively clean by sweepers, both male and female, who also carried out the more unpleasant tasks. Our duties consisted of attending the operations, dressing and bandaging the wounds. The cases brought in were mostly due to accidents, some in the mills, but mainly on the roads, where the fast-moving military traffic had greatly increased with the arrival of the American Army.

I attended three mornings each week, setting off immediately after breakfast in a cycle rickshaw and returning in time for lunch. I liked the work and wasn't put off by the blood and gore and often unpleasant smells. There was a sense of some achievement in seeing someone who had been badly hurt eventually able to walk out of the gate. The numerous cases kept us busy. One I recollect was of an old man, who had stepped on a rusty nail. He was brought in with his foot swollen beyond recognition, completely black. The surgeon decided to operate in an attempt to save the foot. In the small operating room were Mary, Lexy, Mae and me. The man, placed on the table, was given a general anaesthetic. We stood watching the doctor take a scalpel and begin to slash the foot. Immediately a terrible dark mass started to flow from the wounds accompanied by an appalling smell which was difficult to bear. It was the hot weather and there were no punkahs. Through the open window an army of black flies flew in. Soon, Mae, turning deathly white, was forced to leave the room, to be followed by Lexy. Mary remained, assisting the doctor. I stood with a bottle of ether, taking occasional sniffs in a futile attempt to kill the smell. With the operation over the man was carried into the adjoining room and from that moment the process of healing began, slowly, at times with setbacks and little hope but eventually with signs of improvement. It was touching to see the old man trying to express his gratitude, clasping his hands together, bowing his head. It took many weeks to heal, but in the end we saw him leave the hospital, limping a little – but walking on both feet.

Another case stands out in my memory of a young boy who had fallen from a tree. His forehead was deeply cut, exposing, but not breaking, the bone. This cleft, running from nose to the hairline, with the skin and flesh puckered on either side, was filled with red clay, leaving the poor child badly disfigured. The first objective was to remove the clay. This task fell on Nan, who, with loving patience, little by little, removed the clay, thereby exposing the bone. The next more serious move was to put the boy through an operation to try to draw the puckered skin together leaving in the end a straight scar, but removing all the disfiguring features. I never saw the operation nor yet the outcome, but heard later that it was successful.

My work in the hospital was interrupted by the strange case of a woman brought from her village with a swollen stomach, caused by an enlarged bladder. The poor woman was unable to pass water. With the appalling ignorance found at times in the villages, a hot poultice had been applied to her stomach aggravating her condition and causing great suffering. We gathered round her. The application of a catheter and a succession of kidney trays each time filled to overflowing brought instant relief. The poor soul in her gratitude tried to kiss our hands, but unfortunately the same treatment had to be carried out daily. A high temperature developed followed by a puzzling rash. I was the only one in the group who had small children and the doctor could not be sure that it wasn't infectious. I simply could not take any chances of perhaps carrying an infection to the twins and decided to pull out for the time being.

The woman died soon after I left. I hoped to be able to return to the hospital at the beginning of the year, but Ron refused to even contemplate such an idea. In any case other events intervened and in the end I never went back.

On 31 October 1943 our twins reached their fifth birthday. Earlier they had been enrolled for Dundee High School to begin their education in the autumn of 1944, but with the war still continuing it was impossible to plan ahead. Meanwhile we decided to send them to a small school run by a Miss Graham in Barrackpore. Miss Graham, a graduate of Oxford University, was a missionary entirely devoted to helping the poor Indian Christians. She was known to be quite a character, forthright and a bit eccentric. Tall, a little on the heavy side, she never wasted time on her appearance or used any kind of aids to beauty. I can still remember seeing her striding along the Barrackpore Road in a loose-fitting dress, girdled round the waist, a large straw hat, wispy hair, and bare feet in open sandals.

In her little school there were only about ten pupils including the twins, Alistair Doig and little Ann Chapman, the daughter of one of the assistants in Kinnison. The others were children of the Europeans, living in Barrackpore or in the nearby mills. Their ages varied from five to ten and they sat together on stools placed beside small desks under the roof of the porch outside the bungalow. All were taught at the same time with Miss Graham well able to deal with the different stages.

Every morning the twins with Pir Mahomed used to set off on a cycle rickshaw and were collected in time for lunch. On other days I would go to pick them up and usually arrive a bit early so as to enjoy sitting for a while in the garden.

The garden was delightful – quite neglected with a great variety of flowers and bushes – the heavenly blue of Plumbago against a pink Hibiscus, a magenta Bougainvillaea climbing up the pillars of the porch, rare green-yellow orchids tumbling out of a basket on a wall. In the corner of the garden grew a handsome tree laden with sweet litchis, which Miss Graham used to sell to the market.

I loved that garden and at times felt as if I was transported to a bygone India and could almost visualise a lady in a white crinoline stepping lightly across the lawn. The bungalow with the garden must have been situated here since the days of the Indian Mutiny and perhaps even before. Here was the touch of real India with her haunting atmosphere, the kind I had read about – how I would have liked to live in this old place in spite of its lacking all the modern conveniences laid on in our house. I used to sit, a bit away from the porch, waiting for the class to finish, listening to the voices of the children repeating the alphabet or reciting some little rhyme. The garden harboured many animals – chattering little squirrels cheerfully scampering up and down the trees, the inquisitive face of a monkey would suddenly appear peeping through the branches, a couple of mongooses chased each other around the bushes.

When the lessons were over, the cycle rickshaw then took us back through the noisy bazaar and into the other world of a jute compound.

In November our neighbours Phil and Bob Campbell were transferred to another mill in the group where Bob was promoted to be a manager. I missed Phil and the fun we had with her. A graduate of St Andrew's University she was blessed with a sharp wit and could always raise a laugh at a party even if it was at the expense of some other person. What did surprise us was her obsessive fear of germs and infections which appeared to be completely out of character. When invited to tea she invariably held the cup with the handle turned round and sipping from the edge which she hoped had not been in contact with other lips. The first time I saw her at this caper in my house, I was a bit put out, but later when invited together by a mutual friend and seeing our host present a good impersonation with the teacup and peering into every sandwich as Phil was wont to do – I realised that this was just her way. She did not object to being teased and laughed against herself. I remember her telling us how, on one occasion when having dinner at home, she decided to have another potato and told the bearer to bring back the dish and on finding that for some reason the bearer was taking his time she left the table only to discover him standing in the bottle khana and laboriously scraping off tea leaves and some unpleasant items from the potato which had been thrown into the refuse bucket. Certainly one had to be careful, especially with the cooks, for only too often in the eyes of the servant if the germ wasn't seen it was not there.

With Phil and Bob leaving Kinnison, their flat remained empty and that year as Christmas drew near, we mothers got together and decided to hold a party for all the children in Kinnison and those from neighbouring compounds in the vacant quarters, with the parents subscribing towards it.

As the great day grew nearer, Edie, Bella – one of the ladies from Kelvin – and I departed for Calcutta where we spent the whole day running from shop to shop arriving back laden with parcels and quite exhausted. A Christmas tree, the nearest to northern pine, was erected and decorated with coloured lights, a large star, gold and silver glass balls, sparkling tinsel and whatever.

On Christmas Day, in the afternoon, some ten children and all the mothers arrived at the house. We sat down to tea, sandwiches, cakes and sweets. This was followed by mounting excitement as the best was still to come. The climax came when Santa Claus – alias Jock Bryson – one of our young men – a resplendent figure in crimson cloak and hood and a snow-white beard almost down to his waist, arrived in a rickshaw. He entered the room bowed down by an enormous bag bulging with presents.

The night before, Isa, our neighbour, had advised the twins to put down a glass of milk and a biscuit in front of the fireplace. Now, as Santa was distributing the toys and calling out each name, George, hearing his name, came forward. The child – his face white, and trembling in every limb – gathered all his courage to inquire, 'Did you get the milk and biscuit?'

'Yes, my lad, indeed I did and enjoyed it,' replied Santa, not having the faintest idea of what it was all about.

The party was a great success and a special delight for the little ones who had not seen Santa Claus before and were thrilled to meet him.

Back in our house we settled down to enjoy a peaceful Christmas evening. Ron, after a heavy day followed by a hot bath, was in his chair enjoying a half peg. Beside him stood a Christmas tree which I had decorated and lit small candles such as I had seen during childhood in Russia. Our twins were playing with their toys. I, sitting relaxed, was not thinking about anything in particular when suddenly my attention was caught by the tree bursting into flames. Ron's first reaction was to throw his half peg on to the fire. To me it came like a flash that Ron just having had his bath the towel was bound to be damp. I ran to the bathroom, grabbed the towel and threw it over the tree, by now burning like a torch with the flames licking the curtains. Behari, the sweeper, came running with a bucket of water and in the end we were lucky to get off with only damaged curtains and a soaking carpet.

It was a lesson never to use naked flames on a tree, a lesson always to remind me of our last Christmas together with the twins in India.

The New Year of 1944 began quietly. There were no more celebrations in Calcutta as from the start of the war with Japan we never left the children alone with the servants in case of an air raid which might have prevented us from reaching them. Entertaining was restricted to having and visiting nearby friends only.

Prior to leaving for the army, George, afraid that his car would be requisitioned, left it in Ron's care. In spite of petrol rationing the car was a great boon. Occasionally, on Ron's day off, we went with the twins to Calcutta where we would spend the day in the Swimming Club, meeting friends, swimming together or attending a film and returning home in the early evening. There was also the Barrackpore Club where we exchanged books and met other people. Being within easy reach of the compound it enabled us to have an occasional evening there on our own. On account of the petrol shortage there were times when we hired a cycle rickshaw. To travel through the park was always a pleasant experience. How many strange scenes these stately trees must have witnessed, some difficult to imagine such as when in bygone days the Governor of Bengal and the ladies in his household used to ride on elephants along the banks of the river.

I myself remember an unusual happening, shared with Ron one late evening when we were returning from the club in a rickshaw. The night was dark, cool and still. Far ahead we suddenly noticed something glowing with unusual brightness and on drawing closer were halted by the astonishing sight of an enormous tree completely enveloped by a mass of fireflies – trembling, shimmering and fusing into a glorious scene of dazzling splendour. We sat for a little while absorbing this enchanting phenomenon, such as we had never seen before or since and even now, after all these years, when recalling some happy moments in our lives in India we ask each other, 'Do you remember that tree in Barrackpore?'

There is a memory of another run through the park – totally different. It so happened that our younger twin, Michael, suddenly became ill after eating a rice pudding. In spite of our Dr Ghose calling several times and prescribing various medicines, Michael continued being very sick, until Ron in the early hours of the morning, searching through the medicine cabinet, came across a tin containing Glucose D with the instructions that it could effect a cure for sickness. We tried it as a last resort. Immediately the vomiting ceased. Michael fell asleep and slept for hours.

As the tin was almost empty and it was important to have another we decided that George and I would go by cycle rickshaw to the soldiers' canteen in Barrackpore where it was possible to purchase various medicines. We duly arrived there and being fortunate in procuring the tin turned back on our homeward run through the park. There we were suddenly overtaken by a frightening storm accompanied by lashing rain and lightning. The rickshaw wallah was pedalling for dear life, bits of branches and leaves were falling over our heads. I held my little boy tight, both of us utterly terrified. At times the lightning lit up the darkness and it seemed to me that behind these swaying trees something uncanny perhaps was lurking. It was a great relief to see the lights in the bazaar and to realise we were near people. We arrived in Kinnison still clutching our tin and drenched to the skin. I may add in the passing that from that day on our Michael has politely declined rice pudding.

A second daylight air raid took place at the beginning of the year. Bombs were dropped on the dock area causing much damage and some casualties.

Overall Calcutta got off lightly. We suffered no hardships compared with other theatres of war. The tea and mah-jong parties continued with a variety of home-baked cakes gracing the table. I enjoyed them all, never dreaming that somewhere far off in the siege of Leningrad three of my relatives were dying of starvation. We were short of certain consumer goods. The days when we could pick and choose dress materials in the market were over. I remember buying material sold for cutains in Hall & Anderson and having a presentable dress made.

We carried on in the usual old style never suspecting that a great upheaval was due to take place shortly.

The American Airforce decided to take over both mills in Kinnison for the purpose of overhauling aeroplane engines and other items. With the mills went the quarters in the compound. The machinery in the mills had to be transferred to the adjoining mill known as Standard. All the staff, married and single, were forced to double up in Standard where the quarters were not only smaller but the compound also was much restricted with slit trenches in front of the quarters being built up of earth and cinders.

Prior to the take-over, the anti-aircraft battery, stationed in the Beehive, left, leaving the Americans with their usual efficiency to turn Monty's old residence into a flourishing canteen. All kinds of innovations were laid on – giant electric toasters, machines that turned out doughnuts by the hundred and so on. In front of the Beehive, where once stood the aviary housing rare birds, barracks were built for the American technicians. All the houses and roads in Kinnison were renamed – Rose Villa became the Waldorf Astoria and so on. The top floor of the Island House was now occupied by the attractive 'hostesses'. We used to see their blue-clad figures hurrying somewhere, no doubt on their way to bring a little comfort to a lonely GI and help him with his home mail.

We were the last to leave. On that day after three hours' notice when I was frantically packing my dresses and underwear an American officer entered my bedroom and sat down on what was known as the 'long-sleever' – a chair with long arms on which to rest your legs.

'I guess', he announced stretching out his legs, 'this chair is to be mine.' Not troubled by any inhibitions he continued talking while exhibiting a lively interest in my activities and keeping up a friendly conversation.

Outside a lorry was waiting. All our belongings, toys, clothing, pots and pans were thrown in and we moved to our new quarters which, having been divided, were small, with the bottle khana alive with cockroaches large and small. After a great deal of cleaning, scrubbing and painting, we settled down in our new abode.

We were permitted to use the road through Kinnison to the adjoining Kelvin compound and the children still gathered beside the swimming pool. Alistair with his ayah and baby sister in her pram came along each morning. The boys continued swimming in the pool and at times were joined by the Americans. The children liked the GIs who talked to them and gave them sweeties.

Great changes were taking place in Kinnison. To us, accustomed to a more restricted way of life, the free-and-easy style of the Americans was at times quite astonishing. I remember how once when strolling with Ron past our former house we saw through the wide open bedroom window a young woman sitting, half-dressed, on my bed combing her hair. On another occasion, walking back from Kelvin after visiting Edie, I had to pass what was now the Waldorf Astoria. Standing in the open doorway of the bottle khana was the startling sight of one of the officers completely naked explaining something to the bearer. More amazing than anything else was the scene of an American playing tennis with one of the bearers – a scene to send shudders through the British Raj.

In the mills the Indian traditions were likewise facing a shake-up. The sergeant in charge of the workshop, seeing the workers departing at the end of the day, stopped them to inquire, 'What about sweeping the floor?'

'Sahib,' came the answer, 'we not sweepers – we no sweep.'

The reaction was simple. 'You not sweep today – you not work here tomorrow.' They swept.

What really shook the whole district of Titaghur, where we lived, was the episode of the tree. In the vicinity of Kharda jute mill stood a holy banyan tree beside a tank (pond). This tree, venerated for generations, was unfortunately on ground required by the Americans for the construction of warehouses. A *sadhu*, or holy man, always sat in the shade of the tree, giving advice to and receiving homage and contributions from the local population.

The American proposal to remove the tree and fill in the adjacent tank, met with strong opposition. It was impossible and unthinkable to move this holy tree. No one had dared to do such a thing before and would not do it now – an opinion shared by the sahibs. The Americans, however, solved the problem. With their customary down-to-earth approach, they gave the sadhu a sum of money and told him to go and buy himself another tree.

On the appointed day, crowds, including the Fraser family, collected to witness this desecration. It was widely expected that some dire calamity would follow. All stood silently watching a young GI arrive with a bulldozer and calmly approach the tree. There came the sound of roots torn asunder, branches breaking – up went the tree and crashed into the tank. Nothing happened – no lightning struck the ungodly offender. The crowd dispersed.

The Americans, in spite of their unconventional ways, were quite popular, especially so with the Indians many of whom were employed in Kinnison and other American depots and were well paid for their work in comparison to those working in jute mills. Yes, the Americans were here – and a good thing too for where would we have been if it wasn't for Uncle Sam?

Life in Standard was not pleasant. From the trenches, built up by cinders and lying close to the quarters, dust filtered through the jilmils and settled on all furniture and floors. Our precious almond-green carpet and beige suite took on a dirty-grey tinge all of which was quite depressing.

Ron with his usual energy had thrown himself into this great upheaval assisting in the transport of machinery from Kinnison to Standard and the migration of some four thousand workers. To keep up with the production Standard mill worked on shifts beginning at 4 a.m. and ending at midnight. No one was happy, neither the staff nor the workers. The advent of the hot weather did nothing to ease the situation.

During my whole sojourn in India I went inside the mill only once when it was working. My first reaction was to rush quickly through and out the opposite door, but some inner voice told me not to hurry. Amidst the haze of heat and dust I saw women in damp grey saris, wisps of jute sticking to their hair, poor worn faces clammy with sweat, yet smiling to me in a friendly manner. Men were standing at their looms and the sahibs walking up and down, with shirts clinging to their bodies, gave me a cheerful wave as I went by as if they were strolling about in some park on a pleasant day. To me, the deafening roar of the machinery, unbearable heat, the pervading smell of jute all conspired to create a special hell – a hell I took great care never to enter again.

Meanwhile all over India people were celebrating the Holi festival held in honour of Kama, the God of love, a time of sexual licence accompanied by wild excitement in the bazaars as people rushed around with brass syringes squirting crimson and other coloured dyes over each other. Our friend, Jimmy Stewart, when travelling home from the head office through the bazaar, received a squirtful in the open window of his car and arrived home in a fury – his suit ruined by pink splashes. No one previously would have dared to throw dye over a European, but now attitudes appeared to be changing with the Indians growing bolder. This being a Hindu festival Pir Mahomed never took the children through the bazaar. Clashes and riots had been known to take place when someone, deliberately or otherwise, squirted dye over a Muhammadan.

By now we had endured four hot seasons with no prospect of any holiday. It was beginning to tell on the children who suffered from 'prickly heat' and boils. During the cold weather there had been breaks when we spent a weekend with the Hebentons in Lawrence, or with Mae and family in Belvedere jute mill, but now with Ron tied up in his work we confined ourselves to short runs on a Sunday morning around the Barrackpore park with the twins. We were often joined by

Alistair and the two little Indian children of one of the assistants. The children enjoyed these little runs all happily chattering together in Bengali or Hindi.

In May a letter arrived from Scotland. We were reminded that the twins, enrolled for Dundee High School, were expected to be present at the start of the autumn term beginning in September and if by some chance they were unable to leave India, their places would be cancelled and offered to other parents anxious to have their children join the school.

After a long and heart-searching discussion we reached a decision. I would travel with the twins to Scotland with Ron accompanying us to Bombay to see us safely aboard the ship. Meanwhile Edie and Aikman also came to a similar decision. Edie and the children would likewise set off for home with Aikman escorting them to Bombay. We planned to leave early in July. Already several wives and mothers, faced with the same problems, had embarked for Britain and arrived there safely.

The first objective was to have a supply of warm clothing. In Rankin's, the well-known tailor in Calcutta, two coats were made for the boys out of a length of Harris Tweed. My favourite darzi ran up some shirts and pyjamas all of which saved the clothing coupons due to be issued on our arrival in the UK. I bought some wool and knitted against time socks and sweaters. The days were now passing quickly and all too soon we were into June.

One morning, when Ron was resting during his break and I with my knitting was listening to the radio while the children were playing at my feet, I suddenly heard the startling announcement that on the morning of 6 June Allied troops had landed on the beaches of Normandy. I could not believe it – my ears were deceiving me, I thought, but then, shortly, the same exciting news came through again. I ran to the bedroom, but Ron, like myself, at first thought that I must have been mistaken until he heard it being repeated once more. This was D-Day – the day for which we had been praying for so long. A wave of optimism swept through us all with some believing that peace was in the offing – perhaps in a month or two. They were wide of the mark!

Our passages were booked with the firm known as Mackinnon Mackenzie. Owing to war conditions we were not told the date of sailing nor yet the name of the ship.

A crate was made in the mill to hold our belongings and certain items of which there was a scarcity at home such as rice, chocolate powder, tins of hampie and so on. I was also determined to take back a collection of Russian books originally brought out of Russia with memorable last-minute messages written on flyleaves. These precious books had to be saved before they were completely ruined by humidity and insects devouring the pages. As there was a ruling that all foreign books had to be inspected I had to take them to the censor's office. There the head of the department, on seeing the books, asked me if I could speak, read and write in Russian. When I told them, I could, he informed me they were short of translators and would I be willing to postpone my journey and accept the post of a translator as at present they had to send Russian letters, etc, to Delhi where they were dealt with by a Polish lady. I naturally refused the offer and told them, in turn, that it was a pity they did not think about this earlier, as on my arrival back to India in 1939 I had received a notice to report to the Police Headquarters in Calcutta along with all those born in foreign countries. If they had thought of checking on all the records compiled at that time I could have been usefully, and gainfully, employed for years but now it was too late.

By the end of June with the arrival of the monsoon everything was packed and ready. It was then there occurred an unexpected hitch. For some considerable time, Ron's vision in his right eye was affected and gradually getting worse. He had attended the eye specailist, Lieutenant-Colonel Kirwan, who could not understand the cause in spite of numerous, varied tests. On his retirement the practice was taken over by a Major Somerset who, when Ron went to consult him, likewise could not understand the reason for this affliction but at the same time warned Ron that if the sight in that eye was to be saved an operation to remove a cataract had to be performed without any further delay. The operation took place a few days later in a private nursing home in Calcutta and might have been successful had not inflammation set in, caused, according to Major Somerset, by some virus, but believed by Ron to be the result of the draught from the punkah getting under a corner of the bandage on his eye.

As I was due to leave in a matter of days Ron was allowed to go home, but as further treatment was required there was no question of his travelling with us to Bombay. Faced with the daunting prospect of a journey with the twins on my own I was relieved when Edie and Aikman suggested we should travel together in the same compartment.

On the eve of our departure I had occasion to go into the twins' room where Pir Mahomed was clearing away their toys. I noticed he was weeping and, thinking that perhaps he was worried over the loss of employment, I hastened to reassure him that Ron had already arranged with some of his American friends to provide a job with a higher salary that he was getting from us.

'The sahib told me so,' Pir Mahomed replied sadly. 'It is not that. I have been with the babas for three years and now I won't ever see them again.' In India this was the lot of loyal servants and as I myself was not very happy there was nothing I could say.

Early the following evening we all collected in Howrah station. Memory has kept only a few scenes like odd pieces out of a jigsaw puzzle: Ron standing with the black patch over his eye; Jimmy Stewart's smiling face – no doubt expressing his sympathy with Aikman in charge of two women and four children; Jim Dakers with Mae and Pat and some other people beside them; Edie and Aikman with the children; friends seeing them off; baskets of fruit being carried into the compartment.

I have no recollection of the train setting off. Our compartment with six bunks was on the whole roomy and it being the monsoon not as hot as it might have been. Perhaps because there was no outstanding event during our journey, it is barely remembered. Aikman was in charge. The boys did not fight, baby Sonya was good, we all got along, ate our food, divided the fruit, sang songs with the children such as 'Ten green bottles hanging on the wall' and when that went down to 'One green bottle hanging on the wall' we started again until all became tired.

It was only when the trains steamed into the station at Bombay, that my troubles began and Aikman sadly got involved. It so happened that when Edie and Aikman booked the passages through Thomas Cook their accommodation in Bombay was arranged at the same time. In my case the booking was done through Mackinnon Mackenzie who advised me to report to their office in Bombay where all would be arranged on my arrival. In the station it was agreed that Aikman would kindly wait with the twins and my bits of luggage while I went on to Mackinnon Mackenzie and, having fixed my accommodation, would return to pick up my luggage and the twins. It did not turn out that way. On my arrival at the office their representative immediately phoned the Taj Mahal Hotel only to be told that on account of a large conference being held in the hotel not a room was to be had. Further phone calls to several hotels also drew a blank. I returned to the station to explain the situation. Edie with Alistair and baby Sonya were by now in their hotel. At this point Aikman suggested that he would wait while I tried some other places. I did so, but nowhere could I find a room or any place to put me up. In desperation I went back to Mackinnon Mackenzie. They resumed their efforts. This time to the YWCA and even the station where in the waiting room it was possible to find accommodation, but again there was nothing – the only place was the station itself. To sit and perhaps sleep for days with the twins on the station, beside beggars and the usual motley crowd, was something I could not accept. I became desperate.

'Please,' I begged the senior man of the two sitting together, 'try the Taj again.'

'I have already phoned and they are completely booked,' was the cold response.

'But,' I argued madly in despair, 'that was some time ago – someone may have left and even died since then.'

At this moment the other man with a shock of red hair and compassionate eyes, appealed to his neighbour. 'Please, Bill,' he said, 'do try again – you might be lucky.' The first man with an angry glint in his eye lifted the receiver.

'Tell them,' I said, 'I am willing to sleep under the stair if need be – anywhere but the station.'

After a short conversation he turned to me. 'You can go there, Mrs Fraser,' he announced, 'but be prepared to share the room with other women.' And with these words he went back to his papers. The kinder man rose and shook hands. 'Good luck,' he said, a warm smile lighting up his face. I hurried away and throwing myself into the waiting taxi sat there sobbing with sheer relief.

In the station Aikman was still waiting with the twins beside him. For how long – an hour, two hours? I never could tell. I know only that the sight of him standing there has never been forgotten – and what could a mere 'Thank you' have conveyed?

The room in the Taj Mahal Hotel was situated in the high turret above the left wing, facing the sea. A lift took us up to the top floor from where we climbed a spiral staircase leading into a large room divided by an archway. There were some ten of us women and four children. All the ladies were pleasant and for the next few days we all got along well together. The room was well furnished with comfortable beds and to me, after the terrible anxiety and prospect of having to live in the station, was heaven itself. In the adjoining luxurious bathroom, we bathed, changed our clothing and were all set to go down to the dining room. On our way we were stopped by a lovely Parsi lady dressed in a magnificent sari and dripping with jewellery. She was curious to know if the boys were twins. We had a pleasant conversation together, slightly marred by one of my sons inquiring in a loud voice, 'Who is this ayah?' Thankfully she only laughed and continued talking.

We chose a table close to the orchestra and dined in style. In this enormous room of dazzling lights, sparkling candelabra, exotic flowers, fruits piled on sideboards and snow-white tablecloths, was a mass of people ambling around or dining – beautiful ladies in rich saris, European women in full evening gowns or like myself in plain dresses, Naval and Army Officers, Indian gentlemen in well-cut long coats, handsome Sikhs with colourful turbans, a multitude of servants hovering between tables, tending all wants. To the children all this was new and terribly exciting especially the appreciative applause to the orchestra which, imagining it was some kind of ritual, they earnestly joined in, prompting smiles from the adjoining tables.

Outside the monsoon was in full swing with the torrential rain confining us to the hotel, which was no hardship as I was only too thankful to have a roof over my head.

On the scond day Edie and Aikman called with the children. Their hotel turned out to be a disaster – lacking in comfort, but with Bombay bursting at the seams there was nothing they could do. On the third day, however, we were all told to report to the docks for a medical examination prior to boarding the ship. We duly gathered there and after the usual procedures went aboard.

Some of the passengers had friends seeing them off and as the ship was lying alongside the pier they were able to converse with each other. We knew the name of the ship but were not allowed to divulge it.

When Edie and Aikman were exchanging their last few words I also joined in to say goodbye and at the same time told Aikman to ask Ron if he still remembered the ship he had travelled on when he had come home on leave in 1931. He did remember. The name of the ship was the *Maloja*.

On the *Maloja*, owing to the war, conditions were far from perfect, food was poor, the ship overcrowded. On board was a contingent of Indian soldiers and French refugees who had travelled from French Indo-China and having reached Bombay were now on their way to Algiers. Then there were people like us, many of whom we recognised.

The cabins had all been reconstructed to accommodate more passengers. In our cabin there were two bunks on each of the four walls. On my right was a cheerful pregnant blonde travelling with her two little daughters. She introduced herself by her Indian surname adding, 'Just call me Rosie, everyone does.' It transpired that her Indian husband was a scientist whom she had met and married when he was a student. They had spent the first six years of their married life in England, but shortly after the outbreak of the war had left for Delhi where her husband had been offered a post with the government. There they had lived in a large rambling house and while she did not mind being in India, apart from the heat, she found no joy in the communal style of life, a bossy mother-in-law and 'them rats running across the rafters through the night'. Rosie was of Irish origin, but spoke in what I took to be a Lancashire accent. Her elder girl, Sheila, eight years old, was like her mother, fair skinned with blue eyes, but the small sister, aged three, who slept in the bunk below Michael, was a dark lively child named Nalini – Hindi for Lily – and according to Rosie the double of her Indian father. After four years, Rosie came to the conclusion that she had had enough of India and that the child she was carrying should be born in England. Completely uninhibited, good natured with a keen sense of humour, often earthy, but still funny, Rosie was easy to get along with, even if her terrible untidiness aroused irritation at times and infuriated the steward, who in trying to tidy the cabin, would push under our pillows panties, socks, brassières and whatever he picked up from the floor. With her easy-going philosophy Rosie had decided to make the most of this difficult passage and soon found something more entrancing to occupy her mind which involved her vanishing from the cabin for some hours through the night.

A different cup of tea was our other female passenger, who cast a blight over the cabin. Strange by nature and in appearance with tar-coloured hair, cropped short, and a pale face devoid of all expression she chose at all times to remain inside her own silent world. She was also travelling with a young daughter – a peevish, sulky child who never played with other children of her own age, such as Sheila, who was a pleasant little girl always eager to please, nor yet with any of the other children. Mother and daughter sat and walked together on deck and when coming face to face with Rosie or me made not the slightest sign of recognition or passed the time of day. Throughout the whole of our passage on the *Maloja*, a matter of two weeks, she hardly ever uttered a word and treated the rest of the occupants as if they were not there. We never got to know her name, where she came from or where her final destination might be. On one occasion when the girl was ruder than usual to Rosie, from whom she nevertheless, a few minutes earlier, had accepted sweets, her mother in defence of her child's behaviour told us that her husband had died a year earlier and her daughter had never got over losing her father. To me such blatant rudeness seemed a strange way to express grief. On one other occasion when the exasperated steward was gathering Rosie's belongings and at the same time expressing his displeasure in no uncertain terms our 'Smiling Morn', as Rosie had named her, also joined in by raising her

Kinnison, 1942.

The first home in Lawrence, 1937.

A picnic with cousin Mae in Barrackpore park, 1941.

Dundee High School F.P.s' reunion, Peliti's Restaurant,
Calcutta, 1928.

The best holiday we ever had. Darjeeling, 1942.

The twins and Jetty Ayah, 1940.

Ladies' tennis party in Kinnison.

A dangerous journey in an old box in Switzerland, 1949.

Miss Graham's school in Barrackpore, 1944.

The view of the Hooghly and jute barges looking up the river from Kinnison.

The Island House known as the Jheel Khooti.

Leaving India in 1963.

Beside a waterfall in Thailand, 1964.

Ron with two of the girl workers in their tribal dress, Thailand.

In the garden of Bangsen.

*The monument to the Queen and her children, drowned
at Bang-pa-in.*

The summer palace, Bang-pa-in.

The entrance to the cemetery at Kanchanaburi.

The bridge over the River Kwai.

The cemetery at Kanchanaburi.

eyebrows and in a high affected voice exclaiming, 'Did I hear you say you were Irish?' It was a great relief when during the latter part of the journey we were separated and did not encounter her again.

Edie's cabin was a few paces along from ours. We were able to keep in touch, often sitting together on deck with the boys playing nearby. Travelling with little babies is always difficult. Edie had her hands full with baby Sonya, but later she became acquainted with two ladies who, I believe, were teachers and who proved to be of great help to her. I also was kept always on my toes with the twins. Without Ron's steadying influence they knew exactly how far they could go with me and spent the time inspiring each other in thinking up some new ploy to torment their, by no means long-suffering, mother.

Passengers were kept apart from the soldiers and in the evening all doors were closed with orders forbidding anyone to go on deck for a breath of fresh air. The black-out continued. It was an open secret that Japanese submarines were stalking in the Indian Ocean which with the monsoon still in force was often very stormy. What between various ailments and sea-sickness many were suffering some more than others.

There was a brief respite when we halted at Aden. There, according to some of the passengers, we took on board the crew of a cargo ship, carrying peanuts, which had been sunk by a Japanese submarine.

We were now approaching the Red Sea with the promise of further heat and discomfort. In our cabin were two electric fans placed in such a way that the benefit from them only reached six bunks, the other two, occupied by Michael and Nalini, receiving nothing at all. In days gone by when travelling through the Red Sea people used to go on deck at night and sleep on chairs. Now with the soldiers being there this was not permitted. No sooner did we sail into the Red Sea than our crowded cabin became like an oven with the two children suffering more than anyone else.

Rosie lifted Nalini and after placing her on her own bunk left the cabin. I did likewise with Michael and went up to join the other women in the saloon where the two powerful punkahs brought some relief. After three such nights, broken by having to pay frequent visits to the cabin to check if all was well, this terrible sea was thankfully behind us.

Earlier, rumours abounded that the contingent of Indian soldiers was on its way to take part in landings probably in Italy, in which case the civilian passengers would be taken off the ship and placed in a transit camp. The rumour proved to be true. One day we were told to be prepared to leave the ship the following morning and to take only the barest necessities with us.

In the late evening as I was gathering all our bits and pieces and pushing them into a hold-all, Rosie came over. She presented me with a book, *The Sun is My Undoing*. 'This is a parting gift from my friend,' she said. 'I never read but thought perhaps you would like it.' I had no idea who 'my friend' was but gratefully accepted the book and read it with great pleasure.

The following day we disembarked and landed on a sandy beach near Suez. There we sat with our babies and children waiting for transport and wondering what was in store. After some time open lorries arrived. We travelled standing; Edie holding Sonya and the boys at our feet. All I remember of that drive was the expanse of the desert sands and the merciless rays of the sun beating down on our defenceless heads. In a little while a sea of tents appeared surrounded by a wire fence. Someone had laughed and said, 'All hope abandon ye who enter here,' but of course it was not like that at all. This transit camp was in the capable hands of the ATS and run with great efficiency. The commanding officer was a small, competent woman who spoke several languages and was assisted by other members of the ATS with the addition of one or two foreigners, including a Yugoslavian. All the work was done by Italian POWs. We were accommodated in our own tents, provided with clean beds, towels, showers and given a meal. There were also instructions to tuck the netting securely under our mattresses to guard against sandflies, which apart from transmitting sandfly fever could also bring on boils. Finally we were warned we would be awakened in the early hours of the morning to continue our journey to Port Said.

In the early evening after putting our children safely in bed, Edie and I decided that a little reward for all our travel would not go amiss and thereupon departed for the adjoining canteen where we relaxed for some minutes over a glass of something prior to returning to our respective tents.

On entering my tent I was horrified to find it empty. There was no sign of the twins. Terrified out of my wits with the thoughts of horrible possibilities of what could happen to my boys I ran around in the now gathering dusk calling out their names and eventually found them sitting, quite unperturbed in one of the last empty tents close to the perimeter. They had quite calmly set off to inspect the camp in the spirit of some adventure, for which they were spanked and put to bed by their relieved and yet infuriated mother, who having given vent to her feelings sat down and wept, full of regret.

In the early dawn we were aroused, and, after a brief breakfast, provided with soya-bean sandwiches and oranges for the journey, set off on the next lap. It was still dark with the sapphire sky spangled with stars when we scrambled into the bus. Everyone was cheerful, but what I remember best is the happy voices of the children singing in full voice as we careered on to the station. There we boarded the train with our soya sandwiches and oranges meant to sustain us until we reached Port Said and boarded the other ship. In passing I may add we never saw the French refugees again probably because they were *en route* to Algiers.

After travelling perhaps for an hour the train halted in Ismalia where a rather officious officer appeared on the scene and ordered everybody out to wait on the station for the next train to take us to Port Said. Not seeing any place to sit I settled on top of my hold-all with the twins beside me. Great activity went on around us. A train carrying a contingent of Polish ATS steamed into the station. The girls hanging out the windows were laughing and joking with each other, obviously being transferred to another front or going on leave.

In front of me another little drama was being enacted between a young woman and officer standing talking together. This young woman, one of our passengers, had told me that she belonged to an organisation whose aim was to spread love and friendship throughout the world; a statement which reminded me of my husband's view that there were too many people wandering around the universe creating trouble. Now this young woman in her large straw hat was having a lively discourse with the officer when suddenly, squeezing in between them, appeared a horrible little urchin intent on selling what are commonly known as 'dirty postcards', a practice well known in the East, and in this case accompanied by obscene gestures. The normal response would have been for the officer to take the little wretch by the scruff of his neck and kick him out. Instead they continued talking in loud affected voices pretending they did not see the boy and both getting redder and redder in the face. I sat wondering how this scene would end, when fortunately for them it was interrupted by the same officious officer appearing and telling us to get back in the train.

We were once more in the same train but this time travelling in another compartment. Although lucky to find seats beside the windows, there was little in the desert to catch the eye except the strange sight of a ship moving through the canal giving the impression of it sailing on land, which the boys imagined was actually happening. The journey continued for some considerable time. Too soon the soya sandwiches and oranges were eaten and we were ready to eat more, but it was not until the late afternoon that our train steamed into Port Said. We had been on the road from the early hours of the morning. Tired and hungry we followed the throng of weary passengers walking from the station to the docks and up the gangway of our next transport – a Western Ocean liner, the *Britannic*.

Safely aboard we were fortunate to be allotted a three-berth cabin all to ourselves – a great boon after the cramped conditions on the *Maloja*. The call for the first sitting to the dining room was also very welcome as by now the soya sandwiches and oranges were only a distant memory with everyone being ravenously hungry. Considering the wartime conditions we found the food satisfactory and it continued to be so throughout the voyage.

In the early evening, with the exhausted twins sleeping soundly in their bunks, I went up on deck to join the other passengers hanging over the railings, hopefully scanning the unloading of the luggage brought in a barge from the *Maloja*. After a great length of time, anxiously watching every box, I was rewarded with the sight of my crate being hoisted, but continued keeping my eyes open for Edie's which eventually turned up. Not all were lucky. The trunk of one officer disintegrated in mid-air as it was being lifted scattering all his belongings – jackets, boots, shirts, cap, underwear, etc. – back into the barge and sea. A lot of people found this most amusing even though the poor devil had lost all his possessions.

I hurried back to tell Edie that all our boxes were safely aboard. Her cabin was situated quite near my own where she was busily engaged with the baby.

The following day saw us sailing at full speed through the calm waters of the Mediterranean. I had already travelled in one of the first convoys at the start of the war, but never dreamt that I would be privileged to take part in one such as this. It was immense – each ship appearing larger than the other with the barrage balloons swaying above as if accompanying some fantastic pageant. There could only have been very few who did not feel the awe-inspiring majesty of this momentous scene, unlikely ever to come our way again.

Fascinating to watch were the planes leaving the aircraft-carrier and vanishing like silver-winged seagulls into the clouds only to appear again and, swooping down, miraculously land on the heaving deck.

Amidst the great number of people aboard the *Britannic* the civilian passengers were a mere handful, all the others being a random selection of the various services: the Eighth Army returning home after a long spell in the desert; Australians; Poles; Free-French; nurses; and the Polish ATS, the same girls whom we had seen leaning out the windows of the train in Ismalia. There was also a group of soldiers often seen in the early mornings engaged in strenuous exercise on deck. To my curious inquiries as to who these men might be I was informed that this was a special Jewish contingent.

A rather important passenger, with an aura of mystery about him, occasionally seen strolling up and down the Captain's deck, was the German Commander of a submarine sunk by the Royal Navy. The crew, confined below deck, were in transit along with their Captain to a POW camp in Britain. One of my twins, fascinated by this mysterious prisoner, attempted to reach the Captain's deck by climbing the steep stairway and was almost at the top when I caught him. This enabled me to catch a closer glimpse of a handsome, fair-haired man with a proud countenance standing thoughtfully gazing out to sea.

The whole ship was under the control of the RAF, represented by the senior officer, named North, whose rank I cannot recall.

During the morning boat drills, when each group of passengers stood on their allotted space on the deck, he and the Captain of the ship went on their round of inspection halting to check if everything was in order – lifebelts, torches and whatever. In our group there were men and women including four mothers with children. During one such inspection the commanding officer asked the men if, in the event of our having to take to the lifeboats, any of them would be prepared to assist a mother with her child. This, he pointed out, was purely voluntary, but at the same time he would call out the name of each mother and whoever was willing to come forward and stand beside her. There was no scarcity of volunteers, until my name, being the last, was called, and only one man stepped out. He was a young officer, a Captain Stevenson, who came forward and asked me, 'Which one will I save?' I remember saying, 'Take the heavier one – I think I will be able to hold on to the lighter boy, Michael, if we have to go overboard.'

From that day Captain Stevenson always took his place beside me and the twins. We often had to stand for some considerable time waiting for the inspection. The Captain, not given to small talk, used to read a little book the title of which I remember was *St Joan*. One evening as I was putting the twins to bed there was a knock on the door and Captain Stevenson appeared on the scene. 'As my cabin is a bit away – I had to find the quickest road to reach you should the necessity arise.' With these words he left me. A few days later the alarm bell went in the late evening. I immediately began to dress the twins and there all at once was Captain Stevenson. Cool and collected he picked up George. I took Michael and together we followed the throng of people on to the deck only to be told that this was a false alarm to test us. There was certainly no panic.

Throughout the whole journey each one of us, including the children, had to carry lifebelts attached to which were a torch and a beer can filled with water. The purpose of the torch was to show where we were if we should land in the sea and the beer can to keep us from dying of thirst. Royal Air Force personnel were on duty all over the ship keeping a sharp watch to check if we all carried the correct equipment.

The beer cans, not being filled with proper corks, were always leaking and the batteries in the torches constantly being exhausted, which involved going down to the purser's office and having them replaced. One day, George, playing a few yards away from me, came back to tell me that a 'very nice Uncle' examined his torch and then replaced it again. What the 'very nice Uncle' had done was to remove the child's battery and replace it by his own finished one. Furious as I was there was no option but to go down to the purser and ask for a replacement. His earthy comment on the offender does not bear repeating.

From what I remember the weather was kind to us and as in the *Maloja* our little group would sit on deck with the children playing near us. The lads from the Eighth Army, some of them being Scots, liked to talk to us and on hearing that we were on our way home from India used to say, 'You people in India have taken General Wavell, the best General of the lot.'

I got to know the girls in the Polish ATS who, I discovered, were on their way to Scotland. Some of them were sappers who had to deal with mines. When I asked one of them if she was not afraid her simple answer was, 'Yes, I wept with fear.' According to them it was only the Polish ATS who did this dangerous work – no other service women were allowed to do so. Their commanding officer was a young attractive blonde who wore a close-fitting, well-cut uniform. She and the Colonel of the Polish contingent used to stride together round the deck – she holding high her little proud nose. Her condescending attitude irritated the other girls but one of them who had lost her husband in the war was more tolerant. 'She is very young,' she once remarked. 'One day she will grow up.'

I was once sent for by the purser. Puzzled by his summons I went along to his office, where he explained that in the sick-bay was a young Polish girl who was seriously ill, knew very little English, but could speak Polish and Russian. The medical officer, not able to communicate with her, suspected that she had TB and wishing to ask more questions approached the purser to get in touch with someone who could help him. The purser, who, through my passport, knew that I was born in Russia, sent for me to ask if I could meet the doctor.

The girl, although ill and weak, was glad to talk to me and told me that she had a Russian mother and a Polish father but did not know if they were dead or alive. None of her answers, however, to the questions posed by the doctor, through me, confirmed his fear that she had TB. I did see her again and was pleased to note later that she had fully recovered before the end of the voyage.

All mothers who have had to travel alone with small children aboard a ship, whether in peace or war, know how demanding the darlings can be, that constant vigilance is of paramount importance and relaxation is rare and precious.

Little boys have the amazing ability, if given half a chance, to vanish in the twinkling of an eye as they did unfortunately in my case when they disappeared from the toilet room. On a ship carrying thousands of passengers anything can happen. I had rushed around searching, calling, asking, until quite by chance, when passing one of the lifeboats, I heard the familiar voices and noticed that a corner of the tarpaulin had slipped off and there inside the lifeboat were my two tormentors happily engaged in some ploy. How they succeeded in scrambling into the lifeboat without tumbling into the sea was a miracle for which I was too thankful to be angry.

Shortly after the incident with the lifeboat an epidemic of German measles broke out. One after another of the children became infected and were taken to the sick-bay, then Alistair, and Michael five days later, went down as well.

Meanwhile the convoy, having swept round Ireland, was sailing down the west coast of Scotland. Some of the ships, rumour had it, were due to dock in Scotland. To the Scottish passengers and especially the mothers with their sick children this would have been a godsend, for in a matter of two hours after docking, and more than likely with the permission to take the children out of the sick-bay, we could have reached the comfort of our homes.

I remember standing on the deck and hearing Rosie, my cabin friend of the *Maloja* calling over. 'Have a look at my Ireland, Mrs Fraser, see the sun shining upon her, see how beautiful, how green she is.' I was not concerned with Ireland, all my hopes were concentrated on the *Britannic* landing in Scotland. I saw a ship in front, leaving the convoy to turn left followed by another and then, with us behind it, prayed hard we might be next – but no, it was not to be – the *Britannic* went on sailing straight ahead to dock in Liverpool in the late afternoon.

Sometime later we were notified that all the civilian passengers would disembark the following morning. There were additional strict instructions that we were to take with us only what we were able to carry and once ashore were to proceed to the Customs shed where all the rest of our baggage would be waiting to be examined and then handed over for us to continue our journey.

As the problem with Michael had to be resolved I went to the sick-bay, but found my way barred at the door by an officious nurse who informed me that apart from the children who had recovered sufficiently to leave the ship, the others, including Michael, were to be taken by ambulance to the Fazakerley Hospital. 'You should not go in to see your child,' she had added in a terse manner. 'You would only upset him.'

'He would be, if I didn't,' I rejoined, just as tersely brushing past her. Michael was unhappy because his friend Alistair was going home and he wasn't, but when I told him that he was to have a ride in an ambulance, a new and rare experience, he cheered up considerably.

As no one was allowed to leave the ship a few of us went up on deck in the hope of seeing the children leaving in the ambulance. In gathering gloom on the landing stage was seen great activity. Jeeps, lorries and cars were coming and going. We watched a group of shadowy figures climbing into a military vehicle and wondered if perchance they were the German prisoners. I was to hear a strange story later. It transpired that when the German prisoners and their Captain were rounded up to go in a military truck to the POW camp the Captain refused to travel with his crew and insisted that as the commander he had to travel alone. A chauffeur-driven car arrived into which he condescended to enter. On hearing this story I was reminded how a group of men, women and children had to travel standing up on an open lorry across the desert sands to a transit camp.

Meanwhile we did see the ambulance arriving and the children brought down on stretchers. It was difficult to make out to whom each child belonged. As the ambulance began to move away one of the mothers standing beside me became upset. I myself felt heavy-hearted. What a sad homecoming it was with one child being taken away to hospital, the other one not looking well and I not knowing if I might be stranded for some time in this strange city.

Through the night George was restless and I slept fitfully after packing and planning what I could take and what had to be left behind. In the morning my five-year-old boy and I, both laden like donkeys, walked down the gangway. The Customs shed was packed with passengers milling around, sorting out their luggage. I saw Edie with the children and a friend who had arrived to meet her. We spoke together for a little while. She would be going to Arbroath to her people and I to my mother's home in Dundee. We were to meet again once we settled down.

After depositing our baggage in the left luggage in the station we adjourned to the nearby Station Hotel where I found the only room available was one for four persons. Fortunately another memsahib with a little girl appeared on the scene and was only too glad to share the room with us.

The first thing I had to do was to phone Mother, who, thankful that we had arrived safely, looked upon the delay caused by German measles as a matter of minor importance.

Anxious to see Michael, we immediately, after a quick spartan lunch, set off by taxi to the Fazakerley Hospital. The road to the hospital was long and it was there, as we travelled, that I saw for the first time the devastation caused by the war. I had seen the mast of a ship sunk in the dock and some damaged buildings, but never thought that such intense destruction, stretching endlessly on both sides of the road, was possible – and still remembered – the empty shells of houses with bits of rags flapping in the wind, the ruins of a church, broken tombstones in the churchyard, the remains of what may have been a café – the poster advertising a brand of cigarettes clinging to the wall – all stern reminders of how little the war had touched our lives in India.

I had to leave George in the lodge of the hospital before I could enter the ward where I saw Michael, who was now recovering and on the whole quite cheerful but desperate to get out, especially when the nurses expected him to eat a rice pudding.

There was a message in the lodge from the doctor saying she wished to see me. She turned out to be a warm friendly woman who, after asking me some questions, told me that by all the rules, George, who she was certain was coming down with measles, ought to remain in the hospital. At the same time she added that seeing me as I was, badly in need of a rest, she had decided, if I promised to travel in a compartment by ourselves, to allow me to take Michael out of the hospital the following afternoon. This would allow me to make arrangements to leave the next morning and arrive back home in Scotland by the evening. 'It is where you should be as soon as possible,' she had concluded.

Although thankful that our situation was now resolved there was still the nagging anxiety over my little boy who had patiently trotted beside me the whole day in spite of feeling ill and was now looking white and drawn.

Back in the hotel, exhausted by the day's happenings, we retired early to bed as did my room-mate with her child. She left in the morning and shortly after her departure Ron's sister Kate arrived from Dundee having been sent to give me a helping hand.

In the afternoon I left George with his fond Auntie and set off once more to the hospital to collect Michael. In this crowded hotel the two vacant beds in my room came in handy and the four of us spent a restful night.

The promise to the doctor of travelling in a separate compartment did not materialise. The times were such that all trains travelled packed with passengers in compartments and corridors. In the morning as we prepared for the last lap of our journey it was agreed that Kate with the twins would try to find an empty compartment while I attended to the baggage. She did eventually find one, but only until the next station when some other passengers crowded in. In the early evening we duly arrived in Dundee where we were met by all the welcoming relatives with hugs and kisses. Two loaded taxis took us to my mother's house where she, in her usual style, had prepared a lavish supper at the cost of saving up her rations for this eventful day.

George, however, by now was quite ill and immediately on arrival I put him straight to bed and called for the doctor.

While I was busy myself with George I heard my younger twin in the dining room regaling his grannies and aunties with some extraordinary tales, during which his flights of fancy were carrying him back to India where he and George were often left alone while 'they', his parents, went off to Calcutta and the tigers would arrive in the bedroom and prowl around them. 'It was all very frightening I can tell you,' was his dramatic conclusion. The grannies were delighted.

The doctor arrived and confirmed that George had German measles. And so began my life once more in Scotland. Five years earlier, almost to a day, we had left for India in gloomy darkness, fear and uncertainty. Now I was back to a land of austerity, ration cards, clothing coupons but with an atmosphere of quiet optimism, the certain knowledge that the dark night was almost over and although we were still not out of the wood, peace was not far away.

As for me – two years would pass before I would see my husband and the twins their father. This was the start of endless separations – something every married woman, from the day she lands in India, realises is bound to happen should she have children. Terrible and sad as it is, it has to be accepted – there is no alternative if the children are to be educated in Britain.

3

SCOTTISH INTERLUDE

During the early days of our sojourn in Scotland nothing went well for us. The children, exhausted and ill, became susceptible to further ailments. Measles was followed by whooping cough. During this dreadful illness, lasting two months, they not only missed the opening date of their first year at school, but succeeded in passing the infection to my mother who became seriously ill, and also to their grandfather, who, being a dentist, was greatly handicapped but fortunately was able to recover in a matter of two weeks. By the start of November, however, these harrowing weeks were over. The boys started school, Granny recovered and life became normal.

Meanwhile the war, which many of us fondly imagined was drawing to a conclusion, still continued. There was the tragedy of Arnhem, the frightening V-bombs causing death and destruction and the prolonged Battle of the Bulge.

Food at times was a problem. The scanty ration of meat did not go very far, but was augmented by tins of spam brought in my crate from India along with tins of fruit, cocoa, rice, etc., all of which was a great boon. In Dundee there was also a game and poultry shop known as Roger's, where it was possible to buy pigeons, an occasional cut of venison, partridges and chickens. Pigeon pie was a welcome dish, as was rabbit, although one often had to stand in a long queue to obtain it. Fresh eggs were scarce and dried egg powder, although useful, was a poor substitute for the real thing, but Mr Roger came to the rescue by offering gulls' eggs. There is a common belief that these eggs have a 'fishy' taste, but that is not the case. I found these large eggs were very useful and excellent for baking. What was missed most of all was the taste of fresh butter. The weekly allowance of two ounces per head was enjoyed for a mere two days before having to fall back on margarine, but that was a small matter, as overall we did not do too badly and certainly much better than in other parts of the world – we were quite lucky.

The weeks kept slipping by with Christmas drawing nearer. A party had to be planned even if the familiar figure was too far away to take part in it.

Through Ron's sister Kate, who had taught in Deeside and knew a farmer's wife who bred turkeys, I was able to order one. The turkey duly arrived – an enormous, beautiful bird, so large it was only with great difficulty and after I had chopped off parts of the legs, that I succeeded in pushing it inside the oven.

We had a glorious feast complete with trifle and a plum pudding with lucky threepenny bits hidden inside. Presents were exchanged. Toys were difficult to find, but after searching around I was fortunate to buy a few second-hand Dinky replicas of cars and lorries, a great rarity which delighted the twins.

With Christmas dinner over, all adjourned to the sitting room where in the corner stood a Christmas tree filling the room with the delightful scent of pine. The night before, the twins and I spent a happy time decorating the tree with sparkling tinsel, colourful glass balls, stars, gnomes, fairies, and golden walnuts – all carefully stored by Mother throughout the years.

With recollections of the experience of our last Christmas in Kinnison, I fixed small candles on the tree taking great care that they could not possibly fall over or come into contact with a branch above them. After all, I reasoned, during my childhood numerous candles were lit on our tall Christmas trees, year after year, and nothing happened so why not now? The candles were lit brightening up the corner with their soft light. The twins sitting on the floor played with their toys, the elders talked together about the past and present and the events happening around us. It was a pleasant peaceful evening and in this way passed our first Christmas in Scotland – sadly without Ron.

The following evening the candles were lit once more. Leaving Mother sitting at peace with her knitting I went off to give the twins a bath and it was then while I was drying them that we suddenly heard my mother's despairing cry, 'Come – please help – fire, fire!' In the sitting room the Christmas tree was a blazing torch, the flames trying to reach the ceiling. Memory immediately jolted me back to the Christmas in Kinnison when a damp towel smothered a fire. I ran into the bathroom, threw the towels into the bath and rushed with them into the sitting room. The scene that followed beggars all description. There was Mother with a cushion beating out the flames. The glass balls on the burning tree were exploding with the sharp crack of a pistol shot; cotton wool snowflakes – now giant fireflies – flying round the room and alighting on chairs, rugs, everywhere; the twins, stark naked, running in all directions, skirling hilariously; gnomes, fairies, stars vanishing in flames. In the end it was the wet towels that quenched the fire. We opened the window and dropped the smouldering tree into the garden. It was nothing short of a miracle that the whole house wasn't devoured by the fire. Poor Mama's hands were blistered but overall we were lucky to get away with burned towels, cushions, rugs and a scorched sofa.

Never again have I had candles on a tree.

With the Christmas and New Year festivities behind them the boys were back at school. Although late starters they had not been long in settling down and being accepted into the noisy circle of their classmates.

The elation of entering the magic world of school, dressed in their blue blazers complete with badge and proudly bearing their new schoolbags, had soon evaporated. School was not quite what they expected. School was for ever and there was no way of getting out of it. School sometimes was fun – and sometimes it wasn't. At times the teacher was nice and at other times she wasn't. And there was the strap, nobody liked that.

When asked by curious aunties and grannies how they liked the school there was the usual short non-commital answer: 'It's all right'.

There was a strict rule that the children had to be escorted to and from the school by an adult. I got to know some of the mothers and renewed an acquaintanceship with those whom I had known previously. Sometimes after leaving the children we would adjourn to the nearest café, where over a cup of coffee we would chat together for a little while.

The children had to be picked up at one o'clock. On one such occasion I remember the teacher saying to me 'What I have to do, Mrs Fraser, is to instil into your twins that C is not for Calcutta, C is for cat, and B is not for Barrackpore.' Shades of poor Miss Graham – all that she taught now had to be forgotten!

I have found that at times children, in their innocence, casually referring to some incident can reveal the reason behind it. Michael one day happily announced, 'We are going to be invited to Anthony's party,' and added, 'we like Anthony – he's like us, not one of the "kissy boys".'

'Kissy boys,' I echoed quite intrigued. 'What does that mean?'

'The "kissy boys",' Michael explained, dispassionately, 'are those whom the teacher likes to kiss before they leave for home. She never kisses us.'

The inference was obvious. 'I am glad', I said 'you two are not among the "kissy boys".'

By the third year their class teacher was Miss Jean Brown, no doubt still remembered by many. On my inquiries as to how they liked their new teacher the answer was a classic of its kind. 'She', Michael said, lifting his finger to emphasise the point, 'is the best one of the lot. She hates us all the same. You can bring her a pound of tea and she would still hate you.' I have often wished I could have met Miss Brown who, on retiring, opened a little tea-room in St Andrews. I am certain that with her deep understanding of little children she would have appreciated this rather unusual compliment. She would have known that Michael did not mean that Miss Brown hated anyone, but in his own way had tried to convey that she was at all times fair and would never have stooped to accepting any bribes even if it was the rare pound of tea offered by a fond mother currying favour for her child.

In the spring came the long-awaited news. Peace was imminent. Germany had collapsed. The Russians were in Berlin.

On 8 May I was walking home with the twins, passing gardens all decked out in golden daffodils and crocuses in every hue. Peace in Europe had been declared, the day was bright and the very earth seemed to be exuding gladness and the promise of better times – of friendship between nations. I was sure that the old enmity between Russia and the Western Allies was over. How could it possibly be otherwise – they had fought together and Russia, who had lost millions of her sons fighting for every inch of her blood-soaked soil and without whom the outcome of the Second World War might have been totally different, surely deserved some recognition.

In some of the windows, flags were seen flapping in the breeze. We followed suit and hung the flags of Britain and America, but, unable to find a Russian flag, we tore up a piece of sheeting on which the boys painted a crimson hammer and sickle and hung it beside the others. There they were all fluttering together celebrating their joint victory. I was well pleased with myself until some time later when it was brought home to me how much I had been mistaken.

In spite of all the rejoicing there was still the problem of defeating Japan and the nagging question as to what was happening to the prisoners. From the day when Singapore fell not a word had been heard from Ron's brother George. Not knowing if he was dead or alive his mother in her desperate anxiety resorted to visiting a renowned fortune-teller, known as Mrs Wilson, and would come home comforted by the assurance that her son was alive and would return. Mrs Wilson certainly possessed the strange and at times uncanny ability of being able to prophesy certain events. She was in a class by herself and was often visited and sent for by people in high places, even from as far as London.

One morning, shortly after VE-Day, on receiving my usual letter from India I noticed unfamiliar writing on the envelope and immediately became alarmed. The letter was from Edith Penny who wrote saying that Ron had developed typhoid and had been removed to a nursing home in Calcutta. For the next three weeks I was plunged into deep anxiety with the despairing knowledge of complete helplessness in being so far away. The relief came when once again I saw the familiar envelope and knew that Ron was on the road to recovery. He had no idea where he picked up the bug, but the annual compulsory anti-typhoid injections, administered by our mill doctor, undoubtedly saved his life.

In July, with Mother and the twins I went to stay in a small village in Perthshire known as Logierait. We travelled by train to Ballinluig and from there walked across the bridge and along a winding path to the cottage where we had booked three rooms for a fortnight, complete with board and attendance. The two sisters who looked after us were friendly women, the rooms comfortable, the food plain and whole-some with plenty of fine home baking.

The cottage and garden lay close to a road leading to a POW camp. Every morning we used to see a group of prisoners marching past on their way to work and in the early evening returning, at times, singing in unison, as they walked along, a sight that always fascinated the boys.

The days were warm and sunny. We spent many hours beside the river where not a soul was to be seen and the only sound was the gentle murmuring of the swiftly flowing river and the occasional call of some strange bird. The twins splashed close to the shore, or searched around for what they imagined were precious stones. I and even Mother, when it grew quite hot, would remove our stockings and go in wading. One morning to our amazement we saw in a small pool close to the river a fair-sized salmon lazily circling around. It seemed as if it might be an easy catch. Already I was visualising a princely feast complete with lettuce and tomatoes. The salmon had other ideas and as I cautiously approached the edge of the pool there was a mighty swirl of water, a silvery flash – the salmon leapt into the river and vanished.

Climbing back up the steep wooded bank was always hard going, especially for Mother, but she never gave in and by clutching at bushes, branches and ferns would reach the top unaided.

Beyond the cottage was a small hill where masses of raspberry bushes grew. In my early childhood there was always a great delight in gathering wild berries and mushrooms, a delight shared by many people living in northern regions. I can still remember strolling in the wood, and the pleasure when spotting the mahogany top of a mushroom, hiding under a birch, followed by another and still another until my basket was overflowing with these sturdy specimens far tastier, when cooked, than any I can buy nowadays.

There was a lovely fragrance in the woods and a strange, almost uncanny, silence, broken only by the sweet cooing of a dove or the shrill cry of the capercailzie, and, of course, the customary drawn-out call of 'Ah –ooo,' between all my friends, the necessary precaution against losing touch and becoming lost in our deep northern forests.

On the eve of our departure from Logierait we went up to that little hill to gather raspberries. It was early evening with the sun rolling to the west, the air still warm. I had never before in Scotland seen so many wild raspberries – hanging in crimson clusters, tasting so sweet and there for the picking. The twins kept running around, filling little containers and emptying them into a bucket. The following day we returned home and on our arrival, Mother, who had saved up her sugar ration, immediately began to make jam and made enough to last us for the best part of the winter. The jam turned out a rich crimson colour with a lovely flavour, and as every countrywoman knows is always much superior to anything made from cultured berries.

On 6 August the Americans dropped the atomic bomb on Hiroshima and another three days later on Nagasaki and – five days later – Japan surrendered. Terrible as the effect of these bombs were, they saved the lives of the remaining starved and tortured prisoners, for it was widely believed that Japan was planning to have them all executed.

With the end of hostilities Ron's brother George, who had been on the infamous 'Death Railway' in Thailand, was flown to Calcutta along with his brother officers and housed in Belvedere, the Viceroy's residence when in Calcutta. Ron immediately left for Calcutta and on reaching Belvedere found George was waiting for him. The two brothers were reunited after a separation of ten years. George, terribly thin and drawn, was quite cheerful. George spent a week or two with Ron occasionally accompanying him to the Barrackpore Club but most of the time joining his brother officers in Calcutta where they were all making the most of their new-found freedom. Ron was invariably awakened in the small hours of the morning and regaled with all the details of some wild parties.

George rarely referred to his captivity and only once, when explaining away the deep scars on his back, remarked casually that they were the result of an interrogation after a secret radio was discovered by the

136

Japanese guards. What he did say was that on seeing so many around him dying of cholera and sheer starvation, he became determined to survive, ate everything that he thought could be edible – lizards, snails and whatever all went into the pot and were boiled up.

With his stay with Ron over, George went on to Bombay and thence to London.

Back at home in Scotland the family were eagerly awaiting their son's arrival. Ron's mother, happy with the outcome, had gone to Mrs Wilson to tell her that what she had foretold had proved to be true – to which Mrs Wilson added a further prophesy: 'You will hear your son's voice before this month is over.' Granny Fraser returned to the house hopeful but a little puzzled.

It was now 29 September and the last that she had heard was of George staying in Calcutta.

The following night there was still no word and as bedtime approached Ron's father, who had been enjoying a nightcap, stood up and said, 'Your spaewife has been wrong this time.' Just then the telephone rang. Granny eagerly snatched the phone and heard the familiar voice say, 'It's me, Mother, I'm speaking from London and will be leaving for home tomorrow!'

In the morning the welcome news was passed on to Kate who taught in Bridlington Girls High School. On being granted two days' leave she immediately hurried off to catch the train for Scotland. The train duly steamed into Broughty Ferry station and on stepping out on to the platform Kate was amazed to see her brother leaving a compartment a few doors along. They had both travelled on the same train without being aware of the fact. My father-in-law, blessed with an endearing calm manner which often disguised any emotion, was waiting in the station. 'There you are,' he said, as he approached them. The car took them to the house. Inside all the other relatives had gathered. Each window was ablaze with lights and fires burned in every room.

Six months later there was a wedding in the Fraser family. George had known his bride, Annette, prior to leaving for the East. She was very likeable with a delightful sense of humour. It was a happy wedding attended by many friends and relatives, including the twins and myself. Shortly after their honeymoon they left for the Middle East, where George resumed his position as an accountant with the Anglo-Iranian Oil Company.

Sad to say, twelve years later, George died suddenly. Annette with her two young sons returned to Scotland where she had to face up to the daunting task of bringing up her boys single-handed. In spite of many difficulties she succeeded. Both sons are doing well and are happily married. Annette lives alone, but she still has the same sense of humour and has remained one of my closest friends.

Shortly after George and his bride left for the Middle East, glad news arrived from India. Ron was at last being granted the long-awaited leave. He flew from Calcutta on a flying boat, a novel experience he much enjoyed in spite of some adventures when first forced by a storm to land on a lake in Gwalior and further delayed by an accident as they taxied to the moorings in Cairo, which, although not serious, delayed the journey by four days. After finally landing in Poole harbour Ron went on to Edinburgh where it was decided we would meet. It was almost two years to a day when I last saw him seeing me off in Howrah station in Calcutta and now there he was standing on the platform at Waverley station scanning all the people pouring off the train. We were joined the following day by George Stevenson, now demobbed and enjoying his leave prior to embarking once again for India. Two days were spent together seeing a bit of Edinburgh but most of the time we just sat talking in the hotel exchanging our news and making up for lost time. We travelled back to Dundee with George in his car. The twins, eagerly awaiting our arrival, had been running up and down the street looking out for us, but now, as we arrived and George left us, they suddenly became shy and tongue-tied.

Soon Ron's parents arrived. Granny was a bit overcome on seeing her elder son after an absence of seven years, but also appeared to be curiously agitated and had to have a cup of tea to soothe her nerves. This, my father-in-law calmly explained, was because he had somehow succeeded in knocking down a light on a traffic island. The heavy light went up in the air and fortuitously landed on the roof instead of crashing through the windscreen and perhaps disturbing Grandpa's habitual sang-froid!

My mother had prepared a hearty meal. With the incident brushed aside by the greater excitement of Ron's arrival we all gathered round the table.

To celebrate their father's arrival, bicycles were bought for the boys. The following morning Ron began the arduous task of teaching the twins to cycle and after spending the whole day running up and down the Kingsway, taking each child in turn, had the satisfaction of seeing them able to go off on their own.

A week later we hired a taxi and set off, complete with bicycles, to spend a month in the peaceful surroundings of Glen Clova. We put up in a guest house, formerly the manse, run by a Mrs Cameron who was of a friendly disposition and a good baker. We were quite lucky with our fellow guests, all were agreeable and friendly. They were a young doctor with a wife and child; a couple from Forfar whose lively twins were company for ours and a Sports Editor of a well known newspaper and his wife who appeared to be the aunt of the famous writer, A. J. Cronin.

It rained each day, but during the dry spells we borrowed bicycles from Mrs Cameron and cycled with the twins around the glen. In the evening, when all the children were asleep, some guests went fishing while we and the others, including the Sports Editor and his wife, who had a rich fund of amusing stories, foregathered in the little parlour and had a lot of fun together.

One day Ron's parents unexpectedly arrived and spent the day with us. During their visit, Grandpa, who had bought another second-hand car, offered us the use of his old Humber until the end of Ron's leave, when he intended to sell it. Ron travelled to Broughty Ferry with his parents and having collected the Humber returned in the late evening. The car proved to be a great boon. Occasionally, with the twins safely in bed and after asking Mrs Cameron to keep an eye on them, we would get into the car and set off on a visit to my mother or Ron's parents where we would have a welcome snack and a drink. I have happy memories of driving back in bright moonlight, singing as we sped through the deserted country roads. At times some small animal or a cat on the prowl would dart across in the beam of the headlamps. These drives seemed to have a magic of their own and will never be forgotten.

On the day before the end of our holiday the rain we had suffered all these weeks suddenly ceased. The skies cleared, the sun came out. We decided after lunch to climb up to Loch Brandy lying at the top of the hill behind the local hotel. We were joined by the other twins and their parents. The going, although hard, was pleasant accompanied by the humming of insects, the fresh smell of damp earth, grass and heather. Suddenly, in front of Michael who had been jumping from hummock to hummock, the thin dark ribbon of an adder flashed like lightning and vanished in the undergrowth. In spite of many years in India this was the first time I had seen anything resembling a snake and strangely it had to happen in Scotland.

Following a long strenuous climb we reached Loch Brandy - a brooding haunting lochan beside whose dark waters I would not care to find myself alone. It was on this shore while aimlessly strolling around I was astonished to see a cloudberry, better known to me as maroshka, nestling in the marshy undergrowth. The habitat of the

maroshka is in the sub-Arctic regions which I did not think included
Scotland, but realised that the high altitude must have provided a
similar environment. Everbody, infected by my eagerness, joined in
the great search for more maroshkas, but in the end the result was
a mere handful, yet it pleased me very much. I was reminded of a
holiday on the shores of the White Sea where once stood the ancient
isolated Pertominsky Monastery, now, alas, a prison camp. There
was also a dark pool surrounded by a lush carpet of the golden
maroshka and there also might have been seen a little girl kneel-
ing with her basket, eagerly gathering the berries – a long, long
time ago.

The next morning, we packed our luggage into the car, tied the
bicycles to the back, said goodbye to Mrs Cameron and our various
fellow guests and then departed for Dundee.

We spent part of Ron's leave with my mother and the remaining
weeks with Ron's parents. The car came in handy. Although the shortage of petrol did not permit long runs, we were able to drive to places
nearby, visit friends and join in occasional dinner parties.

Meanwhile in India, on her last year of the Raj, the dark shadow of
the partition was drawing closer. People arriving home on leave were
talking of the ghastly outrages already taking place in Calcutta, of the
sudden outpouring of hate between the Hindus and Muslims revelling
in sadistic killings of men, women and children. They spoke of seeing
masses of bodies floating down the Hooghly, the satiated vultures
unable to rise from the bloated corpses.

To the average Briton in India, the partition of the country was an
unmitigated disaster, perpetrated by a group of Indian and British
planners, who, with astonishing optimism, disregarded the age-long
enmity between people of opposing religions, opened a Pandora's box
unleashing an awesome horror culminating in a death toll of over a
million innocent souls. Six million refugees crossed the new frontiers
seeking safety amongst their own kind, but all too many, caught up
in stations, helpless in their carriages, were slaughtered to the last
man, woman and child.

Here in Scotland we were enjoying the last remaining days of Ron's
leave. By now we were into late September with the days unusually
bright and warm. The autumn scent of asters and chrysanthemums
was in the air and in the Frasers' back garden, the lush Victoria plums
were begging to be picked.

One sad dark evening Ron left for India and after his departure the
boys and I returned to my mother's home. The twins did not say very
much. Two and a half years were to pass before they would see their

father again – meanwhile it was decided that I would remain with them for at least another year.

On Ron's return to India he was promoted to manager in one of the mills in the group named Lansdowne. This mill was situated near the Dum-Dum airport and was also close to the Salt Lakes – a breeding ground for mosquitoes. There was no river, but instead a canal edging the outskirts with a branch leading into the mill jetty. The semi-detached house was spacious. In the other half lived the head office salesman, Jerry, a friend of Ron. The compound was small. There were two tennis courts between the manager's house and the married and single quarters. All the houses overlooked a lawn, laid out in flower beds and flanked by a high wall. There was also a small garden beside the salesman's house. As there was no other garden the ladies often sat there beside a Gul Mohur tree growing in the corner.

The killing and burning still continued in Calcutta and district. The working of the mill was frequently interrupted by rumours and actual killings. The Muslims who lived in Ultadanga, about half a mile down the railway line leading to Calcutta, would often be afraid that they were going to be attacked as they returned home after the mill shut down at night. They appealed to Ron, who then phoned up an army captain working from the main police station in Calcutta and requested him to provide an escort from Ultadanga station along the road leading to the main road. As instructed by the captain, Ron led the odd hundred or two workers down the line and formed them up under the railway bridge where a lorry full of British soldiers and the captain were waiting. Led by the lorry, proceeding at walking pace, Ron and the workers followed and as they approached the little lanes leading to their *bustees* (mud houses) the workers dropped out and eventually only Ron and the escort were left. The captain would wave a cheerful goodbye – 'See you tomorrow, Mr Fraser' – and Ron would walk home alone. Although these trips were repeated several times no one ever threatened him.

One evening as Ron and Jerry stood on the tennis court they were horrified to see an arc of fire behind Ultadanga. They feared all the Muslims were being slaughtered, but the next morning were relieved to learn that the Muslims had been warned in time to allow them to escape to Park Circus in Calcutta with what they could carry.

In Park Circus the position was critical. Jim Dakers – Mae's husband – travelling through Park Street found himself between two fires. On one side of the street were Muslims, on the opposite Hindus, both attacking each other with bricks, stones and whatever. Jim didn't have to tell his driver to hurry. The car went through the barrage of missiles at full speed until they reached the safety of Chowringhee. Jim was later to recall he had not been so terrified in all his life.

As so many of the workers living in Park Circus were too frightened to come to their work it was decided to bring them and their families to Landsdowne. A fleet of lorries and taxis went to and fro bringing them to the mill. Some of the taxi drivers were Sikhs, who were Hindus of a special branch of Hinduism, but also great haters of Muslims – yet there they were arriving with women and children and not even charging them full fare. When Ron expressed his surprise one of them said to him, 'Sahib, today it is them – tomorrow it will be us.'

The workers and their families were accommodated in empty jute godowns. There, behind the safe walls of Landsdowne, they happily settled down. All conveniences which they did not have before were now laid on for them – water, latrines and the canal nearby where they could bathe and the children played. As there was always the risk of cholera and typhoid all had to be inoculated. Ron, with the resident doctor, went along to the godowns, where the women, terrified of the injections, tried to hide, while their children, already inoculated, gleefully pointed out where their mothers were hiding under the charpoys, and shrieked with delight on seeing them being dragged out to be forcibly inoculated. They stayed in Landsdowne until after the partition and then gradually left to build their own little bustees.

In Scotland the winter of 1946-47 would be remembered by many for the heavy snowfalls and frosts, lasting well into the spring. To the children the novelty of such deep snows was a source of great activity: the exciting battles with snowballs, the sledging, and the digging of mysterious tunnels to an imaginary igloo – an adventurous ploy, the danger of which was brought home to me when I went looking for them and discovered to my horror that the muffled voices I was hearing came from the 'igloo' on top of which I was standing.

We had a white Christmas and New Year, a plump turkey and trifles and the usual gathering of relatives. With the festive season over the boys returned to school and the normal daily routine was resumed.

In the early spring of that year a letter arrived from Finland. Earlier, when at long last the war was over, I wrote to Archangel once again in the hope that this time I would receive an answer. To my Aunt Marga I expressed the hope that she and her family had survived the war and now with our two countries having fought the common enemy together there would be no barrier between us and we could meet again. I also sent a letter to my Uncle Yura inquiring if he had received the booklet he had asked for with the instructions on the breeding of silver foxes. Again there was no replies to my letters.

I then wrote to my cousin Marina in Finland. Marina had changed houses but the Finns with their meticulous sense of order found her new address. The news from Finland was shattering. They were all dead, Marina wrote, and had died in 1938 during the height of Stalin's terror. There were only two survivors: Marga's daughter Liza, and Yura's son, Alexei. After the initial shock and grief I turned in bitter anger on myself. How could I have been so naive as to imagine that the all-consuming monster could ever have changed and how foolish it was to harbour thoughts of a new benign relationship rising out of the ashes. I was not alone in this. Better and far wiser men were taken in by the smooth face of evil to the point of handing over on a plate more victims to be killed and tortured. Not all the news from Finland was bad for although the family had suffered great hardships and my Aunt Olga, Marina's mother, who had been ailing, died, all my cousins survived, which enabled me to keep up a correspondence especially with one who bore the same Christian name as myself and who had married and gone to live in Paris.

In the halcyon days in Russia before the First World War, each summer two of my Aunt's numerous daughters used to come to spend their holidays with us in Archangel. The last time I saw Jenya and Zlata, two of my cousins, was in the tragic summer of 1914. Now with Jenya living in Paris there was every hope that another reunion might come our way some time in the future. When and how this would take place I had no idea. I knew only that it was bound to be and looked forward to that happy day.

During that same spring Ron's parents went to live in Edinburgh. Ron's father, who was a dentist, decided to retire and move to Edinburgh where he was born and spent his early childhood. The night before their removal a heavy snowstorm swept over the countryside. In the morning all the streets and gardens lay under a pall of snow. I went along to help and do a little last-minute tidying in the house. It is always sad to walk through rooms which once resounded to the voices of a happy family, where parties, dances and Christmas gatherings took place, but which were now cold, empty shells. It was a bad time of the year to move, but with the coming of warmer weather they settled down quite well in their new surroundings.

In the late summer a telegram arrived from my brother, steaming across the Atlantic on the *Queen Mary* with his young wife and two small children.

My brother, Alistair as he was called, and I, brought up in Arctic climes, were later fated to travel and live in the tropics – I in the steamy heat of Calcutta and he in Venezuela where he held the post of Field Manager with the British Controlled Oilfields. Unlike the system in India his leave used to take place every two years, the last one being in 1938, unfortunately missed by me having to join Ron in Lawrence.

Prior to the outbreak of the war all employees of the British Controlled Oilfields sailed to and fro between Europe and South America aboard the ships of the Royal Netherlands Shipping Company. With the start of the war many of these ships were sunk with tragic loss of life. This resulted in the banning of all future leaves to Britain. Permission, however, was granted to all members of the staff to travel to any part of the American continent if they wished to do so.

One of Alistair's colleagues, an Irishman called Johnny, suggested that if Alistair cared he could join him and spend his leave with his married sister who lived in New York. They duly arrived there and spent their leave with Johnny's sister Mary, a loving and hospitable woman, and her husband Tom. Mary had a son and two daughters, both attractive and friendly girls. The younger girl, Nora, and my brother fell in love and a year later, Nora, braving a flight to Venezuela during the war conditions, duly arrived in Maracaibo where she was met by Alistair. After their marriage they set off for the oilfields in the depth of the Venezuelan jungle. Now four years later they were on their way to Scotland.

The telegram arrived in the evening with instructions for me to meet the boat train due in London the following forenoon. With barely a minute to spare I caught the night train and arrived early in the morning. After booking a room in the King's Cross Hotel, where I knew we would have to spend the day prior to leaving Scotland, I set off to meet the train. It duly arrived and a great multitude of passengers poured out rushing past me. The thought that I may have missed them threw me into a panic. Amongst the hurrying crowd I noticed a young man walking along with a rather nonchalant manner. Anxious, in desperation I approached him in the slender hope that he might be able to help me. 'Tell me,' I said, 'did you by chance meet a man and a lady with two small children?'

He glanced at me with barely disguised contempt at such stupidity. 'Lady,' he rejoined coldly, 'the *Queen Mary* is a large ship and carries thousands of passengers – there are numerous men and women carrying children,' and without a backward glance he continued walking.

More people kept pouring out and then at last with great relief I recognised my brother with a baby in his arms and a young attractive woman holding a little girl by the hand. My brother and I were always close, the result perhaps of having shared so many troubles and griefs during our turbulent childhood. To meet him once again after an absence of ten years was quite overwhelming. We spent the rest of the day in the hotel. I found my young sister-in-law amiable, generous and blessed with a fine sense of humour. We became great friends and have continued to be so throughout the long years that followed.

In the morning we arrived in Dundee where we were welcomed by Mother and the twins. Mother's flat was bursting at the seams. There we were: baby Kathleen, five months old; Sheila, aged three, a wise and lively child; the twins; Mother; and me – but somehow we managed to squeeze in. They had brought with them a large crate packed with all kinds of goodies – tins of ham, sausages, cheese, salmon and sweets. We were living it up for the next eight weeks and longer. Life was brisk – relatives and friends kept calling – a car was hired and trips arranged into the country. The days sped by and before we realised it the end of their leave arrived. They left for the United States early one morning in October and the house suddenly became empty.

After my brother and his family left I was faced with my own departure for India. The boys were going to be cared for by my mother. Although I knew they would be left in safe hands, the thought of having to say goodbye to them was difficult to bear.

It was arranged that Phil Campbell, my friend of Kinnison days, and I would travel together. We planned to meet at the West station in Dundee, go on to Liverpool, where we would spend the night in the Adelphi Hotel, and the following day board one of the Anchor Line ships, which would take us to Bombay.

When the appointed hour of my departure drew near, Mother, the boys and I arrived at the station. We were joined by Mae and Pat and their dog Misty. Phil was already there waiting and as the moment arrived for the final goodbyes she hopped into our compartment and sat there waiting.

We mothers, living in India, are conditioned to accepting these farewells, yet when the moment comes it can be heartbreaking. I was afraid I would break down and upset the boys, but as the train was on the point of leaving Mae came to the rescue by drawing the twins' attention to her dog. They turned to play with it – the last I saw of my children as the train started to move was them running with the dog towards the exit.

The following day we boarded the ship, the name of which now eludes me. It was described as one of very old vintage with only the sails missing to complete the picture – but the cabins were comfortable and the cuisine good. My cabin was shared by two ladies, one of them elderly and the other Vi, of my own age, with whom Phil and I kept in contact after our arrival in Calcutta. We made friends with two tea planters and their wives and found in them kindred spirits. They were good fun and one in particular had a rich fund of jokes and stories – some perhaps risqué, but still amusing.

The voyage was mainly uneventful, but when approaching Cape Finisterre we ran into a dreadful storm. The poor old ship shuddered and creaked, pitched and rolled. The sea came through the ventilators into our wardrobe and soaked our clothing. Vi, lying on the bunk below the porthole, was also drenched. To my surprise she suddenly struggled up and reached out for her lifejacket.

'Why are you doing this?' I asked her.

'The ship is bound to go down,' she said in resigned tones, 'and we might as well be prepared.'

'Please believe me,' I tried to comfort her, 'I once went through a far worse storm than this and survived.' I was remembering my own frightening experience on a small trawler rounding the Kola Peninsula when many years ago we were escaping out of Russia. Vi appeared to be reassured and climbed back into her bunk.

By morning, to our great relief, the wind lessened, but later we heard that we passed a French trawler flying a distress signal and on arriving in Malta were told that another French trawler had gone down with the loss of all hands.

Those who travel across the many seas find all ships are the same. Romances flourish only to die a quiet death at the end of the voyage. The sea air seems to make some people cast off all inhibitions. There was a sweet young thing with an angelic countenance, on her way to be married, who had a passionate love affair with a member of the crew and on arriving in Bombay threw her arms round her fiancé.

On the whole the journey was not so boring. We had a lot of fun with our tea planters whom we were to meet again when they came down from the hills to Calcutta, but it was good in the end to see the Ballard Pier and recognise in the waiting crowd the welcome presence of the familiar figure.

Ron had arrived to meet me with plans for us to spend a day or two in the Taj Mahal Hotel and have a look around Bombay, but found it was impossible to get in anywhere except into a dingy hotel, offering no comfort. We left the next morning to board the train which once again took us across the broad expanse of India to Calcutta and Landsdowne.

4

OLD HANDS IN NEW INDIA

Ten years earlier, almost to the day, I had arrived in India at the beginning of the last decade of the British Raj. Now I was back at the start of the first decade of Indian Independence.

On 15 August 1947, the day of Indian Independence, Ron was instructed by the head office to organise a ceremony involving the striking of the Union Jack and hoisting the flag of India. Ron found it impossible in his heart to do so and relegated the honour to the burra babu (head clerk). Crowds had collected. There was general rejoicing and no trouble. At the conclusion of the ceremony Ron said a few words expressing the hope of continuing friendship between Britain and the new India. There was an enthusiastic response and the crowd gradually dispersed.

I was not enamoured by Landsdowne and still had vivid memories, when once invited to dinner in the same house, of seeing the walls grey with mosquitoes and how we ladies had to sit at the table with our legs in pillow slips, our arms covered by cardigans, in spite of the intense heat. Things had improved since then. Ron, ignoring the displeasure of the head office, had the windows and the veranda enclosed by netting. There was also the weekly custom of spraying all quarters with Gammexine powder, which certainly removed the mosquitoes but was not exactly a health-giving exercise and annoyed the ladies having to clear away the powder from their suites and carpets.

I missed the life in Kinnison, the easy access to the adjoining compounds, the Barrackpore Park and the club there. We kept in touch with our friends, although Aikman and Edie were now transferred to Chittavalsah in the south of India and we were not to meet for some years to come.

Jimmy Stewart still resided in Kinnison. Soon after my arrival he gave a luncheon party to his friends. The guests were Phil, Bob, Jimmy Mechan, George Stevenson, Ron and I. Jimmy, a meticulous host,

147

had two of the main dishes brought from Firpo's. The lunch went off
to a fine start with soup, fish followed by steak and kidney pie, usually
served hot, but on this occasion, to my surprise, cold. I observed a
glance of displeasure from Jimmy in the direction of the bearer, but no
one passed any remarks. The *pièce de résistance* was a rich trifle carried
in hot with the melting jam and cream all mixed up together. As it was
an obvious mistake, we all treated it as a joke, but our host was furious
and rising from the table dashed into the bottle khana from where an
angry mixture of Hindustani and English reached our ears. It
transpired that the dishes from Firpo's were handed to the cook with
the strict order to place the trifle in the fridge and the pie into a hot
oven; the cook merely reversed the instructions – something by no
means unusual in India. Sometime later I was invited to tea by one of
the ladies in Lansdowne. There the sandwiches offered were, to my
astonishment, filled with sweet whipped cream and flavoured with
vanilla –quite odd, I thought, and not very good, but said nothing. The
cake, however, a cream sandwich, did not appear on the table. My
hostess was infuriated with the cook, having ordered him to make a
cream sandwich – an order he obeyed literally. And who could blame
him – a sandwich is a sandwich!

These strange incidents often happened but in India, I learned in
time; nothing was surprising.

One day a very pleasant Indian gentleman called on us. He was
immaculately dressed in an *achkan* (knee-length coat) and sporting a
Gandhi cap. Fine looking with honest eyes and an earnest manner he
made a good impression. His mission, he explained, was collecting
funds for the opening of a small centre in the nearby village which
would provide free milk to the children suffering from malnutrition.
He had already been round the compound and all had responded
generously as did we. I was most enthusiastic in conveying my
appreciation that at long last something was being done for the children and also expressed the wish for more young men like him and
for other villages to follow suit.

As he was leaving he bowed in a gracious manner and asked me if
I would be so good as to come to the village and preside over the
opening ceremony of the milk bar due to take place a week later. They
would all be so honoured, and the children delighted, he added. After
some hesitation and Ron showing a certain reluctance I agreed.

The following week, on a hot and sultry day, Ron and I set off for
the village. Ron was not enthusiastic and tried to put me off. The road
was long and dusty, he pointed out, and a storm was brewing. I turned
on him in anger. How could I possibly break my word, I argued, and

what would the Indians think all standing there waiting for my appearance, if we never bothered to turn up?

The only way to reach the village was to walk along the railway track, standing aside for each passing train. After some three miles we scrambled down the rough embankment and continued on our way until we came to the village where we were met with curious glances and barking dogs. The friend who was to meet us and direct us to the milk bar was conspicuous by his absence nor was there any welcoming crowd all eager to meet Mrs Fraser. Questioning the villagers Ron discovered there was no milk bar and no one had heard of the charity or the collector. It was one of the biggest sell-outs I had experienced in India. It has to be said the man was clever. He had succeeded in fooling not only us but also the Muhammadan labour officer attached to the mill, a man not easily fooled, especially by a Bengali Hindu.

We climbed the embankment and began our weary trek to Landsdowne. With that a duststorm broke out covering us in grime and cinders. By now I was crippled by a blister on my heel. A heavy downpour followed through which unladylike expressions might have been heard. We arrived in Landsdowne soaking wet and filthy – to the unconcealed delight of Shamsher Ali, who had warned me that the memsahib should not believe a word of what a Bengali Hindu had promised. Actually, it was not just the futile trek and the fact that I had been taken in that upset me but that this rogue had succeeded in shaking my faith in human nature.

Life in Landsdowne continued and although the place did not appeal to me I gradually got used to it. There had been an addition to the household during my stay at home which enlivened the daily routine. On the day of my arrival, as I stepped out of the taxi, I was met by three dogs barking a shrill welcome.

It so happened that Mae and Jim, prior to departing on leave, asked Ron if he would take care of their bitch Bonny, a cross between a Labrador and a spaniel. Jerry, living in the adjoining house, owned a very smart little terrier named Jock who, in due course, became enamoured with Bonny and, although half her size, with amazing agility succeeded in fathering on her four healthy puppies. Ron found homes for two of them, kept one and named him Glen; Jerry, adopting the last one, called him Johnny. Both dogs were alike – black with white dickies. Twice the size of their father they were not endowed with the same intelligence, but were friendly and loyal. Bonny meanwhile was duly returned to her owner. The dogs usually accompanied me when I went strolling around the compound or by the canal where, to the children living in the godowns with their mothers, the dogs were a great attraction. I visited the godowns and met the women. In spite of cramped conditions they were amazingly cheerful, and gathering round me asked many questions. Who was I? Did I have any babas? I told them I had two sons – both born at the same time, to which their response was *'Bahut accha hai'* (That is very good) – boys were always more welcome than girls who expected their parents to provide a dowry for them when they married. Although Calcutta was now comparatively peaceful, the women still felt safer living in the godowns. In other parts of India the troubles still continued.

We were now into the fateful year of 1948 when the whole of India was shattered by the dreadful news of the assassination of Mahatma Gandhi on 30 January. Many feared that if the murderer was a Muhammadan it would start another killing of innocent victims, but he turned out to be a Hindu which avoided another bloodbath. Mahatma Gandhi was a man of peace and was on his way to a meeting when the assassin shot him. He died instantly.

There were four ladies in the compound but the one I got to know best was my own contemporary whose Christian name was Grace. We both had two children at home. Grace's son and daughter were older than the twins and her girl at the time was attending the College of Domestic Science at Atholl Crescent in Edinburgh. We often sat beside the tennis courts or in the corner of the small garden. We liked to talk about our children. It was a topic more interesting and closer to our hearts than any other and whiled away many empty hours. Grace was a member of the Calcutta Amateur Operatic Society. She was endowed with a beautiful voice – true and completely effortless. I used to think that had Grace been given a chance in her youth she would have gone far, but the times in these 'good old days' were hard and difficult.

On occasions we used to go to Calcutta together, usually by train. We had to walk along the railway line to the station of Ultadanga where we boarded the train which took us to Sealdah station and from there by taxi into the centre of Calcutta. After some shopping and lunch in the Swimming Club, we would return by the same road, walking along the railway line carrying our purchases.

· The other way to reach Calcutta was by taxi which involved having to send a durwan to bring the taxi from the main road. Travelling between Calcutta and Landsdowne was often awkward. The part that I liked best was when on drawing closer to the compound we drove along a narrow road beside a wide strip of water. On the opposite bank surrounded by palms and greenery were a couple of bustees. From there a finger of land ran across to the road and close to it spreading over the water like a carpet were the heavenly blue, wild hyacinths.

150

Occasionally the graceful figure of an Indian woman carrying on her head a *chatti* (earthenware pitcher) would be seen crossing the causeway accompanied by a little dog. It was an idyllic, simple scene perhaps worthy of an artist's brush. The place always held a certain fascination for me. I remember once, when driving past, seeing an old man standing in the water and with folded hands earnestly saying his prayers – nearby was a small boy relieving himself and further along a young woman, filling her chatti, as usual oblivious of any germs lurking in these waters. On another occasion, during the rainy season when the pool and causeway were flooded, I saw the little dog, quite undaunted, swimming across and on reaching the road giving himself a little shake and continuing jauntily on his way to the bazaar.

The bazaar which we had to go through presented a different picture. I just cannot remember seeing anything worse than this terrible place of squalid, poverty-stricken broken-down bustees all huddled close together, the foul drains smelling to high heaven. At the end of this bazaar was a level-crossing over which we had to cross before we could reach the compound. Often there would be a railway engine barring our way, which we suspected was done deliberately, and we were forced to sit and wait until it was the driver's pleasure to move away and allow us to get through. Once while waiting in the car, glancing casually around, I was stricken by the pitiful sight of a small boy sitting on the side of the road, close to a pile of refuse where lay a dead dog. He was scraping the inside of a banana skin and licking his fingers, but on another day I found some consolation on seeing a very old man, sitting apart from the fetid garbage, surrounded by a group of small children to whom he appeared to be telling a story. The earnest eyes of the children, listening with rapt attention, and the kindly face of the old man presented a poignant and unforgettable scene that rose above the surrounding squalor.

The name of the bazaar was Dakhindari, renamed 'Dark and Dreary' by the jute wallahs.

As time went by I gradually learned that the average Indian's life is ruled largely by astrology and superstition. I remember one of our Indian friends, named Prabhu, regaling me with all the portents – lucky or unlucky – where cows, goats, cats and dogs all played a part. He was also a firm believer in the paranormal – the evil eye, haunted houses and ghosts. In me he found a ready listener as I likewise harboured my own special beliefs – on no account to arouse the wrath of the jealous gods by gambling with fate or taking anything for granted and at all times never to allow a black cat to cross my path or allow this harbinger of evil, friend of witches, to enter my house.

Certainly, from all that I have heard, India has always been to me a land of mystery, enchantment and strange happenings. I once had what I believe was an uncanny experience concerning our dog, Glen. The mill was being electrified at the time, with motors replacing the old steam engine. As the work entailed could be done only when the mill shut down at night, Ron often felt obliged to supervise the changeover. I disliked being left alone, but having no other option consoled myself with having Glen for company.

Late one evening after Ron had departed for the mill I settled down to read with Glen lying at my feet. In a little while I noticed he became restless and for some reason kept staring into the opening leading into the dining room. Thinking that perhaps there was a cat or some other animal I went into the dining room but seeing nothing returned to my seat. Glen, however, refused to be pacified. He rose and stood in the opening, moving his head from side to side as if he was seeing something odd and puzzling, suddenly emitting a low growl, his birse rising. He retreated, obviously scared stiff. It was enough for me. 'Come!' I called to him. We both rushed out into the darkness – anything was better than being inside the house – and continued running past the astonished durwan and then into the mill. Ron was standing on a raised platform where a motor was being installed. Glen immediately climbed up but, unable to descend, had to be carried down by Ron, who curtly dismissed our incident as a piece of superstitious nonsense.

Sometime later, however, Ron had to admit my fears had some foundation as one evening when he was in the house Glen was again seen watching something in the dining room while growling and refusing to settle down. The house was not old and had no history of anything untoward ever having taken place there, but this strange manifestation occurred from time to time. We could find no explanation for it and eventually came to the conclusion that animals, especially dogs, have a finer perception of things unseen than we do.

With Ron now being promoted to a manager we received one day an invitation from the directors to a cocktail party – aptly re-named by Phil as the 'Menials' Ball'. The invitations were sent out every cold season to all the senior members of the various departments in the company: jute, paper, coal, travel, etc.

I cannot say I was enamoured by these functions. There, dressed in all our finery – the men in dinner jackets – we would gather in the house and garden of the Managing Director. With glass in hand we moved from group to group, meeting a few friends, acquaintances and strangers from other departments. There was the customary small-talk and a little laughter. The wife of one of the directors or the Director himself would say, 'How nice to meet you, Mrs Fraser,' or 'Glad you were able to come along,' – the usual superficial pleasantries which I was daft enough to believe were sincerely meant.

The best moment came when it was all over and we together with our close friends were on our way to Firpo's or the Grand Hotel where we enjoyed a good dinner and watched the performance of a first-class cabaret.

As each cold season followed another we attended these head office gatherings only if we happened to be in the mood for them, at times preferring to see a film followed by dinner in town.

I am reminded of an incident which took place years later when we attended one of the annual parties. The hostess, wife of the Director, had gushed over me with great warmth as we stood together in her garden. The following morning I went to Calcutta to do some shopping in what was known as the 'Good Companions'. I saw the same lady bending over some hand-embroidered articles lying on the counter. 'Good morning Lady —,' I greeted her in a friendly tone. She raised her head and stared coldly straight into my eyes and turned away without the slightest sign of recognition. I never allowed myself to make the same mistake again. All this took place a long, long time ago – the lady has vanished from the scene and no doubt is lording it over the angels. I have to add that the women were more prone to indulge in this stupid behaviour than were the men. Some women appeared to be acutely conscious of their position – no matter at what level. The men rarely bothered.

From the early days of my Russian childhood, spent in the Arctic regions, where on a wintry evening, sitting with my elders around the table, I listened spellbound to the voice of my young uncle reading the wondrous tales from our Russian classics, there formed in my being a great love for books. In the years that followed – years of ups-and-downs – there was always the consolation in moments of grief to be transported to another world and to forget the present if only for a little while.

The first book I read in Scotland after being taught to read and write English was *The Rosary*, a romantic tale, followed by others in a similar vein until I gradually moved on to the classics.

I knew little about India. It was only after I was married and went to live there that I acquired some knowledge, mostly through the books found in the Barrackpore club library and later in the Bangkok library which offered a rich selection from all corners of the world. The shelves were full of books written by the retired members of the ICS, ex-Viceroys, their wives and army officers. I never came across anything that might have described the lives of the countless men and women connected with commerce and especially the important jute industry in Bengal. Of course, there was no comparison between the two communities.

The members of the ICS were men of high scholastic qualifications dedicated to the service in India. In spite of ridiculous snobbery and stupid protocol, we have to recognise their achievements – roads, railways, the freedom of speech and the gift of the English language. They were the people, often referred to as the 'Heaven born', who, through virtue of administering law and order all over the country, truly knew the real India.

Yet at times I have wondered just how much some of them knew about how the other half of the Europeans lived and have been astonished to read, more than once, a statement alleging that all the European women and children at the onset of the hot weather hur- riedly departed from the burning plains for the pleasant hill stations. From my personal experience this was far from the truth. During the five years, when our children lived with us near Calcutta, there was only one break in the cool hills of Darjeeling. We were not alone in this. Hundreds more were like us.

With the exception of tea planters who had a pleasant outdoor life in the tea gardens, the other Europeans involved in cotton, paper and jute led a different style of life in the plains. Dundee being the centre of the jute trade in Britain practically all the Europeans connected with jute in Calcutta, or in the mills, came from Angus or Fife. They came from various backgrounds and, although the magic of India beckoned, all had the realistic down-to-earth approach – simply to improve their lot and make some money.

At one time India offered the opportunity to reap a rich harvest. The mansions in West Ferry and district of the nabobs from India testify to the truth of my statement, but these times were long since past and the same mansions by the end of the Second World War were divided and subdivided. It was still possible for some to acquire riches – my late Uncle Henry, a broker in Calcutta, was doing quite well for himself until in his early thirties death overtook him in the year of 1919 – but it was not as easy as it used to be and became more difficult as the income tax rate increased to a high level.

As long as the Raj remained, young men continued flocking to India eager to take up their places in the ICS, army, offices and mills, but no matter what position they held there was a pattern common to them all. No one, with few exceptions, remained in India until overtaken by old age. Old men and women were rarely seen in the European community. Men usually retired when in their fifties and lived out the remaining years in the land of their birth. The companies in any case did not encourage anyone to stay beyond the age laid down by the firm when they could claim their provident fund.

I remember one of the ladies once saying to me, 'I like India but would not care to die here. All I want after we retire is to have a little bungalow and spend the rest of our days at home.' She did not ask for much, poor girl, but died before they were due to retire, and her husband married again.

And that was another aspect of life in India. In spite of up-to-date medicines in the treatment of diseases which in the past filled the cemeteries around Calcutta, there were still cases of unexpected deaths taking place – particularly tragic when they occurred close to the date of retirement.

Nothing was permanent in India – certainly not our homes, carpets or furniture. We were moved from one compound to another and, as each leave came round, commuted between Bengal and Scotland like birds of passage. There were always some kind of vague plans and hopes especially amongst the ladies that after we retired something permanent would be found at home. That little word 'after' kept lurking at the back of our minds. We were given to collecting little things – embroidery of all kinds. The 'Good Compoanions' in Calcutta was such a tempting place which offered beautiful tea-cloths, luncheon sets, guest towels and whatever. A Kashmiri shop in the market sold furniture and various articles in solid walnut wood. I treasure to this day a set of peg tables with coffee table to match all finely carved and much admired by my friends. There are ornaments and brass ashtrays, for example, reminders of our times spent in the East.

I remember one lady in particular who kept collecting all her time in India a great variety of things for 'after'. No Chikan wallah, visiting the compound, was ever chased away with a sore heart and by the time when the day arrived for her departure she had succeeded in gathering a pile large enough to start a linen shop at home.

Overall, apart from certain drawbacks, such as the sad separation from the children, life had a brighter side to it. There were friends, comfortable quarters, gardens, flowers and the joy of the cold weather. It was pleasant to rise in the morning secure in the knowledge that the breakfast was prepared, the beds would be made, the house cleaned, lunch and dinner cooked and served.

It is only now in our declining years in Scotland, when confronted by the endless stream of chores, that I am reminded of those blissful hours of ease and have to admit in that respect life was good in India – a statement heartily endorsed by my husband who, until we finally retired from the East, had successfully avoided all forms of domestic tasks.

In Landsdowne I found the hours passed slowly. During the weekends we usually set off for the Swimming Club in Calcutta where we would meet our friends – Edith and David Penny, the two Jimmies, or whoever – and from there go on to one of the cinemas and later finish up with dinner in Firpo's. Occasionally there was a performance by the Calcutta Amateur Theatrical Society, known as the CATS, or the Operatic Society, both of which we usually supported. There was also an exchange of visits between friends which at times stretched to weekends. Through the week when Ron was hard at work I often would set off on my own to meet my woman friends in the Swimming Club. There we played mah-jong, or went shopping, or just simply sat talking together and after a cup of tea returned to our respective homes.

The highlight of each week was the arrival of the familiar envelope with the laboriously scribbled notes inside: 'We are having good fun in Glen Clova – Grandpa is here with us. He has caught the largest salmon you ever saw. Will write again. Love Michael'; or 'Granny took us to the pictures last week. We saw *Bonny Prince Charlie* – only he wasn't a bit like Prince Charlie. The battle was exciting. Love, George'. The writing changes gradually from child to a boy, to a youth, to a student. I keep them all – each one a sad reminder of empty days.

The little garden in the compound served to while away the idle hours. Assisted by an enthusiastic mali I planted pink hibiscus, rare blue plumbagoes, sweet-smelling jasmine, in all the corners I could find. Two shades of Bougainvillaeas were soon climbing over the arches of the porch and on the banks of the canal were planted several Gul Mohurs – the spreading umbrella-like trees with their rich clusters of crimson blossoms.

Years later I had occasion to visit Lansdowne. The Bougainvillaeas over the porch had vanished, but the Gul Mohurs had flourished and beneath the spreading branches of one of them an old woman was resting in the shade.

George Stevenson came one evening and brought his two little dachshunds, Sherry and Whisky. As George was going on leave to Scotland we were committed to take care of them for the duration of the next six months. Sherry, small, with a silky black coat, was quick and very wise; Whisky, tan coloured, fat and slow to think. Between Jerry's Jock and Johnny and our three we shared a lively pack. Not a rat or a single stray cat was allowed to survive in the compound.

Dogs can be quite amusing, at times almost human in their behaviour. Jock often called on us and was in the habit of settling down close to Ron's feet. His two sons, Johnny and Glen, would never have dared to claim this special place, but one day when Jock arrived he was surprised to see the spot which was his prerogative occupied by a small black stranger. Jock did not even hesitate, but simply sat down on top of Sherry. Sherry, indignant but uncertain as to what the outcome might be if he displayed his objections to being sat upon, and not wishing to lose face, immediately, with an expression of grave concentration, began to dash around the room pretending he had to catch a lizard on the wall, an objective far more important than just sitting at anybody's feet. The lizards, high out of reach, were contemptuously making clicking little noises – their equivalent of cocking a snook. Soon Jock, who never prolonged his visits, decided to return to his master. Sherry, on seeing that the coast was clear, gave up the hunt and, moving casually to the now vacated place, settled down there for the rest of the evening.

Both dogs being highly intelligent had a healthy respect for each other. In dealing with stray cats, Jock was the master. He never hesitated as most dogs do, but attacked before the poor cat had time to think. Sherry was unrivalled when it came to burrowing under seemingly inaccessible places and ferreting out a rat.

He overdid his zeal one day when we took him with us to the Barrackpore club and he vanished into the foundations. A grating had to be broken before we would get him out. He emerged covered in filth and smelling to high heaven. It transpired he had succeeded in getting into a deserted jackal's lair. He paid dearly for his venture, for although he was thoroughly scrubbed there and then, an infection set in on his tail and removed every hair from it. We were a bit worried as to what the effect would be on his owner of seeing his dog with a hairless pink tail. Fortunately, after several visits to the vet, where the drastic treatment, borne patiently by Sherry, effected a cure, we were greatly relieved to see the hair growing over his tail in time for George's arrival. These little incidents provided a welcome break in the daily routine and furnished me with something to write about in my weekly mail to the boys.

In due course George returned from his leave in Scotland and called on us to collect his dogs. During the evening as we sat talking he told us that while at home he had at long last found someone he wished to marry. We were delighted to hear his news. He had been an eligible bachelor far too long and it was time for him to settle down.

We enjoyed hearing all the latest news from Scotland, especially as we ourselves were looking forward to our own leave due to take place in a few months. Plans were made that this time on arriving in Scotland we would take off with the twins for a holiday to some part of Europe not visited by us before. Hours were spent in pouring over travel brochures of all the various countries, but in the end it was the one from Switzerland that caught our attention. It depicted a delightful little village named Axenstein situated above Lake Lucerne. In describing all the amenities, the owners of the hotel had also mentioned that Queen Victoria herself had once visited Axenstein and expressed her admiration for the place. Although not quite sure as to the truth of such a statement, we decided if it was good enough for Queen Vicky it should be good enough for us and duly wrote to book our accommodation.

In early June of 1949, with the hot weather still in full swing, and after the usual gruelling journey across India, we arrived in Bombay and boarded one of the Anchor Line ships, the *Cilicia*. The voyage was uneventful. There were some people we got to know who helped to pass the time and with whom we kept up later, but who gradually vanished out of our lives and memory.

We disembarked in Liverpool, where we boarded a train to Dundee and in due course arrived at my mother's house. The boys came rushing to meet us. They had been running up and down the street looking out for the taxi long before the time it was due to appear. Ron had not seen his boys for three years, I for two. Now there they were taller and a little older. Once again for just a little while we would be a united family.

A few weeks later we were on our way to Switzerland. The train journey was broken in Edinburgh so that we could spend the day with Ron's parents who, in the evening, came to the Waverley to see us off. We had no idea that in spite of the war being over for four years there would still be this great congestion when travelling. Crowds were milling in the station and it was only with the greatest difficulty that we succeeded in scrambling into a compartment together. It was shared by other passengers including a group of young ATS on their way to London. One of them, a pretty little blonde, sitting next to Ron, soon fell asleep and having nestled up close to him, slept soundly all night with her golden head resting on his shoulder, a situation I suspect he quite enjoyed. I, however, was not so lucky sitting between George, who slept with his head on my lap, and a fat man who had obviously been imbibing and was now breathing heavily down my neck.

From London we joined the boat train to Dover and crossed over to Calais from where we continued our journey by train to Lucerne. The compartment on the French train was comfortable and we enjoyed congenial company with two housewives and their husbands who talked in half English and French and asked many questions: 'Where did we come from? What did my husband do? What was his salary?' They in turn informed us that their husbands were employed by the Railway and all of them therefore were travelling free on their way for a short holiday in Switzerland. We left them at Lucerne and boarded one of those delightful steamers which sail on Lake Lucerne moving across from shore to shore disembarking or collecting passengers from all the little towns and villages. The landing stages were busy. We could hear laughter and lively exchanges between the passengers and the crew in a language we could not understand. The day was perfect. Azure skies, bright sunshine, picturesque tidy villages nestling close to the shores of the peaceful lake and behind them the wonderful vista of hills and mountains – a far cry from the exhausting heat and dust of Bengal.

We disembarked at the little town of Brunnen where we were met by the hotel porter who was sent to meet us from the hotel. A funicular railway took us up to Axenstein, a place we were pleased to discover to be even lovelier than our expectations. We were welcomed by the owners Gustav and Sophie, standing at the entrance of the Park Hotel, a homely residence which specialised for families with children. The rooms were comfortable and well furnished. Our two adjoining bedrooms, overlooking the lake and hillside, were likewise well appointed. The cuisine was excellent and quite astonishing to us after the austerity of Britain.

The adjoining Grand Hotel was, as the name implied, an imposing edifice. Inside, the spacious, luxuriously furnished reception rooms, with their tall gilt mirrors and crystal chandeliers, still held the charm of a long-lost world. At one time the hotel catered for the wealthy aristocracy from all parts of Europe, but now, forced to adapt to exist, the doors were open to tourists arriving in busloads to stay the night and depart the following morning.

As both hotels were owned by the same family the residents in the Park Hotel were allowed to enjoy the amenities of the Grand Hotel. We liked to go over in the evening to listen to the music played by the orchestra, composed of three young men from La Scala, Milan. I remember seeing there an old aristocratic-looking couple, dressed severely in black, sitting a little apart at a small table playing out a game of patience while listening to the music and looking as if they had stepped out from the previous century.

Both hotels, with terraces in front, overlooked the lake. Many of the residents liked to sit there over a cup of coffee as we did on occasions and we became acquainted with a pleasant American lady who spent hours painting the view of the opposite shore of the lake.

In the grounds of the two hotels a tree-lined path led to a fine swimming pool and near by was a golf course. There was also a clubhouse which had catered for swimmers and golfers. Inside could be seen the trophies, photographs and silver cups won in golf competitions with engraved names, many of these were of officers on leave from various regiments in India.

A short distance away was the private residence of Gustav and Sophie, which was let for the summer to a retired high-ranking Belgian officer with his wife and little granddaughter Christine. Van Stoppen, as he was called, was a proud handsome gentleman, a fact of which he was well aware. To their house, much to the annoyance of the elderly wife, were constant arrivals of attractive young women each of whom, after a week or so, would depart only to be followed by another. According to Sophie they usually arrived carrying a small plastic bag but departed with a large trunk filled with clothes and all kinds of goodies.

A winding path through the wooded mountain led to Brunnen. Half-way down we usually halted to admire the beautiful statue of Mary with little offerings of flowers in front of her. I found the descent quite pleasant but the climb back exhausting and usually returned by the funicular railway.

Brunnen, lying close to the shores of the lake, was a thriving little town overflowing with hotels catering for tourists. We enjoyed going down on occasions to look around, do some shopping and finish up by having some refreshments outside a small restaurant. There was one occasion when we joined the bathers on the beach and went swimming. Ron hired a small rowing boat and took us well out on to the lake. It was most enjoyable but as the beach was very crowded we preferred to swim in the private pool of our hotel where we were joined by some of the residents and their children and spent many happy hours with them.

One lovely summer day we decided to visit the Frohnalp, situated behind Axenstein with a deep valley lying in between. There were two ways to reach the mountain. Either from Brunnen and thence by tramcar to a funicular railway which would take us to the top. The other course was to cross from Axenstein in a flimsy metal box suspended from a cable – a contraption originally meant for carrying supplies, but often used by people and strongly recommended by

Sophie as a great time-saver, completely free from danger. We followed Sophie's advice. Accompanied by our Belgian friend Van Stoppen we set off across the meadows and duly arrived at a small platform where inside a hut a young woman was controlling the electric motor driving the cable.

We had understood that our friend was to accompany us on our trip but it turned out that he had only wished to escort us, and on being asked replied, 'Madam, I fought in the First World War and through the whole of the Second and received several decorations for bravery. I have not the slightest intention of risking my life inside that horrible little box. I wish you a safe journey.' With these sweet words he departed back to the hotel.

As only two persons at one time were allowed to travel Michael and I scrambled into the box and sat facing each other. It began to glide slowly, gently, gradually increasing speed. We were enjoying the new sensation of seeing the wonderful scenery gliding past and were almost half-way when there was a sudden stop and the box began to sway violently from side to side. Michael, white faced, kept asking, 'Will we be saved? Will we be saved?' Numbed with fear I could not answer. Far below I could see the houses, cows grazing in the meadow, the silver ribbon of a stream – while we, high above, were trapped inside this swaying cage. After two or three agonising minutes which seemed like hours the box started to move once again and eventually reached the platform. It transpired later that it had been travelling too fast and the young woman had to ram on the brakes. It was an experience neither Michael nor I wished to live through again.

Ron and George arrived next. Nothing untoward happened to them. From the cable-car terminus we went up to the top of the mountain by chair-lift. On the way up we were meeting people coming down, all very cheerful, carrying little bunches of flowers, waving and greeting us in a friendly fashion. We spent some time at the summit having refreshments and later just sitting on the mossy ground enjoying the magnificent panorama spread before us – the mountains, lake, valleys. Below us, bright-coloured splashes lay on the sunlit slopes where masses of blossoms in all shades and hues grew between stones and boulders.

On returning to the platform we found a group of local children swinging and turning somersaults on the guardrails of the platform. One false move could have sent them flying into the void but they appeared to be quite unconcerned. There were also some visiting schoolchildren who were waiting to cross but politely allowed us to go in front of them. Michael and I set off for Axenstein with some trepidation but this time, with no hitches to scare us, we were over safely and quickly.

Ron and George were to follow, but a girl and her young brother asked to join them. The girl assured Ron that the car often took four persons. The extra load, however, proved to be too heavy. On approaching Axenstein the box came down on the soft ground of the slope and was dragged along leaping and bumping with George shouting, 'Let's get out, Papa, we've gone far enough – let's get out and walk,' which was quite impossible. The box eventually reached the platform. The young woman operating the contraption was not in the slightest bit perturbed; to her, sitting in the hut, smiling sweetly, it was all in the day's work.

These two little adventures are still remembered and talked about to this day.

All the children staying in the Park Hotel came from various parts of Europe, yet when playing together got along surprisingly well – such as on one morning when they had gathered round a table on the terrace and were happily engrossed in some card game. There were the two little German girls and the delightful granddaughter of Van Stoppen, a pleasant French boy, André, and our sons. Sitting a little apart we could hear them laughing and talking in their own tongues and by some means perfectly understanding each other. I remember thinking what a pity it was that some of the politicians did not follow the example of these children.

Shortly before our departure great celebrations took place on Swiss National Day and by evening reached their highest peak. In the soft darkness under a starlit sky the little steamers came sailing down the lake ablaze with lights. On the opposite shores at Righi, where the Declaration of Independence had been signed, Bengal fire was lit, intermittently illuminating the hillside in all the hues of a rainbow.

Axenstein, not to be outshone, joined the festivities in a grand way. The dinner that night was very special with the *pièce de résistance* being a sweet served on each table in the style of a castle with the Swiss flag, fluttering on the tower. Later all the guests foregathered on the terrace in front of the Grand Hotel.

The evening started with the National Anthem being played which at first I fondly imagined was British and perhaps a compliment to the British guests such as us. I was mistaken. It was the Swiss – the music being the same as our own. It was followed by all the anthems of the different nations – including British, French, American and so on. With the anthems over, fireworks began at which Gustav excelled himself. This magnificent display in all styles and forms spread across the sky, dimming the very stars and in the end presented the faces of his grandparents, the original founders of the hotels.

In the late evening, with the children packed off to their beds, dancing began in the ballroom of the Grand Hotel where we were joined by one of the local farmers who, quite impromptu, with great skill and brilliance, presented the Swiss National dances with one of the ladies, which was much appreciated and loudly applauded. In this free-and-easy gay atmosphere the dancing continued until the small hours when we finished up in the bar with champagne and caviar.

It was after seven o'clock in the morning when we were climbing up to our bedroom with the twins coming down the stairs to meet us.

We left two days later and never saw Axenstein again. It was a memorable holiday which, along with the one in Darjeeling, proved to be the best we had ever known.

Fifteen years after, our son Michael, perhaps nursing nostalgic memories of the place, revisited Axenstein. He found there was nothing. The Park Hotel was now a convent. Of the Grand Hotel no sign was to be seen. It had been demolished some time earlier. The pool, where once we had spent so many happy hours, was likewise destroyed, half filled with refuse. Only the walls remained of the abandoned clubhouse rotting and falling apart. A door hanging askew creaked eerily on broken hinges. The cups and trophies, witnesses of past glories, had long since vanished. A haunting sadness hung over the whole place now empty and desolate. A little information was gleaned from an old man in the village. Gustav was living alone in one of the small houses in the district, but no one knew where Sophie had gone. 'What was the reason for this dreadful destruction?' Michael had asked. The answer was simple: 'No tourists!' Switzerland had become too expensive – everybody was now going to Spain.

Meanwhile, having said goodbye to Axenstein, we embarked for Paris to a reunion with my Russian cousin, Jenya. This meeting was arranged prior to our leaving for Switzerland as we felt we could not miss the opportunity of seeing her on our way back through France.

The last time I had seen her and her sister Zlata was when they were staying with us, on holiday from Finland, during the summer of 1913. It was the custom for some of my Aunt Olga's numerous daughters to visit Archangel each summer. Not having any sisters, I always enjoyed meeting my cousins and especially Jenya and Zlata as they were of my own age. I remember Zlata as a golden-haired little girl with dark eyebrows, thick eyelashes and eyes as black as cherries. It was a rare and lovely combination of which my Aunt was very proud. Determined to keep this golden shade Aunt Olga used to shampoo her daughter's hair, never missing a week, with an infusion of dried camomile flowers. All the other girls were dark haired and pretty, including Jenya who was always rather quiet with a faintly pensive expression.

There is a vivid memory of that hot summer's day in 1913 when my Aunt had arrived with Jenya and Zlata and we were all talking with babushka in the garden. Being rather bored with having to listen to adult conversation the girls and I had quietly slunk away to hide behind the raspberry bushes where we proceeded to eat up all the berries meant for jam-making and later received a good telling off from our angry babushka.

Now after thirty-six years there would be a reunion and with Zlata as well, who was by a happy coincidence on holiday from Finland and staying with her sister. It was arranged that both Jenya and Zlata were to meet us at one of the stations in Paris. Wondering if we would recognise each other after this long lapse of time, I suggested that they should wear something which would catch my eye, such as a flower on their dresses.

The journey from Brunnen was uneventful. We had boarded once again the steamer and enjoyed our last sail on the lake to the town of Lucerne where, in a little restaurant close to the lake, we had a splendid lunch. With a few hours to spare prior to boarding the train for Basel, Ron and Michael went sailing around the lake in a pedalboat while George and I had a look at the town and did some last-minute shopping in some of the wonderful shops which offered a great selection of rare and beautiful things, alas too expensive for our pockets.

On arriving in Basel we found the station crowded with tourists, many carrying skis, sharp pointed sticks and kitbags, all jostling and pushing with complete disregard for the safety of other passengers. It was only by tipping a porter that we were able to scramble into the train at all. We shared the compartment with a young couple who, ignoring our presence, embraced each other hotly, to the wide-eyed astonishment of the twins who displayed a great interest in the proceedings, until someone popped his head into our compartment and announced that there was a vacant one next door. Our loving friends promptly vanished, no doubt to continue their lovemaking in a little more privacy while we settled down on our own and feeling rather tired soon fell sound asleep.

In Paris, the following morning, a great mass of people poured out on to the platform. Crowds were also standing in the station. 'How could I possibly recognise my cousins in this swarming multitude?' I asked myself, and then I noticed two middle-aged women standing quietly scanning people. I saw no flowers, nothing to guide me, but some strange instinct drew me towards them. 'You are Jenya and Zlata,' I said to them in Russian. 'Da,' they answered and threw their arms around me.

A taxi took us to Jenya's home in the district of Billancourt where we were met by her husband Pyotr Pelekhine, a sturdy well-built man with strong features and a friendly manner, who bowed and kissed my hand. Their five-year-old son, also named Pyotr, but nicknamed Masik, a lively child strongly resembling his mother, came running to meet us. Pyotr Pelekhine, better known as Petya, had fought in the Tsar's army during the First World War and later in the White Guards against the Bolsheviks. After the tragic collapse and the takeover by the communists he succeeded in escaping to France where he joined the large community of Russian émigrés. He had had a varied career in Paris – from taxi driver to garage owner and finally at the end of the Second World War running, along with Jenya, a small, successful factory manufacturing fancy goods much in demand by the fashionable shops in Paris.

As well as Zlata staying in the house, there was Petya's sister, Tamara Tersetta, with her beautiful daughter, Alichi. Tamara's husband, Egon Tersetta, had been the resident agent in Bulgaria for the Italian shipping line, Lloyd Triestino. They owned a beautiful home on the shores of the Black Sea, but when Bulgaria was overrun at the end of the war by the Red Army Egon was arrested and tried by what was known as the 'People's Court'. At first condemned to be shot, the sentence was later commuted to solitary confinement for life. Tamara with young Alichi, left completely destitute, had by various means – most of the time walking – eventually succeeded in reaching her brother's house in Paris. They were now assisting in the work of the factory. Egon by now had served four years of his sentence. Both Jenya and Petya told us privately that they did not think he could survive much longer, as it was known that Egon's health had broken down. Tamara, however, firmly believed that eventually her husband would return – a faith in the end rewarded by Egon regaining his freedom.

We gathered round the table spread with various *zakuskis* (hors-d'oeuvres), meat and vegetables with the inevitable bottle of vodka. We were joined by Katya, Jenya's great friend, and her husband, André Lemoulinier, a congenial type with a fine sense of humour, both to become close friends.

Later other members of the Russian émigrés called. There was the tall Cossack, Vladimir Grigoryevich, who owned a taxi in which he later took us sightseeing around Paris.

Princess Volkonskaya arrived. A member of a well-known old Russian family she had stayed on in Russia after her relatives had fled, but during the Second World War at the time of the dreadful siege when thousands were dying of starvation she had succeeded in getting out of Leningrad by crossing the frozen surface of Lake Ladoga, clutching her little boy in her arms, to the enemy lines where she was imprisoned but some time later was released to join her brother living in Paris. The princess, in spite of having to struggle for her very existence, was a very joyful friendly person. Delighted on discovering that we were from Scotland she told us that at one time she had had a Scots nanny who used to sing Scottish songs to her and of whom she cherished fond memories. In the years to come I used to see her sitting at the table beside Jenya laughing and joking while eking out a living for herself and her young son by painting rare designs on scarves and shawls. Her son, I may add, achieved a successful career and was a source of pride and joy to his mother.

On that day of our arrival we went out after lunch into the sunny little garden. The twins, dressed in their kilts, were asked if they knew any of the Scottish dances and on discovering that they did were persuaded to dance. The two boys got up and on a small patch of the garden with great precision and style presented the Highland fling with Ron and I substituting the music by chanting the beat – 'Diddely-dee-Diddely-dam.' Rapturous applause followed the ending. From that time on all my Russian friends used to refer to the twins as 'Les petits Ecossais' – and the Highland fling as the 'Diddel-dee' dance.

With the dancing over André very kindly took the twins and Masik to visit the Eiffel Tower. They returned thrilled with their outing. The boys got on very well together with Masik assuring us that Michael, whose knowledge of French consisted of two words, spoke perfect French.

In the evening, with the children in bed, we gathered round the table talking well into the night. We talked of many things recalling the distant scenes of our childhood, of the great family gatherings that used to take place in the house, of all the incidents that happened sometimes strange, sad, or happy. Each topic began with 'Do you remember?' and usually centred on our long-lost world, the heart of which was babushka. At one point Tamara sitting beside Ron whispered to him in English, 'Everything revolves around babushka.'

The Pelekhine family for generations have been involved with diplomacy. Their grandfather, at one time a member of the Russian Embassy in London, acquired an English wife. Through her grandmother, Tamara could still converse in English much better than her brother Petya who remembered only a few words. Most of the conversation was in Russian, with some French from André which Ron understood, but unfortunately I found difficult to follow.

In the Billancourt district lived many Russians. One morning Jenya took me with her to do some shopping in a nearby shop. I was amazed to see a small Russian woman, with her fair hair in a pleat wound round her head, still adding on an abacus with great speed and efficiency, Russians serving and Russians being served. All the food was Russian style and everybody spoke in Russian. For one moment I was transported back in time, once more in a shop, overflowing with nice things to eat, standing beside my mother and hopefully expecting that the young man serving her will offer me on the edge of his knife some tasty bit – perhaps a morsel of smoked salmon or a little piece of ham – but, of course, that shop has long since vanished as has everything else.

I had not realised before our visit that there was such a large minority of Russians in France. According to Petya when the war of 1914 was going badly for France the Tsar transferred millions of his soldiers to the Western Front and in this way saved France from being defeated. France, remembering this gesture, opened her doors to the masses of fleeing Russians after the Revolution.

As the years went by I became acquainted with many members of the Russian émigré colony. All had known better days but with their inherent fortitude faced up to a long exile fighting for survival in an alien land. Cheerful and resourceful they were eking out a living by driving taxis, painting scarves, writing stories for the Russian journals, running restaurants and shops.

We spent three days in Paris touring around that lovely city with Jenya and Masik in Vladimir's taxi seeing the sights – the Sacre-Coeur, Notre-Dame, and even an ancient prison where one could still see the terrible instruments of torture used on helpless prisoners and which young Masik later said he would remember for the rest of his life.

All too soon these memorable days were over and we were on our way to Scotland. Jenya and Zlata came to the station to see us off. I was to return again and again. The time had arrived when travelling by plane was more convenient than the slow voyage by sea. I made a point, whenever possible, to stop over in Paris even if only for a few days. That little house in Billancourt drew me like a magnet. I never laughed so much anywhere else and liked nothing better than to sit at the table talking and listening for hours to all the tales that carried me to other places, other times. There the air was different. Everything was simple, no pretensions, no affectations. All worked too hard to waste time on such fatuous nonsense.

The factory was flourishing with additional staff being engaged, but it was Jenya's talented etchings, created in silver on gold, depicting delicate scenes, flowers, butterflies on powder compacts, cigarette and jewellery boxes, that brought in the demand and financial reward which enabled them to acquire an old farmhouse with outbuildings and a good piece of land in a country village, thus realising a dream they had cherished for many years. It was a place Ron and I were also due to visit and enjoy in the future.

Only six weeks remained of Ron's leave on our return to Scotland. Summer was good that year. Sunny warm days continued to the end of September with the sweet autumnal scent of chrysanthemums, asters, ripening apples in the gardens.

Ron golfed each day. There were meetings with friends and occasional dinner parties. We also called on George Stevenson's fiancée with the gift he had asked us to deliver to her. She turned out to be an attractive friendly girl with a fine sense of humour, who in due course quickly adapted herself to the life in India.

The boys were back to school. New blazers, books, jotters, pens, paint-boxes had to be bought and the old routine of homework took over, with Ron supervising until his departure. The boys by now had accepted the sad fact, that unlike most of their schoolfriends, they would have their father for only a few months with long intervals in between.

In October Ron began to pack his trunks. It was decided that I would accompany him as far as Liverpool and see him to his ship. On the day of his departure the weather changed abruptly. From the darkening skies rain poured down in torrents, never ceasing. He said goodbye to the boys in the house as it was too dismal for them, or anyone for that matter, to come to the station.

After a dreary train journey we arrived in Liverpool and put up in the Adelphi Hotel. There in the evening we dined together – the last dinner for a long time to come. The following day Ron saw me off at the station prior to embarking on the ship. In the past I had always accepted each separation with some fortitude, knowing there was no other course, but this time I left Ron with a heavy heart.

I had a carriage to myself and sat there still overcome by a deep depression, combined with a strange inertia, at times dozing or staring indifferently at the passing bleak rain-soaked countryside. On arriving in Dundee I was met with the same driving rain. A taxi took me home. There the boys bounded down the stair to meet me. Their glad welcoming faces uplifted my spirit. Mother in her usual way had prepared our evening meal. The four of us gathered round the table. And so began another winter.

I kept myself occupied during those bleak days. A lot of time was spent through the week each evening supervising the boys' homework which was increasing as they grew older. In helping them I was relearning myself what I had long since forgotten.

I made a point of meeting once a week some of my women friends, grass widows like myself, home from India. Our meetings usually took place in Draffens where over a cup of tea we idled away a cheerful hour or two exchanging the latest news.

There was also a visit to Arbroath, where Edie like myself was at home with the children and living in a pleasant flat she and Aikman had bought some time previously. The boys were delighted to meet again their old playmate Alistair. Sonya had grown into a pretty fairheaded little girl and was now attending school. As Edie and I had not seen each other for quite a while it was good to meet again. We spent a happy day talking of this and that and recalling again the troublesome journey we shared together with our children when travelling home from Bombay over oceans and seas swarming with enemy submarines.

In the early evening, after a hearty meal, we set off for our train journey home. It had been a glad reunion and a refreshing break in the unvaried style of our daily life.

The winter was long and weary that year, but one day, out of the bare grey earth, snowdrops appeared, to be followed by crocuses in all their hues and the gladsome sight of an army of daffodils nodding their golden heads. Spring had arrived.

With the coming of brighter days I decided to rent a cottage for two months during the summer in a place known as Ballachragan, situated on high ground above the long road leading from Dunkeld to join the main road from the Sma' Glen to Aberfeldy.

A few days prior to our departing for our holiday, Jimmy Stewart and Jimmy Mechan, both on leave, called at our house. Jimmy Mechan, who owned a car, kindly offered to take us to the cottage – an offer I gladly accepted. On the appointed day both friends arrived, never dreaming what lay ahead of them, for not only was there a mass of bits and pieces but two additional passengers in the shape of the twins' school friend, Scott Stewart, and his younger brother Ian. The four little boys and I, after some struggling, succeeded in squeezing into the back. The boot of the car was packed and a trunk had to be tied to the roof. The journey started with Jimmy Mechan at the wheel, his corpulent friend beside him nursing on his lap a large hat box, the top of which, being level with his nose, created a situation he did not relish and made no attempt to disguise his displeasure. We eventually reached Dunkeld where, in a little country tearoom offering home baking, we halted for a cup of tea. From there, after the boys had devoured everything bar the table, the journey continued on the road out of Dunkeld. To the right of this road a dirt track led up to the cottage. The two Jimmies, helped by the boys and myself, removed the contents of the car and arranged them the best way we could inside the cottage. My warm invitation to them to remain with us and partake a supper of ham and chicken was spurned by my bachelor friends, who all too soon departed in search of something better to revive their flagging spirits.

Not having had the opportunity to inspect the cottage prior to my decision to rent it I had to depend entirely on the description sent to me by the owners. There was no disappointment. The cottage turned out to be even better than I expected. During the war it had been occupied by a lady from Dundee who made several improvements. Hot and cold water was laid on and all the fittings and furniture were in good taste and comfortable. There was a genuine air of antiquity about the cottage. It also had the unique distinction of a small press built into the stone wall beside the fireplace, which I took to be a safe, but was actually used for keeping salt in a dry condition, a custom of a bygone age. There were three bedrooms, a spacious living room, a larder and presses.

The cottage belonged to a Miss Anderson and her brother who lived in the adjoining farm. Kind and thoughtful, they supplied me with chickens, rabbits, eggs, milk and cream, all of which I highly appreciated. Nearby grew masses of wild raspberries. The boys used to gather them. Sweet and juicy, with Miss Anderson's cream, they provided a delectable dessert. With all these luxuries not readily available in the town, we were living it up.

There were, however, two drawbacks. Between the cottage and the Andersons' farm there lay a large field, which made me feel a bit isolated. The lighting consisted of oil lamps and candles. The soft lamplight was pleasant in the living room, but we found the candles in the bedrooms rather awkward.

On the first night of our arrival, after I prepared our meal, I made up the beds for the boys in the large bedroom, arranged our belongings and finally organised my own small bedroom. Exhausted by my labours I fell into bed and slept soundly until a bright shaft of sunlight and the hungry voices of my children woke me up to start another day. It was a different story the following night.

At this point I have to go far back to Archangel, when one winter evening the family and I, nine years old, had gathered round the circular table to hear my young Uncle Seryozha read from one of our Russian classics; it was a common practice in the dead of winter. That particular day the cold was more intense than usual. A thick frost lay over the windows in fanciful designs of ferns, trees, mountains and castles. At times the sound of a sharp crack would momentarily halt the reading and someone would remark. 'The frost is hard tonight – the rafters are shrinking.'

I had been nibbling the sweet pine-kernels and, feeling thirsty, asked Seryozha to stop while I went for a drink. Hurrying from the dining room and through the hall I entered a long narrow corridor. On my left was a second door opening to a stair down to the kitchen. At the far end was a window and against the wall a wide staircase leading up to the garret. Under the stair was a sideboard on which stood a row of samovars and a tray with tumblers. In one of the samovars boiled water was kept for drinking. I began to fill a tumbler and with that heard, quite clearly, a voice coming from above saying my name. Holding the tumbler I stepped out and glanced up at the staircase. There, leaning on the banister, was a woman – an ordinary woman, plain faced with no outstanding features. Over her head and shoulders was a small shawl such as was worn by peasants. 'What do you want?' I asked her. 'Who are you?' There was no answer. Vaguely alarmed I repeated my question. She remained silent – and then suddenly smiled, a venomous, frightening smile. Horror-stricken I dropped the tumbler. The sound of shattering glass set off a screaming, such, my father was to say later, as he had never heard from me before. All at once they were all there. The servants came rushing upstairs. 'The woman, the woman,' I kept repeating through my sobs. 'She is hiding in the garret – catch her – find her.' But when my father ran upstairs he found the door was locked and the key hanging on a nail outside.

She was never found, the mystery of her appearance remains unsolved. Yet she has not vanished entirely and still haunts me in my dreams. She comes in various guises, young and pleasant, old and friendly but eventually, suddenly frightening and I awake bathed in sweat, screaming for my mother.

My mother who had been absent at the time of the event, dismissed the whole affair with her Scots down-to-earth approach: 'There is no such thing as a ghost.' She was probably correct. I know only that from that distant wintry evening, throughout the long decades which followed, I have been quite unable to sleep alone, no matter where I go.

On the morning following our arrival in Ballachragan, having fed the children and let them loose to explore the lie of the land, I spent a few hours creating a semblance of order, rearrranging the living room to my own liking and preparing a meal for four hungry children.

In the afternoon my kindly neighbour, Miss Anderson, called with a batch of warm girdle scones. She also explained the mysterious workings of the oil lamps and was generally helpful about several matters. During a pleasant conversation over a cup of tea, we discovered we had a mutual acquaintance in Broughty Ferry. In this way we got to know each other better. She left in the early evening to cross the field to her farm.

After a late supper the boys went off to their bedroom where they proceeded to have high jinks and pillowfights, until a few stern words restored order. Tired out by all their explorations they soon fell sound asleep.

For a while I sat reading prior to going up to my bedroom to settle down for the night. Everything around us was peaceful. Only the lone cry of some bird broke the silence of the night. The evening scent from the flowers in the garden, drifting through the open window, had a soothing, restful effect lulling me to sleep. Sometime during the night I awoke and was immediately overcome by the old fear of an unseen presence in the room. I tried to think of happy things – tried to sleep – but no, the same feeling persisted and at times it seemed as if whatever it was was drawing closer to my bed and even touching my face with the cold tips of its fingers. I had to get out of that room. Fear can sometimes produce a hidden reserve of strength. I dragged the bed out into the hall and from there into the large bedroom.

Four startled little boys sat up: 'What is it, Mummy – what has happened?'

'Nothing has happened, darlings, Mummy just wants to be with you – go to sleep.' And that is what they did and so did I, pacified by the sweet presence of innocent children.

The following morning the bed had to be put back. Helped by the boys the heavy iron bedstead, complete with bedding, was pulled across the hall into the small bedroom. The going was hard. 'How did you do it by yourself, Mummy?' they asked me. 'I really don't know,' I answered.

In one of the presses I found a light folding bed. It was carried upstairs and placed in the boys' bedroom. There I slept for the rest of our stay in Ballachragan.

I loved the days spent in Ballachragan – enjoyed the novelty of being my own mistress. The weather was fickle, alternating between rain and mist and sunshine. Somehow it did not matter to me or the children. They were having a wonderful time diverting streams, building dams, chasing rabbits and generally revelling in all kinds of adventures.

Many of my friends came to see me. Some for just a day, others stayed longer. Cousin Mae arrived one day and after spending the night with me, during which we talked for hours on end, left the following morning. Mae and Jim were now both at home, having decided to retire and leave India for good. Their daughter Patricia was now twenty-one years of age. Attractive, blessed with a lovely nature, she had become engaged to a pleasant young man called Bill. They both came to spend the night with us. During the afternoon they and the twins set off for a ramble in the hills. I joined them for part of the road, but after crossing a burn and landing in the middle, gladly retreated from the scene. They returned, wet and hungry, to a hearty meal and a bright log fire to welcome them. In the evening the twins and I retreated for the night, leaving the young couple to enjoy a little privacy.

Jimmy Mechan and Phil, home on leave, called and spent the day with us. I enjoyed that little touch of India, hearing all the latest news from Phil, who like myself was resigned to staying on for some time with her son. There is always this special link between people who spend half of their lives in India. The day passed all too quickly. I only wished they could have stayed a little longer.

At the end of a week the twins' two friends returned to Dundee. Another invasion followed. My brother, Alistair, and Nora with their three children arrived home on leave from Venezuela. Soon the whole family, including Mother, appeared in a Land Rover to spend some time with me. My brother had especially ordered the Land Rover to accommodate not only his family but the twins and me as well. Looking back I have sometimes asked myself how and where did I succeed in putting them all up – but somehow I did.

We had a glorious time careering all over the countryside, having picnics on the shores of Loch Tay, Loch Earn, on the moors and so on. It was a happy time especially for my mother who had led a lonely life for many years. Most of these days were sunny and warm. It was one of the brightest periods in our lives to which we still refer and like to recall some of the incidents such as the day when returning from one of our jaunts tired and hungry and looking forward to a delectable meal of cold chicken and salad, we had gathered round the table only to find to our grievous astonishment, when the lid of the pressure cooker was removed, the bare skeleton of the hen resting in a mass of revolting grey jelly. We blamed Miss Anderson who on delivering the chicken was evasive regarding its age. Having concluded that the hen must be long past the first flush of youth, we turned on the full works with a disastrous result. We did manage, however, to survive quite nicely on some corned beef and a large dish of luscious raspberries with cream.

After the family left for home, the cottage became silent and empty. The boys and I, now on our own, continued to enjoy our stay. Every morning there was the usual trek to the farm for the milk. On a bright sunny morning the walk was very pleasant. The path lay close to a field of ripening corn – a golden sea caressed by a playful wind. On my left was a clover-scented meadow and beyond it could be seen a clump of dark stately pines near where the boys and I used to gather mushrooms.

Soon to the boys' delight their great friend, Alan Christie, arrived. Alan lived quite near my mother's house and, from the time the twins arrived from India, was their constant companion. No sooner did he appear than the three of them vanished back to diverting the streams and other happy ploys.

We were now approaching the grouse-shooting season. There was quite a stir in the district when the Spanish Royal Family arrived with their entourage and made their headquarters in the Birnam Hotel. They hired the shoot just behind Ballachragan. One day, crouching behind the wall, we watched the shooting party firing from the butts as the beaters drove the birds in their direction. Some flew safely over, others were brought down. I have to admit there was no pleasure in the sight of the helpless birds falling down like stones and some still valiantly struggling to keep up and dropping in the end.

Later in the day, when the boys were on a path behind the farm they saw the Royal party walking past them. HRH Don Juan picked up a dead rabbit and handed it over to George. Speaking in perfect English he said, 'Take this to your mother for the pot.' George obediently brought it to me. I have no doubt that His Royal Highness did this out of kindness thinking that the boys belonged to some poor peasant family such as he might have found in his own country. The rabbit, however, was not fit for human consumption. I told George to throw it over the dyke.

A few days following this incident Ron's parents and his sister Kate, who were staying on holiday in Aberfeldy came to spend the day with us.

On the night prior to their arrival, I decided to bake some cakes. The finished baking was placed on a wire tray and laid on the table in the larder. The larder, situated close to the back entrance, was a spacious room with a stone floor and presses holding dishes.

Having finished my chores I set off for the farm to order a chicken and some cream for the following morning. Some time was spent talking to Miss Anderson while the boys, taking the chance to roam around the farm, accompanied Mr Anderson who left to kill the chicken. I was later regaled to all the grisly details of the poor bird's demise which had apparently been roosting when suddenly snatched from its perch.

The next morning I arose early and hurried to the farm to collect my order. On returning, a heap of sawdust beside the door of the larder caught my attention. I opened the door and the scene which met my eyes beggars description. All my baking, the lovely walnut cake, macaroons and lemon tarts lay strewn over the floor, broken and filthy. The walls were scarred. Broken plaster, more sawdust and the revolting traces of a rat were scattered around the room. The rat having found itself trapped inside had tried to escape through the wall and eventually gnawed its way out through the door. Horror-stricken and terrified in case this loathsome creature was now hiding in the cottage I opened the back and front doors in the hope that it would leave. The boys were sent post haste for Mr Anderson who on arrival had a curious story to tell me. It transpired that when he and his sister bought the Ballachragan farm the henhouse and cowshed went out of use. The rats, finding their source of food cut off, departed *en masse* to another farm nearby. There the farmer, confronted with this invasion, decided to exterminate them and did so with great success as the rats being strangers had not established any escape routes. Perhaps, Mr Anderson had added, there was this one rat which had decided to return to the old haunts. It was a fine tale. I only hoped it was true. Certainly, it has to be said, we never saw another.

To me there is no other creature on earth more vile and revolting than the rat. Although worried sick in case the rat was cowering in some corner, the preparations for my visitors had to go on. In the end, with order restored and a fresh batch of baking set out on the table my in laws duly arrived. The boys had been warned that on no account were they to mention anything about the rat. Ron's mother had an inborn fear of rodents of any kind. The slightest hint of what had occurred would have led to her immediate departure for Aberfeldy.

We spent a pleasant day together with nothing untoward happening. The following morning, with breakfast over, the boys went off to play, but immediately returned, gleefully shouting, 'The rat is in the trap – it's bigger than a cat. Mr Anderson is going to kill it – it's in the wood shed – come and see it!' Although mightily relieved, I declined the invitation.

By the end of August our holiday was over. Alistair arrived to take us home. Crammed into the Land Rover with all our bits and pieces we waved a sad farewell to Ballachragan and took to the road.

My brother's leave was now also drawing to a close. He and Nora had the same problem as Ron and I regarding the education of our children and had decided that their eldest child, Sheila, would remain in Scotland under the care of her granny and me.

This five-year-old, blue-eyed little girl with softly curling, chestnut-coloured hair, was having to part not only from her parents, but from her younger sister and brother as well. I have no doubt she suffered deeply, yet there were no protests or tears. She accepted what was inevitable with a calm fortitude which I found very touching in one so young.

I remember seeing my brother standing at the window watching the small figure with her schoolbag, stepping firmly out beside the friend escorting her to school. 'There goes my daughter,' he had said sadly turning away.

My little niece settled down quite well after her parents departed. We found her slightly American accent and some expressions most endearing. 'Oh you silly coyote,' she would exclaim at times when playing with the boys. There was also the charming custom, which unfortunately she soon forgot, acknowledging thanks by saying in turn, 'You're welcome.' In the beginning I used to escort her to and from the school. On one such occasion I asked her teacher how my niece was doing. 'Sheila', she replied, 'is my smallest and brightest star.' She slipped into our lives as if she had always been with us.

Unnoticed the days and weeks flew by and before we realised it Christmas with all that it means was upon us. It was a happy time for the children – gilding walnuts, decorating the Christmas tree, fixing the fairy lights, sparkling tinsel and hiding behind the beds to tie up Christmas presents for Granny and Mother. A small party was held on Christmas Day with the usual turkey and trifles. A week later the old year died.

It was at the start of the new year that Ron and I after many letters and heart-searching decided that a boarding school would have to be found for the twins. Mother was getting older. It would have been unfair to burden her again with our boys.

We had no fault to find with Dundee High School. The boys were happy there. It was a fine school but there were no boarding facilities. We wanted a school where the boys could become day pupils during our leave from India and hearing that some of the masters in George Watson's College for boys in Edinburgh catered for boarders, I got in touch with the headmaster, who granted an interview during which he informed me that the boys would have to sit a test prior to being accepted. In the spring the twins sat the test and were duly admitted to the school.

The problem of boarding the boys still had to be resolved. It was not easy to find boarding accommodation, but in the end after getting the name of the PE teacher I wrote to him and he readily agreed to board the boys.

Meanwhile, during the summer, the twins, with Sheila and I, left for Braemar where I had rented a villa on the banks of the Clunie. It was quite a pleasant house, well furnished, but the work involved with it was prodigious. On arrival I was confronted in the kitchen with a small gas ring and an enormous old-fashioned grate, which had to be constantly stoked with coal to provide hot water. I laboured hard over this 'Black Monster' as I referred to it, for not only was there the difficulty of getting it to burn and keeping it going but also the weekly cleaning and polishing with black lead, a process quite unknown to me which often led to blackening myself as well.

On looking back what stands out in my memory is the kitchen, the endless cooking and a picnic or two – nothing else.

The boys enjoyed themselves. They had their friend Alan once again and spent a lot of time fishing or resuming their favourite ploy of diverting streams. Little Sheila tagged along with them but was not always welcome. I used to hear complaints from both sides. 'Oh these horrible boysies, Aunty – they tried to run away today,' – or the boys' impatient 'We had to carry her across the burn.'

We took the bus one morning to a place near Balmoral Castle and after climbing through the wire fencing reached the banks of the Dee. The day was hot and sultry. We spent the time having a picnic and wading in the cool waters of the river. At one stage we saw a large salmon wedged between two stones and moving from side to side in the current. We wondered hopefully if it was still alive. Michael, persuaded to jump in to pull it out, after a tremendous struggle during which he slipped and fell, succeeded in crawling out with the salmon in his arms. It was dead – quite dead with a fishing hook stuck in its gill.

From Helsinki came Lulu, the daughter of one of my numerous cousins in Finland. She was a pleasant girl who went hill climbing with the boys and Sheila and joined in all the other activities. We were to meet again many years later in Barcelona where she was happily married to a Spaniard.

177

At the end of a month we returned to Dundee after what had been for me an exhausting holiday.

On arriving home I found a letter from Ron awaiting me. On reading the contents I was shocked and saddened to learn that our friend Jimmy Stewart had suddenly died. A mere year ago he was travelling with us to Ballachragan and grumbling about the hat box sitting on his lap – and now he was gone. He had returned to India in the hope of retiring at the end of his term. There was no warning of any heart trouble. When the attack occurred he was removed to the nursing home where after a few days he appeared to be recovering. Ron had been seeing him each day and on the Sunday was intending to visit him as usual. In the morning he happened to be passing the mill office and on hearing the telephone ringing went in to answer it. He was told that Jimmy had died that morning and the cremation was taking place in the afternoon. It was the usual intimation sent round the mills when anyone died. People died in the morning and were buried in the afternoon. We lost a good friend, jocular, generous.

And now I had to prepare for the twins' departure to Edinburgh which involved having to go there for the final arrangements with Mr Fleming, PE teacher, with whom the boys were to board. Although I was not invited to see the dormitories, the house was spacious and well furnished. Mrs Fleming appeared to be a kindly person and Mr Fleming quite pleasant.

For the next few weeks I busied myself sewing names on each required article. The list was prodigious and everything, of course, doubled. Blazers, shirts, dressing gowns – three pairs of shoes became six. There were also sheets, pillow slips, quilts.

The day arrived when we boarded the train for Edinburgh and in due course arrived at the boarding house. A short time was spent with Mr Fleming who met the boys in a friendly fashion and displayed an interest in George's hobby of studying wild birds.

Everything ran smoothly, yet somehow on this occasion I did not quite take to Mr Fleming. There was no reason to be doubtful but that is how it was. As Ron's parents and sister lived nearby we had tea with them. In the early evening I escorted the boys back to the gate of the house and left them there with the promise to return the following week.

Back at home I was kept busy with the preparations for my own departure to India due to take place in a matter of ten days. This time I was flying to India in the company of two women friends who were likewise going out to join their husbands.

As promised I returned to Edinburgh to meet the boys at the top of Waverley steps. My heart sank when I saw them approaching me with their faces white and drawn. They did not complain when asked how they were getting along. 'We don't like the food,' George remarked. 'But we'll get used to it,' Michael interrupted. 'Yes,' George nodded sadly, 'after all, everything is fixed – we can't go back.'

The day being a Saturday enabled me to take the boys out for lunch and later for tea to their grandparents where I later said goodbye to them all and left to catch the train. I see myself yet, sitting alone in the compartment, much upset, and trying to find consolation in the blessings that the boys, being so near their grandparents, and Aunty Kate, who was to be their guardian, would visit them every week. They also, of course, had each other, which was more than the other boarders had.

Two days later I met my friends in Prestwick airport. It being our first flight, the three of us were nervous. The flight was uneventful. About eighteen hours later we touched down at Dum-Dum airport where our husbands were meeting us. We parted with our friends and proceeded to our respective compounds.

I was back to Mother India – back to the smells of the bazaars, to the scent of Frangipani, to the heat and the rains, to the glorious cold weather, to clouds of mosquitoes and creepy-crawlies, to glad reunions with friends and curry on Sundays.

Very little had changed in Landsdowne. Jerry, being transferred, had left with Jock and Johnny no doubt sadly missed by Glen. The families, sheltered in the godowns during the time of the troubles, had returned to their bustees. Things appeared to be normal on the surface but the memories of the killings prior to the partition still lived – constant reminders of the undying hatred between the two religions.

Another lady was now living in the compound. Yvonne, a young cheerful Anglo-Indian, was the wife of one of the assistants. During the war she was attached to some women's auxiliary corps where her duties consisted of acting as a guide to members of the American Army, showing them round the various temples and places of interest in Calcutta. The other ladies and I were often regaled to her lively reminiscences of these excursions, at times sounding highly improbable, but still most entertaining. At one time our firm did not encourage marriages with Anglo-Indian girls, but with the advent of the Second World War restrictions were eased.

Far back in the days of the East India Company and the slow sailing ships men married Indian women and were actually encouraged to do this as it was one way of having a foothold in India. Mixed marriages were accepted but gradually, perhaps with the arrival of British brides, a gulf was formed between those who were referred to as Eurasians and the true Anglo-Indians, the people who had arrived from the British Isles to take up various positions with no intention of remaining for good in India. Eventually the name of Eurasian was erased from those of mixed blood and replaced by the more acceptable term of Anglo-Indian. The prejudice, however, continued to be held by both Indians and Europeans. This created a certain complex amongst a few which at times during a conversation led them to refer to home as if they had left it the day before yesterday.

I am reminded of an occasion when we were invited to the wedding of one of the staff whose father was a Scot and mother an Anglo-Indian. The bride, also Anglo-Indian, was young, attractive and as fair as a lily. During the course of the celebrations when Harry Lauder records were being played, the bridegroom's mother, an amiable lady, turned to me and with a hint of nostalgia in her voice remarked, 'Oh, but how this reminds me of my home in Hampstead Heath – the heather growing round the doorstep and the pipes playing at the bottom of the garden.'

It must be said that the scornful treatment of the Anglo-Indians was quite unjustified. The British Raj owed a great deal to them. They were the backbone of the railways, police, customs, nursing and at all times loyal to the Crown, but in the end, with the arrival of Indian Independence, found themselves in the tragic position of being in no man's land. Some were able to leave India for Britain, Australia and elsewhere, others were left with no option but to stay on.

It was not only the Anglo-Indians who were hit by the changes in India. The partition had a damaging effect on the great jute industry in west Bengal. In Pakistan where the great bulk of jute was grown new mills were springing up with the consequent loss of trade in India.

Life in the jute mills continued as before, with occasional strikes, some serious, some minor, usually contained.

I was in the habit of walking to the office to meet Ron when the mill closed down for the day. On one such occasion I was dismayed to see a mass of workers crowded around Ron and hearing them calling out 'Marro – Marro,' (Beat him – Beat him). To the right could be seen the members of the European staff making their way to their quarters. Behind them was the young kerani, Douglas Cunningham, who turned and came back to ask if he could be of some assistance – a brave action indeed. I heard Ron talking above the threatening shouts, but, just as I was preparing to run across to the railway in order to reach the station and phone the police, the crowd suddenly began to disperse. Ron's ability to speak freely in Hindustani stood him in good stead. 'You are brave now, threatening to beat me up,' he told them, 'but you forget the days before the partition when I escorted you to your bustees at night like a lot of children and walked back alone.' It worked. The crowd melted away.

Not so fortunate was the outcome in another mill where Jim Dakers was salesman. On his arrival one day from the head office, he was told that a mob of workers had surrounded the manager and the assistant manager outside the mill office. Jim immediately left the house. The crowd allowed him to go through to join the two men, but closed in behind them. The discussions continued until suddenly a stone was thrown from the back of the crowd which hit the assistant manager and knocked his eye out. It was a signal for the crowd to surge forward, but with that the police arrived on the scene. The mob scattered, as Jim was to say later, 'like a pack of rats'. They were saved in the nick of time.

Early one evening when Ron and I were sitting in the lounge, with Glen at our feet, we heard the sound of shots in the distance and wondered idly what was happening. The following morning we learned the full details of what had occurred the day before. We lived in the vicinity of the Dum-Dum airport and on the Cossipore Road leading to the airport was situated the Gun Factory and also Jessop's Engineering Works. A gang of Communist terrorists unsuccessfully attacked the Gun Factory, but broke into the Engineering Works where they brutally killed two of the Europeans by throwing them into the boilers. The other members of the staff were saved by the efforts of the workers who succeeded in hiding them until the murderers took off to create further havoc in the airport prior to escaping over the border to Pakistan. This horrifying account shook everybody – Europeans and Indians alike – but the perpetrators of this loathsome crime were never brought to justice.

Little trivial things at times enliven the drab days. Once, strolling idly in the garden, I found a pigeon lying on the lawn. On closer examination I found it had a broken wing. The bird had obviously been brought down by a catapult and left to die. The first impulse was to find someone to put it out of its misery, but on second thoughts I brought it into the house and tried the best way to revive him. The pigeon recovered, but could not fly again. In the mill a large cage was made to hold him and there in his spacious quarters, fed and watered, he settled down to live for many a long year. I called him Golubchik – Russian for 'little pigeon' – an endearing expression used between humans. Not knowing what his sex might be I took it for granted Golubchik was a cock bird. The cage was placed on the veranda with the door of his cage open so that he could sit on the edge and peacefully survey life in the garden. At times I took him down on to the floor where he trotted around enjoying his exercise to Glen's amazement, who, while watching curiously, never attempted to harm him in any way.

Golubchik turned out to be very intelligent and as watchful as any dog. He paid no attention to passers-by, but as soon as he saw anyone entering our house an urgent warning would be sounded: 'rikitty coo – rikitty coo,' a stranger is around. At times he gently cooed to himself, swaying from side to side. He went with us, wherever we went, and died sadly after some six years.

With the cold weather behind us we were into the trying conditions of April – a time when the spreading Gul Mohur tree once more bursts into a mass of brilliant scarlet blossoms as if offering some compensation for the unbearable heat.

The brightest moments in our lives were when the airmail arrived. The boys appeared to be happy. They never complained – had their special friends in the boarding house; spent Christmas with Granny in Dundee and went sledging with Alan Christie.

Here life went on as usual, with the weekly visit to the Metro or New Empire to watch a film or have dinner with George and Joan or other friends. We missed Jimmy Stewart. Our old companions of Darjeeling days, Edith and David Penny, were now living in Pakistan where David had been offered a lucrative position. They had previously lived in a lovely house built at the start of Indian Independence in the compound of the Khardah jute mill. Semi-detached, with one part for the salesman, the other for the manager, it was designed in the best style of Hollywood and created a great deal of interest in Calcutta. All rooms were spacious and handsomely furnished, bedrooms, air-conditioned with bathrooms attached, an impressive cantilever staircase with special lighting effects.

I remember the house-warming attended by all their friends from the mills and Calcutta. It was a jovial celebration which lasted into the early hours of the morning. I also remember driving home through the bazaars past the poverty-stricken bustees and somehow suddenly aware of the great difference, asking myself, 'Was this grandeur perhaps tempting providence?' I used to know Edith in the days of our youth in Scotland. On meeting again in India we resumed our contact with each other and played mah-jong, attended dinner parties, but now there was one house less for us to visit.

As the four-year term between home leave was now reduced to three Ron was due to depart for the UK in early July. Our plan was to find a furnished house in Edinburgh, so that we could take the boys out of the boarding house. Ron had also arranged to take delivery of a new car in London, the intention being for the boys and I to meet him there and to travel together through England to Scotland.

In April in the midst of all our happy preparations a cable arrived with the tragic news of the death of Ron's father. The news shattered us. Having lost my own father in Russia I was always very fond of my father-in-law, a man at all times courteous and from whom I had never, throughout the whole of my married life, heard a single unkind word. It transpired later that he had caught a chill followed by pneumonia. All efforts to save him proved to be in vain. As it was imperative to send a reply we set off to the Cable Office in Calcutta, but were caught in an unexpected torrential downpour. In pitch darkness with many roads flooded, we eventually reached the Cable Office to send our condolences.

In late May, true to my promise to the twins, I boarded the plane for London and from there to Turnhouse airport near Edinburgh where I was joyfully met by the twins and their aunt. We proceeded to Granny Fraser's house to spend a few hours with them all. With the boys having to return to the boarding house I sadly left them and went on to Dundee to a second happy reunion with Mother and little Sheila. So began another stay in Scotland.

Through my friend Maimie and her husband, John, who were acquainted with the owner of a flat in Montpelier Park in Edinburgh, we were able to rent this flat for a year. The flat, situated on the corner of a cul-de-sac, was on the ground floor with a front and back entrance and a small garden with a solitary crab-apple tree. We considered ourselves lucky. The flat, consisting of three bedrooms, lounge and dining room, was spacious and well furnished. We could not ask for more.

At the end of July I received the scheduled date of Ron's arrival in London and with the twins set off to meet him there. It was arranged that we would travel to London by bus from Edinburgh. Certainly it would have been more comfortable to go by train, but the bus was less expensive and easier for George who had broken a leg recently. Having booked ahead into the Cumberland Hotel, we settled to wait for Ron. After an hour and more had passed beyond the time he was due to arrive we became anxious. I phoned Heathrow and was informed that the plane had been delayed but was due to arrive any minute now. Sure enough to our relief in another hour the familiar figure blew into the room, hot and dusty, and after a quick embrace and a kiss vanished to have a bath. However, he soon emerged and ordered a large selection of sandwiches to be brought to the room. Ron had not seen his sons for almost three years – there was a lot to talk about. At the end of a fortnight we took possession of the flat and began our life in Edinburgh.

We enjoyed our stay in Edinburgh. The gracious capital had a lot to offer in the way of theatres, cinemas, exhibitions and the magnificent Royal Botanic Garden. The shops nearby were convenient as was the delivery to the house of meat, groceries and vegetables. We settled down to a cosy winter of drawn curtains, soft lamplight and glowing fires. For Ron this was his first winter's leave with the approaching Christmas, since his arrival in India in 1927. The boys were back at school, happy at being able now to return each day to the comforts of their own home and receiving some help from their father with their homework.

During the autumn my sister-in-law Nora arrived with the children from Venezuela and put up with Mother. The purpose of Nora's arrival was to settle the other two children, Kathy and Johnny, at school, to buy a house and establish a permanent home in Scotland.

Christmas that year – the first Christmas to be celebrated together since the days in India – passed quietly with only Ron's mother and sister Kate attending.

Shortly after Christmas my brother arrived from Venezuela and the whole family, together with Mother, joined us to celebrate the New Year of 1953. With extra folding-beds and the sofa we somehow succeeded in arranging the sleeping accommodation.

Ron, due to leave for India in the beginning of the year, received a letter from the head office informing him that owing to rearrangement of managerial staff his leave was extended for another five weeks. We were delighted to spend those extra weeks together which passed all too quickly.

After Ron's departure for India, Alistair, with Nora and the family, moved into my flat. It was an opportunity to prepare curtains, carpets and whatever for the immediate occupation of their new house in Edinburgh. It also enabled their children to start their education in the Convent of the Sacred Heart at Craiglockhart. We spent a happy time living together. I can't recall any disagreements – only a lot of fun and many amusing incidents.

In May my brother and his family left to take possession of their new home. I continued, living on my own with the boys until Mother came to stay for a week or two. We were sorry for her. One by one we had moved to Edinburgh; only she was left behind to live alone. In time to come, however, she was fortunate to find a pleasant little flat in Edinburgh where she lived within reach of her family until her death some years later.

Ron and I had decided that I would join him in the autumn. I was preparing myself to accepting once more a term in Landsdowne which never appealed to me, but to my great relief and delight I received from Ron the happy news that he was being transferred to Kinnison, a place where the quality of life was better and where we had previously spent many happy years with the children.

A few months remained prior to my departure during which I had to ensure that the boys would be left in trustworthy hands. Mr Clark, a Latin teacher, affectionately referred to as 'Nobby Clark', was recommended to me not only by some parents, but by the boys who had boarded with him and were friends of the twins. I called on Mr Clark and realised at once that here was a person of integrity and was much relieved when he agreed to accept the boys as boarders.

By the end of July the flat was handed over to the new tenants. Some of the treasures I had collected, such as china and crystal, were packed in cardboard boxes and taken for storage to the garret in my brother's house. Through the years during our lives in the various furnished flats I was given to collecting things for 'after' which were usually packed in cardboard boxes and delivered to my ever-patient brother to be kept in his garret until the happy day when we could move them to our own house. I used to refer to all these numerous packages as 'my cardboard kingdom' and was often teased about it, but which in the end proved to be invaluable.

The last few weeks, prior to the boys starting their term and my leaving for India, were spent with my mother where the boys met up again with their faithful friend Alan and went long runs on their bicycles with him.

We returned to Edinburgh to spend the last day with my brother and also to visit Ron's mother and Kate who lived quite near to Alistair.

In the evening I said goodbye to my sons, spent the night with Nora and Alistair and in the morning left for Prestwick to catch my plane. The boys had been upset, but tried to hide their feelings. It is my firm belief that children who are constantly fated to feel the joys of meeting or the sadness of separations in the end suffer more than the parents.

I spent the night in Prestwick and the following morning boarded the KLM plane for Amsterdam where I duly arrived after a short flight. As the plane for India was not due to leave before the evening, to while away the long hours I took the airport bus into town where I strolled

around the streets taking in the sights of Amsterdam and returned in
time to have dinner prior to boarding the plane. The restaurant was
busy with most of the tables occupied. A friendly waiter directed me
to share a table with a gentleman. After studying the menu and giving
my order to the waiter I pointed out to him that my plane was due to
leave in less than an hour and would he be so good as to see that my
dinner was served without delay.

At this point my table companion intervened. 'Excuse me,' he said,
'are you by any chance flying to India?'

'Yes – to Calcutta,' I nodded.

'In which case,' he informed me, 'you have plenty of time for dinner
as the departure time has been put back an hour.'

There ensued a conversation between us during which I expressed
my disappointment with the general high-handed treatment meted
out to me by KLM and had added that my brother travelling from
Venezuela by the same airline appeared to receive more consideration.
What did my brother do there, he asked me, and on being told that
my brother was the field manager with the British Controlled Oilfields
he inquired if my brother knew a Mr Rappaport. 'Yes,' I said. 'He is
one of the directors.'

Our conversation continued. I happened to mention that by some
strange coincidence both my brother and I although brought up quite
near the Arctic regions were fated to live in the tropics – he in
Venezuela and I in Calcutta. This statement aroused a lively interest.

'What part of the Arctic regions?' he asked.

'The north of Russia,' I answered.

He became strangely curious. 'Do you speak Russian?'

'Yes,' I answered.

He smiled broadly. 'And so you know the Russian language,' he
said, speaking in perfect Russian.

I had the feeling he was testing me. 'But, of course,' I rejoined
rather sharply in Russian, 'I was born and educated there.' From then
on we conversed in Russian only. I told him that I had had a Russian
father who died in Russia and a Scots mother who now lived in
Scotland. In his case, he said, it was the reverse – he had an English
father and a Russian mother. Our talk continued until we boarded the
plane. As we were seated in different parts the conversation could
only continue during the various halts *en route*. We exchanged our
experiences. He with his brother and mother had escaped from
Russia during the time of the Revolution – his father escaping later.
I, in turn, described to him how we had succeeded in getting out via
Murmansk and Norway.

186

I was a little puzzled at times and perhaps misunderstood him, but I got the impression that it was his father who was Russian and the mother English.

He left in Teheran where he explained he was joining his brother who was a civil engineer and engaged in building a bridge. Prior to leaving he handed me his card on which was printed: A. Kay, British Thompson-Houston Company. He also added that he would probably be in Calcutta on business in which case he should like to call on us. I in turn told him that both my husband and I would be only too pleased to meet him. We never met again.

A few weeks later while reading *My Europe*, by Robert Bruce-Lockhart, I read a passage in which the author refers to Aleksandr Kerenski, who was the Prime Minister during the time of the Provisional Government after the first revolution in March 1917 and which unfortunately lasted only until October when it was taken over by Lenin and his Bolsheviks, forcing Kerenski to escape in disguise. Kerenski, Bruce-Lockhart goes on to say, is the father of two brilliant sons, one of whom is employed by the British Thompson-Houston Company and the other a civil engineer who was busy building bridges in Iran.

Everything fell into place. A. Kay was Aleksandr Kerenski, the son of his famous father. Why he didn't divulge this is a bit puzzling to me, but no doubt he had his reasons.

In Dum-Dum airport I was met, as usual, by Ron. We travelled along the familiar Barrackpore Road on to Kinnison and across the little bridge to the house on the island known as the Jheel Khootie, a handsome two-storeyed building facing south-west, the lower flat of which was traditionally occupied by the new manager. Above us lived Phil and Robert Campbell who was now the chief mill manager over all the mills in our company.

The burramemsahibs were always granted a certain licence regarding the decoration of their quarters, but in my case the now-retired burramemsahib had gone to town with outrageous ideas and colour schemes unacceptable to any woman with normal taste.

The walls and ceiling, painted dark green with fluorescent tubes dangling on chains from above, casting a greenish light, gave me the impression that I was setting foot into something akin to an aquarium. Artificial flowers of every kind – daffodils, chrysanthemums, roses – festooned the frames of pictures left behind. My predecessor disliked fresh flowers. The malis who with great artistry used to arrange the flowers in the house were promptly and firmly told, 'Nahin munta' (Don't want), 'they bring beasties into the house.'

Originally there had been a handsome fireplace in pleasing tiling and a solid teak mantelpiece. The tiles for some strange reason were replaced by single tiles each representing the flowers on the carpet. In days gone by during the cold weather the fire was lit occasionally and brought a touch of home to those who gathered round. Now it was blocked by cement, impossible to remove and serving no useful purpose. The flooring on the veranda suffered most. When the old cracked tiling was being replaced the burramemsahib chose a combination of red and pink which presented the appearance, aptly described by one of our wits, of raw minced beef. This was an eyesore endured for the rest of our stay in that house.

On the day following my arrival painters arrived. Walls and ceiling were painted cream, the bizarre tiles skilfully blanked out, the ugly fluorescent tubes removed and replaced by standard and table lamps. With fresh curtains and chair covers, a few ornaments and books our abode took on a more homely appearance. Life in the Jheel Khootie was pleasant with its garden, trees, tennis courts and little bridges crossing the surrounding water.

I was able to renew my acquaintance with old friends, especially with Edie, who was back again and living in Kelvin with Aikman, now a director in his firm. Almost a whole decade had passed since the time we travelled home with our children. Great changes had taken place during those years.

Gone were the days when the durwan guarding the gates to the holy precincts of Monty's house, still referred to as the Beehive, used to allow me with the twins to enter the garden during Monty's absence and how we would timidly approach the aviary to admire the collection of rare and beautiful birds. The aviary has long since vanished. A Club House was built on the same place and named the Honey Pot. The gates stand wide open and anyone who cares can come along to enjoy the amenities offered and bring their children as well. Once a month a fleet of cars can be seen bringing ladies from the various compounds to join in the competitive game of mah-jong with a prize to the winner. I attended on one or two occasions, but did not return preferring the more leisurely pace with my own friends.

Young men continued to come out, followed by their wives and children. New married quarters, modern and air-conditioned, had been built to accommodate them. Far greater benefits than in our time were now enjoyed by the staff. Passages for all men, women and children were paid for by the company. There was also another innovation which allowed free air passage for schoolchildren, up to a certain age, to visit their parents during school holidays.

The twins were a few months over the age limit and were the only border case, others being years older. Ron hopefully approached our head office man who told him to go ahead and have the twins' passports arranged, pointing out that a mere few months would not matter much and was a small reward for 26 years service and having paid all passages for his wife, children and even himself up to 1939, out of his own pocket.

We were overjoyed as were the boys when they heard the glad news and especially so when they discovered that Alistair and Sonya Doig were coming out as well.

We waited impatiently for the final confirmation. It never came. I knew at once when Ron arrived at the house, by the distressed expression in his eyes, that we had been refused this one and only chance of the boys coming out.

Other men, who had barely served one term and in two cases were actually dismissed in the end for incompetence or whatever, had their wives and children out not once but several times.

Here was the perfect example of blind obedience to rules disregarding all other considerations. Even more galling was the fact that in the following year the age limit was increased by a year to suit one of the directors whose child was a year older. Had this new age limit been in force from the beginning the twins would have qualified, and seen the land of their birth.

Through the years, like many more, we had known various injustices, but had to ignore them and carry on as best as we could, but this one has remained forever in our memory. However, as time went on I discovered that fate has a way of squaring things up.

As the twins' hopes of coming out to us were shattered, I tried to think of ways and means by which I could compensate for their disappointment.

My cousin Jenya, in France, had often suggested that we should spend a holiday with them in the village of Rats-Gris where she and Petya had bought a farm in delightful surroundings and were gradually bringing it up-to-date. I gladly accepted this invitation and wrote to the boys telling them that when my leave came round again I would meet them in Paris from where we would go on to the village. Our sons, by now used to ups-and-downs in their young lives, accepted this change of plans and looked forward to an unusual holiday in a village in France. They wrote cheerful letters and, judging by the description of the various capers in which they participated with the other boarders, Nobby Clark was a tolerant man.

I had arrived during sticky September in time for the Durga pujah

soon to be followed with the start of the cold weather by the celebrations of the Diwali in honour of the goddess Lakshmi, the giver of
wealth and good fortune, accompanied by a multitude of lights twinkling in houses and gardens.

As of old it was the season for tennis, dinner and tea parties now
enlivened by the children arriving from home. We also gave a party
for Edie and Aikman with Alistair and Sonya and included young Ian
Gold, the son of one of our salesmen. It was a joyful gathering, in spite
of my own disappointment, with various games being played in which
young and old took part. All too soon the children returned to their
schooling in the UK. Life in India fell back into the old routine.

It was during the cold season when, on reading an advertisement in
the *Statesman* offering miniature dachshund puppies for sale, I went
to Calcutta and returned with my chosen puppy – small, black-coated
and very endearing. I named her Mitzy.

Prior to buying Mitzy I happened to be in Calcutta where I met an
acquaintance who asked me if I would agree to adopt a Siamese cat.
The present owners, retiring and due to leave for the UK in the near
future, were anxious to find someone who could give their cat a
home. I, as Ron later described, in a moment of mental aberration,
impulsively said, 'Yes, just bring her along.' Now with Mitzy happily
installed I unexpectedly received a phone call. Did I still remember
my offer? 'Yes,' I lied shamelessly, having quite forgotten the
incident.

Anna, the cat, was duly delivered to our house. Like all Siamese cats
she was attractive with large turquoise-coloured eyes expressing icy
contempt for the human race in general, including ourselves.

Gradually, getting accustomed to her surroundings, Anna took over
the whole of our house. There was the usual, amusing, mad half-hour
in the early evening when she rolled, turned somersaults, chased
lizards or would leap over chairs and furniture to land on tables
without disturbing a single one of my precious ornaments. She then
proceeded to settle down on the back of Ron's chair behind his head.
Glen, accustomed to sitting at Ron's feet, would timidly try to
approach his place. Anna never allowed this. Although indifferent to
Mitzy, she hated Glen with all the strength of her cat's being. As soon
as Glen drew near the chair she would stand up, arch her back and
emit a terrifying humming sound like a hive of angry bees causing
Glen to retreat hastily into the bottle khana.

By now we had all had our fill of Anna. The cook having to prepare
dainty meals, Sadhu dragging Anna's special box day after day,
Golubchik pining in his cage, Ron because the cat was queening over

his dog and I suffering a guilt complex for allowing her to be brought to the house and poor Glen worst of all.

Things, however, were now reaching a most unusual climax.

One evening Shamsher Ali approached Ron to tell him that he had found the curtain hanging beside Anna's box wet and smelling. We were puzzled. How was it possible for Anna to achieve such a thing? Investigation was called for, but as we approached the bedroom Glen came running out and attempted to pass us. Glen, deprived of all privileges by his hateful enemy, had decided that if she could have a private toilet, then so could he and simply cocked his leg against the curtain. What followed beggars all description. Ron, enraged by such unseemly behaviour, made for Glen; Anna, glorifying in his downfall, leapt on top of him digging her claws into his back. Ron, grabbing her tail, had swung her across the room. Pandemonium broke out: Glen howling, Anna cursing in Siamese and Mitzy galloping round and round the room in a state of wild excitement.

In the end I received the ultimatum: 'Either the cat or I stay in this house – you have your choice.'

I phoned that very same night to our acquaintance in Calcutta informing her that the cat would be delivered to her house the following morning.

Meanwhile life around Calcutta continued much the same. Firpo's was still the place where people foregathered to enjoy a first-class meal. Clubs and places of entertainment flourished. The New Market continued going strong. The numbers of beggars had not decreased, nor yet were the poor any richer. Sacred cows, as ever, meandered freely or reclined on the busy pavements of Chittaranjan Avenue – I counted up to sixty-odd one day while on my way to Calcutta.

The attitude to the Indians, however, was changing – we were drawing closer and getting to know them better, not only the men but their wives as well.

In our parts Barrackpore cantonment remained the centre of various activities, the Club being a favourite haunt of ours. It was pleasant to sit on the veranda, chatting with friends over a drink or two and watching the ever-changing stream of small boats and launches going up and down the river.

It was here in this Club that Ron introduced me to Lydia, and her husband Mac Allcock, with whom I became very friendly. Lydia was half-Russian, half-Swedish. Her husband Mac was a friendly, jovial man concerned with the sale of tractors and land clearing. They lived in one of the old-world bungalows in Barrackpore, travelling daily to and from Calcutta.

Lydia, behind an offhand manner, which did not endear her to many of the ladies, possessed a warm and generous heart. We got to know each other well. The daughter of a Swedish father and Russian mother she had in her youth lived with her parents in various parts of Europe and thus acquired a fluency in seven languages, including Russian, which enabled us to converse with each other when we were sitting alone together. She was an excellent hostess and at Christmas or other special parties could produce a magnificent cold buffet with dishes representative of many countries. Not having any children, dogs were her great love. On arriving at the house, we used to be met with three friendly giants – two Great Danes and an Alsatian, the fourth and the most intelligent dog was a bull-terrier named Burra, who could almost speak. In the house also resided Lucy, the mongoose, a most amusing little creature. The two bearers always wore shoes – something that was never done normally, but this was a protection against Lucy's habit of suddenly darting out when the bearer was in the process of serving a dish and biting his toes, with disastrous results. The bearers used to protect themselves by flicking a napkin. I myself once had an uncanny experience, when on the point of starting to eat my steak, Lucy leapt on to my lap and the meat vanished with the speed of light-ning. Lydia kept Lucy for several years during which time, after a rendezvous in the garden, she produced three babies in the lower drawer of Lydia's dressing table.

As the little mongooses grew older Lucy removed them to the garden from where they never came to the house. Lucy was often seen frolick-ing on the lawn with her children and later returning home, but one day she went out and with her brood vanished for ever.

We used to enjoy visiting Mac and Lydia. The whole menage with all the dogs and mongooses, combined with a free-and-easy atmos-phere, never failed to fascinate us.

There was a memorable Christmas party one year when after a sumptuous dinner all guests received presents laid out under a decorated Christmas tree. The dogs were not forgotten. They all came up one by one to receive their gift consisting of a meaty bone wrapped in Christmas paper.

Our own, more down-to-earth style of life continued as before. I am reminded how once, staying with my cousin in France, during various discussions I was asked if it was true that Scotsmen were supposed to make the best husbands. I had to think a bit before I answered as my experience was mainly limited to the slightly restricted life in a com-pound. Living as most of us did in the mofussil, it was considered unusual for any married man to go off on his own and leave his wife alone. There were exceptions but as a rule all married couples went out together. As most men started work at 6 a.m., or even earlier, at the end of a very hard day, having bathed and changed, they were only too glad to settle down to a peaceful evening with their wives.

During weekends there was often golf or tennis between men friends but in the evening married couples usually got together or went on their own to see a film, dine in Calcutta or whatever.

It was a different story for bachelors or grass widowers, but even they were not given, throughout the working week, to setting off for the bright lights of Calcutta and would foregather for a game of cards, a drink, or a sing-song, such as I heard drifting over the Hooghly when crossing over to Lawrence as I first arrived in India.

Nowadays a lot is said of how long or even short separations are the cause of broken marriages. We may have been made of sterner stuff for we bore our separations patiently and looked forward to our re-unions. Divorces were rare in our community.

Finally, my answer to the question was, 'Yes – in spite of all their faults – they are the best.'

In July 1955 during a heavy monsoon downpour we drove to the Dum-Dum airport, where I said goodbye to Ron and boarded the plane for Paris; the first stage of the plan to meet the boys there and go on to Rats-Gris began.

The journey to Amsterdam was uneventful, but on arriving I was told that due to a strike, the connecting flight to Paris was cancelled and the only option offered was to fly to Brussels where I could catch a plane due to leave for France in a matter of two hours. It was a lovely summer's day. We were flying low, so low as to be able to see clearly the houses, gardens and the faces of the people playing tennis. On arrival in Brussels, however, I was informed that the flight to Paris had been put back by four hours. There was nothing for it but to wait in an airport which offered no comfort and where even the ladies' toilet facilities were indescribably filthy, something one would not have expected to see in a European airport.

I eventually joined the plane for Paris and after a rough flight with thunder and lightning, arrived in Orly airport from where on a crowded bus and standing all the way I thankfully reached the Place des Invalides.

Cousin Jenya, aware that my knowledge of French was limited, strongly advised me to hire a Russian taxi driver. 'There are plenty of them around,' she had written to me. No such driver materialised, but the helpful receptionist while arranging a taxi on my behalf told the

French driver where he had to take me and had shown him my notebook with the written address. The taxi drove on and on until it halted beside a large dark house encircled by tall trees. It was the wrong house. I showed the driver my notebook who, on realising that the mistake was his with a muttered 'Merde', turned back and off we went once more. Finally we drew up beside a high wall with a solid wooden, double gate, which likewise bore no resemblance to my cousin's house. A heated argument followed with me in my anxiety and confusion talking in a mixture of incomprehensible French and Hindustani. At this point the driver, announcing he wasn't going any further, threw my luggage on to the pavement and demanded his fare.

By now it was midnight and not a light to be seen. Terrified at the prospect of being left alone on the pavement, not knowing where to go or what to do, I began to plead with him not to leave me, offering all the money I possessed. Just then a guardian angel appeared in the guise of a French workman. I rushed over to him and asked if he knew a 'Madame la Russe'. Miraculously he understood me, 'Voila,' he said, pointing to the gate. I refused to believe this, but again he repeated 'Voila, Madame,' and opened the gate. There to my amazement I recognised the path and the row of terraced houses with the little gardens in front. In fairness to myself I must add that I had never seen the gate closed during my previous visits.

In one of the windows a light still burned. Jenya and Petya had waited all night and were on the point of going off to bed when I appeared on their doorstep.

There was a final scene where Jenya, horrified on seeing me handing over a fistful of notes, tried to intervene, accusing the driver of bare-faced robbery to which, with bland insolence, my friend replied, 'Madame and I are in perfect agreement,' a statement I did not dispute as I embraced him fondly and sent him on his way.

Inside, now safe in Jenya's house reaction was setting in. I was not suffering from jet-lag, of which I hear so much nowadays, but from mental exhaustion arising from the travail I had undergone, which had left me unable to speak and join in any conversation.

Jenya led me up to the small bedroom upstairs where I collapsed on to the bed and immediately fell sound asleep.

Two days later we were back in the Place des Invalides awaiting the arrival of my sons. I had not seen them for two years and foolishly imagined they would be just as I had left them. I was therefore amazed to see two lanky youths hurrying up the steps and calling over in deep voices.

We all piled in to Petya's car and set off for the Hameau de Rats-Gris where we arrived in the space of an hour and were met by Katya, André and Maska.

Rats-Gris, a picturesque village, lies above the busy road leading to the south. When the Pelekhines bought the farm a large piece of land went with it a part of which sloped down to the slow-flowing river Loing. On the main ground above was the old farmhouse, consisting of two large bedrooms and kitchen and which for some strange reason was named 'Stari zal' (old hall or ballroom). Close to it was a small summerhouse with a tiny veranda.

The only other substantial building was the barn, now converted into a two-storeyed house, with a wide patio overlooking a wooded garden where grew a variety of trees including the sweet-smelling white acacias, much loved by the resident bees which produced wonderful honey.

On the other side of the lane from the house on a large plot of land stood the garage, Petya's spacious workshop and outbuildings. There was also an orchard with many apple trees.

The boys and I were allotted one of the large bedrooms in the 'Stari zal' with a screen to divide it.

During the following days a great throng of friends and relatives began to arrive, the first of whom was Tamara, and her husband Egon Tersetta. They were accommodated in the second bedroom next to us. Tamara's firm belief that Egon would be eventually freed was justified, as after eight years of solitary confinement he was set free. Well compensated by his firm he was fortunate in being able to buy a beautiful house in Genoa. Their lovely daughter, Alichi, had been married recently and was spending her honeymoon in Florence.

The Tersettas were followed by Vladimir Grigoryevich, the Ukrainian Cossack ex-officer, with his wife, whom I knew only as 'Mukha' (the fly), a little woman with a sharp tongue who was known to completely domineer over her giant husband. They had brought with them their flamboyant daughter Katinka, her boyfriend Mitya and a tiny mongrel named Moshka (the Midge). All settled down in the spacious storeroom at the back of the garage.

Last to arrive was Maruska with her two children, a little girl Clodette, renamed Clodettka, and a two-year-old boy, Eugene. They occupied the small summerhouse. Perhaps the most interesting guest was Maruska, employed in the Pelekhine factory and whom Petya described as being invaluable as she combined the light touch of a woman with the strength of a man, two important factors required in the workshop. Maruska was a peasant, the sole survivor of her family during Stalin's ruthless collectivisation in Ukraine. She had seen her father being led away, her mother, sister and brothers dying from starvation, but had survived after being removed to an orphanage. At the age of twelve she was forced to work for a commissar residing in the large house of an estate originally belonging to a wealthy landowner who had long since vanished. Her daily duties consisted of having to drag buckets of water from a well and wash every floor of the house. Maruska, like many peasants, was given to quoting proverbs and similes when describing anything. 'That son of a bitch,' she had said, referring to the commissar, 'had everything bar birds' milk.'

Later she worked in the coal-mines, where, labouring alongside the men, she developed unusual strength for a woman. The start of the war found her driving a lorry with supplies to the front, but as the Germans advanced she joined the partisans, hiding in the woods, destroying railways, bridges and killing when they could. It was hard going in the dead of winter with the bitter frosts, but at the end of a week there was the village, a change of clothing, a wash-up, some food and back to the woods.

The village fell in the end leaving no option but to infiltrate amongst the villagers. A few of the partisans were caught and executed and others including Maruska sent to slave labour camps in Germany. There while working in a munition factory she met and married a Frenchman. Maruska, of stocky build, sallow complexion, the result of years of starvation, nondescript features and hair could never be described as attractive; only the eyes – large, clear grey, lively and shrewd – had a certain appeal. Her strength and agility were prodigious. Maruska was one of the great survivors.

The other survivor was Egon. Tall, handsome, he was half-Italian, half-Austrian. Educated in Vienna, where, as a member of the cadet corps, he and his fellow cadets were often directed to the court of Franz Joseph to dance with the old ladies-in-waiting, a duty no one relished. On one of the rare occasions when he mentioned his solitary confinement, he told me he never allowed his morale to go down, never lost hope and on being permitted to have books taught himself English. Yet this long period of confinement had left its mark. He could not suffer too much talking, too many people, but would go off on his own to sit below a tree with a book or walk for hours on end around the countryside.

What was so delightful about our stay in Rats-Gris was the free-and-easy atmosphere, where everybody did as they pleased. Petya and the boys went swimming in the river and also all three were involved in building a boat – something which gave the twins much pleasure.

Vladimir Grigoryevich, Mukha and tiny Moshka would call for a chat over a cup of tea, while Katinka and her boyfriend Mitya vanished into the woods in the time-honoured fashion according to the old Russian folk-song.

Maruska also liked to call with the covert intention of bringing up the subject close to her Russian heart, which was to buy a piece of land from the Pelekhines, something that Jenya was very much against but which eventually Maruska succeeded in wheedling out of Petya and built a little cottage on it.

At times Jenya, Tamara and I would go off on our own to nearby Montargis where in the locally renowned patisserie we enjoyed a peaceful hour over a cup of coffee and delicious cakes.

Montargis is a charming old town, with many interesting features, and fine buildings, the square with the town hall, a lovely park, shops offering a wide variety of goods and a large swimming centre, where on one occasion the boys and I spent the whole day.

The countryside surrounding Rats-Gris offered many pleasant walks through fields and woods reminiscent of Scotland. Nearby was an old château which aroused my curiosity, standing empty and mysterious with an overgrown garden. No one knew much about it except that it had changed hands several times.

As the time for my departure drew near, Jenya decided to hold a get-together party. The preparations started in the morning with everybody joining in. A large selection of zakuski had to be prepared, and the inevitable bottles of vodka. The home brew was every bit as good as the bought variety and far less expensive. The procedure, quite simple, was left to Tamara who knew exactly what to do. One third of the bottle was filled with pure spirit, sold openly in most chemists. The bottle was then topped up with water, a small sliver of lemon peel and a teaspoon of sugar was added. All this, allowed to sit until the evening, when the lemon peel was removed and the vodka ready for drinking. Some light wine, soft drinks for the children were also added, and along with the zakuski, the table was spread, all set for the celebration.

In the evening everyone gathered together. The party, after a stilted start, went off with a swing – all talking, joking, laughing and on to singing. Vladimir Grigoryevich, a powerful baritone, began with a popular folk-song soon to be joined by all the others. We sang about our mother Volga, the troikas and their drivers, some sad, some gay and the ever popular 'Evening Bells', in which Vladimir and Mukha with her high clear soprano harmonised together while the others presented the effect of ringing church bells.

And then there was dancing to a gramophone. To the strains of a Viennese waltz Jenya and Petya took to the floor. They had always worked so terribly hard, now watching them I was glad to see the expressions on their faces, happy and relaxed. Everybody danced that night.

Maruska got up and, to the accompaniment of some gay Russian music, did an impromptu dance with all the gestures of hands, shoulders and arms. Poor Maruska, who spoke badly in French and was forgetting her own language, could still present the spirit of Russia as only a true Russian could do.

The star of the evening, however, was Egon. Egon, quiet and reserved, went on to the floor and with Katinka as his partner presented the tango, as it used to be done in his youth, with great style and graceful steps. Katinka, a natural dancer, had responded with a slightly provocative air never making a false move. Rapturous applause greeted the end of their delightful performance.

The following morning a dramatic scene took place between Mitya and Katinka. Mitya, madly jealous, accused Katinka of being deliberately sexy while dancing with Egon and in great dudgeon went off to Paris only to return the next day.

In passing I may add, that although for a while Katinka flitted between Mitya and another lover, named Shura, she eventually chose and married Mitya. She turned out to be a faithful wife, a loving mother and a good daughter to her aged parents.

A few days after the party, the twins and I were flying through the clouds on our way to Scotland and on that same day arrived in my brother's house in Edinburgh.

Prior to my departure from India there was an agreement with my sister-in-law, Nora, that I, on my return to Scotland would take over the house and children, to enable her to join my brother, now working for an oil company in Ecuador. This arrangement suited us both as I was spared the bother of having to search for a furnished flat and the expense that went with it.

Shortly after our arrival, Nora left for warmer climes and I settled down with the children for the duration of her absence.

The house, known as Mount View, was spacious and comfortable with a pleasant garden in front and back. Although caring for five children at times was quite arduous, I, being fond of them all, found it rewarding. Sheila, now eleven years old, and her younger sister Kathy attended the Convent at Craiglockhart; my little nephew Johnny, a delightful and most amusing child, a preparatory school.

The boys by now were grown up. Michael, having decided to leave school, was serving an apprenticeship as an electrical engineer with

Bruce Peebles, and George was working hard at his Highers for entry into Edinburgh University.

The winter was hard that year with snow and frost, but in the evening, with Michael away to his classes, George engrossed in his studies, the children and I would gather round the fire and watch the TV until it was time for them to go to bed. I would then settle down to write my weekly mail to India and Ecuador, sew, knit or read. Ron's mother and sister Kate who lived within walking distance, would call to pass the evening with us. My mother came through from Dundee on several occasions and stayed for a little while. I still found time, now and again, to entertain some of my friends. Edie and Aikman paid a welcome visit and we spent a happy day together.

There were birthday and Christmas celebrations and one special party for the girls and their schoolfriends when some ten little girls attended and enjoyed the usual cakes, ice cream and the games which followed.

The weather continued cold and windy well into the spring. In April Ron's mother, who had been ailing for a few days, died suddenly. Sadly, Ron missed seeing her by a mere two months when he arrived home on leave in early June.

Previously arrangements had been made for the two girls to spend the school vacation with their parents. I travelled with them to Prestwick airport and the following morning watched these little girls setting off on their own to Ecuador. Two months later I returned to meet them.

Little Johnny likewise was sent off to an aunt who had a farm in Ireland where he had the time of his life and was quite heartbroken having to leave it. According to what his aunt related later she had also enjoyed his company. One day while talking to him she had remarked, 'Your aunt must be an angel!' to which he solemnly replied, 'She is not an angel. She is a Protestant.'

Meanwhile George at last received the welcome news that having successfully passed all his examinations he was accepted as a student in the Faculty of Law at Edinburgh University.

Our sons, now almost eighteen years old, were quite capable of looking after themselves but as Ron's leave was drawing to a close and I returning with him, we wished to see them settled in comfortable lodgings before we left and were fortunate to find two pleasant elderly ladies, living in Randolph Cliff, prepared to accept them.

The poor dears had no inkling of what they were taking on, as no sooner did we leave, than the twins, free from all parental control, aunts or uncles, joined in the merry life of students and young people,

199

prevalent in Edinburgh and within a short time branched out to share a flat with some of their friends and never looked back.

At the end of October with Nora having returned from Ecuador and taken over the house, we bade a fond farewell to family and friends and set off for India once more, halting *en route* in Paris to see my cousin and Tamara and Egon in Genoa. Finally we joined the flight to India in Rome and arrived in Calcutta in early November.

No special events took place during the next few years. There were the usual leaves, the usual furnished house, the usual brief contacts with our sons. The boys by now were used to these short visits and beyond the necessary allowance for University fees and lodgings were making out quite well on their own.

One benefit, however, we derived from the constant coming and going and that was when, during our flights, we were able to halt in various places at no extra cost and in this way explored a large part of Europe: France, Italy, Spain and Austria.

In India changes continued. Many of our friends had retired, others gone for ever. In 1959 while I was at home Phil called one day. Robert and she had retired from India. They were planning to build their own house, but meantime had rented a bungalow in Monifieth. Phil was her usual witty self. We laughed a lot remembering some humorous situations we shared in India. A week later a friend came on the telephone: 'Did you know,' she said, 'that Phil had died suddenly?' India was not the only place for sudden deaths.

As in Landsdowne, so in Kinnison I became interested in the garden on the island. Several pink acacias were planted, a hedge of crimson poinsettias, heavenly blue plumbagos and a Japanese honeysuckle. I then took into my head to grow papayas, that health-giving fruit, which we had for breakfast every morning. The head mali, seeing a memsahib who was so enthusiastic, responded with the same fervour. We had a long lively discussion about these papayas one morning when Ron appeared on the scene. 'Imagine,' I said to him, 'the mali tells me we can actually grow round papayas – as round as melons, as well as the other elongated kind.' Ron, after exchanging a few words with the mali, who for some strange reason appeared to be agitated, merely retorted, 'Get in that house! Do you know what the poor man was trying to explain to you? That to grow papayas it is necessary to have a male and female tree! There is no such thing as a round papaya.'

The trees were planted and in due course, to my delight, produced beautiful papayas. Unfortunately only a few appeared on our table. Someone also may have liked my papayas, as they somehow mysteriously vanished.

Meanwhile several of the mills were closed down for good. In order to meet the competition from Pakistan and elsewhere it was essential to install modern machinery in the remaining mills and by working treble shift get a satisfactory return on the heavy expenditure involved. The extra hours worked were equal to those that would have been worked by the mills that had been shut down and which were now leased for the storage of rice.

Ron, being deputy chief manager, was often sent to various mills for a few weeks at a time. I enjoyed seeing the other compounds and meeting the ladies there. There was, however, one place named Union South which I did not like at all and where we spent a month. My poor Golubchik during our stay there developed a strange fungus round his beak and in spite of all attempts to cure him eventually died. In this compound, along from us, was where our salesman, Claude Hendry, lived with his wife Edith. In their garden grew some very tall trees and behind the wall a jungle where there were numerous monkeys. Small monkeys can be most endearing, but these were unpleasant and very dangerous. The windows and doors always had to be securely closed, but one day when Edith was in town and the servants resting in their quarters, the monkeys succeeded by some means in getting into the house and there, as our American friends would say, had a ball.

On her return Edith was met with a scene of the most appalling devastation. Everything that could be broken, lamps, crystal, china, rare ornaments was lying shattered upon the carpet and cushions torn to bits with the feathers all over the place. They had also succeeded in getting into the bathroom and breaking into the medicine chest, creating further havoc by scattering the contents over carpets and furniture. Poor Edith, like her precious ornaments, was completely shattered.

It was a great relief to return to Kinnison.

In February 1961 a stirring event took place in Calcutta. During their tour of India, Queen Elizabeth and the Duke of Edinburgh arrived to what was once the old capital. The preparations had been tremendous. All beggars, sleeping and living on the pavements of Chittaranjan Avenue, were removed and the whole length of this wide thoroughfare bedecked with masses of fluttering flags. The road was closed to all traffic, but it so happened that Ron was the last to drive through on his way to Kinnison. Turning into the road to Barrackpore he came upon crowds of people, men, women dragging their children – all running together, and, on asking where they were going, replied, 'Hamlog ki rani atta hai' (Our Queen is coming) – and that after fourteen years of independence!

In the evening all the British community, by invitation from the

201

British High Commissioner, assembled in evening dress, on the race-course in Calcutta to pay their respects to Her Majesty.

When driving slowly in two lines of cars to the assembly point, a car driven by a European and two passengers in lounge suits drew up beside us. In front was the Red flag, with hammer and sickle, of the Soviet Union, an astonishing sight for a Royal visit! What were they doing here, I wondered, but was informed later that the men were from the Soviet Embassy in Calcutta.

From the place where the Queen was due to arrive a long crimson carpet was spread and a nearby table laid out with refreshments. It was a soft, star-spangled night with an air of expectation. People stood in groups talking to each other until interrupted by the voice from the loudspeaker saying, 'Ladies and Gentlemen, please lay down your glasses and put out cigarettes –the Queen is on her way.' Everybody rushed to the table and hurried back to take their places, but with nothing happening drifted away for another drink and a cigarette. After a further delay, however, we received the same order to put down the glasses and stop smoking.

The Queen arrived in an ancient Rolls-Royce, accompanied by the Duke of Edinburgh and Miss Naidu, the governor of Bengal, who was known to tipple and according to a rumour had kept the Queen waiting.

We were all drawn up on either side of the carpet. The Queen dressed in a sparkling beaded dress in pale turquoise shade, and a white mink cape, walked slowly between the guests, halting to exchange a few words with anyone who caught her attention. The Duke of Edinburgh walking behind was his usual free-and-easy self, stopping here and there to have a chat or pass some humorous comment. I had the impression the Queen appeared to be a little tired, which was not surprising, considering the heavy round of engagements she had endured during her tour of India in places hotter than Calcutta at that time of the year. There must have been a strong police presence, but it was by no means obvious. Ron, with a few friends, was standing close to the car in which the Queen with her escorts departed, and could quite easily have touched her.

It was a momentous occasion not only for the handful of British subjects, but, I believe, for the Indians as well who had so warmly welcomed our Queen to their country.

Perhaps more important in our own personal life during that month of February 1961, was the decision, after long discussions, to buy our own house.

As Ron's leave was due to come round in the summer it was decided

I should go on ahead and try to find a house in time for his arrival.

In the early spring of that year, with all our belongings accumulated during the many years packed in crates and boxes, I sailed for home on one of the BI ships from Calcutta. Ron, who was now the chief mill manager over the group mills, saw me safely aboard and settled in my comfortable cabin. After an uneventful journey of four weeks we docked in London from where I went on to stay with Mother, now happily installed in Edinburgh and who was delighted to know that we also were now preparing to settle in Edinburgh.

The search for the house began on the day following my arrival. Michael, who had acquired an ancient Citroën, drove me around, far and near, from house to house but it all turned out to be far more difficult than I ever imagined. There were a few houses, which I would have loved to possess but could not afford, and those that I could were not what I wanted. Michael equally anxious to have, at last, a home he could go to, with infinite patience gave up all his precious spare time and on looking back I know that during those two months we had covered not less than thirty houses.

This fruitless search continued with Ron due to arrive in a matter of weeks and still not a glimmer of hope.

Eventually, just as I was making up my mind to fall back on another furnished home I saw a house for sale that sounded promising and after an inspection made an offer which was accepted. It was situated in the pleasant district of Blackhall and although not quite the answer to my dreams it was a substantial two-storeyed terrace house, with four spacious bedrooms, lounge, dining room and cloakroom. There was a box-room, plenty of cupboards and only the kitchen requiring gutting.

The garden in front was small, but the one at the back was spacious and well laid out with several fruit trees. Adjacent to the garden was a roomy garage where Michael was able to house his beloved Citroën. We moved into our first house in May and on arriving opened a bottle of champagne to celebrate the occasion. The crates were duly delivered as was my 'cardboard kingdom' with all my precious collection of china, ornaments and many useful articles collected and kept in the garret of my brother's house, with the hope that there would be a happy day when I could use them. This happy day at long last had now arrived.

The boys and their enlisted friends with great enthusiasm laid carpets, moved furniture, arranged bedsteads and blissfully proceeded to yank out a fireplace in what was originally a drawing room, but was now a bedroom and where it was planned to have a fitment of a dressing table and wardrobes. To avoid carrying this heavy marble framework through the house, it was decided to lower it into the garden through the back bedroom window. Ropes were duly fixed and I, standing below, was committed to direct the proceedings. The great moment arrived with this monstrosity slowly moving down the wall, when suddenly a great white mass flashed past my nose and disintegrated into a hundred pieces on the lawn. I was very lucky.

In June Ron arrived, but this time we took no holiday but spent the whole of his leave labouring on further improvements – papering and painting until eventually the house took shape.

Ron left for India in November while I stayed on, planning to spend a year with the boys, prior to joining Ron for the last few months of our stay in India when Ron was due to retire and leave India for good.

Fate, however, stepped in once again. In the early summer, Michael announced that, wishing to see a bit more of the world, he had decided to go to sea and after applying to the BI received a reply stating he was accepted, with instructions to proceed to London for a short training prior to boarding one of their ships.

By sheer coincidence, George, who had earlier applied for an appointment with a firm in London, was likewise accepted.

A few days before their departure, a farewell party was organised for all their numerous girl and men friends.

After hurriedly preparing a cold buffet and being aware that elderly people are by no means welcome I discreetly stayed out of sight. The party lasted into the early hours of the morning at the end of which I found a pile of dishes to be washed, a broken wine glass, and a burn mark on one of my peg tables, something that didn't surprise me and could have been worse.

The following evening George left for London and Michael a few days later.

Realising that there would be no joy for me to remain alone in an empty house, I decided to rent it out and leave for India. After numerous applications from prospective tenants, a Jordanian heart-specialist, with a German wife and child, was chosen.

My last week at home was spent with Mother. Poor Mama, I can still remember how happy she was to have me and how she fussed over me as if I was once again her little girl.

Nora with Alistair and Mother came to see me off at Turnhouse airport. Nora was to recall later, how on previous occasions when I was leaving for India, Mother, upset, used to remark, 'I'll never see her again' – but this time, watching the plane departing she was quite cheerful and turning to Nora had said, 'I'll see her soon, she'll be back in the spring.'

A monsoon downpour met me as I stepped off the plane. We drove through flooded roads and on arrival at the Island House I was welcomed by Shamsher Ali and a new, young *mesalji* (a general help to the cook and bearer) and Mitzy and Glen, full of joy leaping around me. This was the last lap in India and we were the last of a group of intimate friends. Even Mac and Lydia, our friends in Barrackpore had left for Patiala in the Punjab, where there were more opportunities for land clearing.

The night of their departure has remained in my memory, as, on arriving at the airport to see them off, we were confronted with an astonishing scene. Mac, in his flamboyant style, had chartered a plane for his personal use. First to enter were all the numerous servants with their brood of children. The household gear, fridges, cooker, and furniture followed next. Last came the four dogs; all having been sedated they walked up the gangway, one by one, with great dignity.

Although missing my old friends I was fortunate enough to become acquainted with two pleasant couples, John and Edith Lyon and Eustace and Joyce Tunnicliffe who were living in Fort Gloster, a place I knew so well from my days in Lawrence, and where John and Eustace were in charge of a new project manufacturing electric cables. We found we had a great deal in common and entertained each other on occasions.

There was also Jean Duncan who lived in Rose Villa, where her husband Jack was the salesman and Myra, Jerry Scott's wife.

We used to meet in the Swimming Club for a game of bridge or mah-jong, where laughing and joking took priority over concentration and where one passing wit described our carefree meetings as 'The Mad Hatter's bridge party'.

On 26 October 1962, the whole of India was shaken by the Chinese invasion through the passes and over the trails that led out of Tibet. India was not prepared for such a war nor were the troops equipped with warm clothing to fight in such cold regions.

The wife of one of our directors got in touch with me to organise a knitting party. The ladies in the compound responded with great enthusiasm. Wool and knitting needles were provided and our meetings took place each week in the Honey Pot Club where we knitted socks, scarves, gloves and whatever.

Most of the ladies were now Indian, and although not all could speak English fluently we all got along with each other. They knitted speedily with one of the ladies producing a pair of socks daily. In no time a substantial pile of garments was accumulated and sent to Calcutta.

The war, however, was now going badly for India, but on 21

November, China unilaterally declared a cease-fire and the war ended as suddenly and surprisingly as it had started.

The knitting parties faded out, but nevertheless while they lasted I was fortunate in being able to get to know the Indian ladies and grew closer to them.

Below us in the Island House in the flat previously occupied by us lived Hari Ghose and his wife Ghopa. Hari, Ron's deputy, was due to take up the position of chief mill manager after our departure. Ghopa was a gentle, serene woman who always wore beautiful saris and possessed impeccable taste. We got along very well together and used to have long conversations about everything in general. Her English was very good, but like many Indians she at times used rather quaint expressions. One day she asked me if I could teach her a little more English. Having once overheard her, when acting as hostess to some VIPs, asking one of the ladies, 'Do you want to go?' – meaning to use the toilet – I said, 'Ghopa, dear, you do not say ''Do you want to go?'' but instead, ''Would you care to wash your hands?''' a statement that rather surprised her. I hasten to add that if some English spoken by Indians may have sounded a bit strange to us, our own attempts at Hindustani must have seemed even more odd to them, but being naturally polite they passed no remarks.

The other lady I liked very much was Mukta, who was the wife of the manager, Sandy Bose. One afternoon when strolling in the compound she introduced me to a lady, walking beside her who was obviously in the last stages of pregnancy. 'This is my sister-in-law,' Mukta said, and added brightly, 'She is loaded.' The sister-in law smiled sweetly and nodded. Mukta and I were also in the habit of having long walks together. She had very definite ideas about the marriage customs in India and was quite indignant when referring to a young woman she knew who had had a runaway marriage. 'What has she got, that girl?' she said. 'Nothing was fresh, nothing was new!'

'Did you know Sandy before you were married?' I tentatively inquired.

'Of course not,' she replied. 'We met for the first time during our marriage.'

'How did you know you would like him?' I continued.

'My father', she rejoined, by now on the defensive, 'would never have chosen a bridegroom if he thought I would not like him!'

I didn't pursue the subject.

The brightest and happiest moments during these last few months of our stay in India were when our son Michael came to spend two weeks with us. He had arrived from home to Bombay where he was instructed to proceed to Calcutta and board his ship the *Bulimba* due to leave for the Australian run.

On the evening of his arrival Ron and I set off for Dum-Dum airport. The night was cool and peaceful. We stood eagerly scanning the starlit heavens for a glimpse of the plane and suddenly saw it skimming across the sky, drawing close and coming down to a perfect landing. Michael was back in the land of his birth. Our Sikh driver Jagendra, a very likeable man, came forward to meet us and was duly introduced to our son. Back in the house after a welcome from the servants and two excited dogs, we sat down to dinner and talked well into the night. The following morning Pir Mahomed called. Pir Mahomed never dreamt that he would ever see again any of his young charges and now, after seventeen years' absence, was quite overcome to meet Michael. The two of them, driven by Jagendra, departed to Calcutta to visit the Victoria Memorial and the Jain temple.

We spent the next two weeks taking Michael around all the places he had once known but now vaguely remembered. There was the old school house in Barrackpore, the Swimming Club in Calcutta, Firpo's, meetings with friends and finally to watch the ever-exciting polo where the Maharaja of Jaipur and his team as usual excelled themselves. More special than anything else was the visit to Lawrence. I had not travelled on the Budge-Budge Road for many long years but saw nothing different. There were still the same bazaars, tea-shops, naked children, pie dogs. It was only when we approached the Albion jetty, great changes became apparent. The house where my cousin Mae once lived was now deserted and already the encroaching peepul tree was sending out its branches through a broken jilmil. The garden, at one time my cousin's joy, and the adjoining tennis courts had vanished.

The tide was high when we crossed over to Lawrence. The mill was no longer working. The godowns and mill buildings were leased out for storage of rice. The compound, known to have been one of the loveliest on the river, was now, like Albion, a wilderness. Gone were the flowerbeds and well-kept lawns where the ladies used to stroll of an afternoon and gone was the garden seat where we liked to sit and talk about the price of bhekti, the darzis, but more often the folks at home.

The married quarters, which had formerly been occupied by Jean, Lily and Alice, were standing empty, dirty and neglected.

With Michael I approached our old bungalow and stood remembering past scenes. A man appeared on the veranda. 'What do you want?' he asked in a high resentful voice. 'Nothing,' I said and added, hoping that he might invite us in, 'We lived here once.' He stared at us in silence and then, abruptly turning away, vanished inside.

Little was said during our journey back to Albion. I never crossed the river again.

We had hoped that Michael might have stayed with us over the festive season, but that was not to be. We saw him off on the *Bulimba* a mere two days before Christmas, somewhat cheered by the knowledge that he would come back before we left for home.

The start of the New Year brought a sad happening. Our dog, Glen, developed a mysterious illness and in spite of all efforts to save him died and was buried on the island under one of my young pink acacias.

One problem remained. All our tacit inquiries for someone to give Mitzy a home proved fruitless. Mitzy was difficult, no one wanted her. To have her sent to Scotland and placed in quarantine was also out of the question as our own position at home was uncertain.

Deliverance came from quite an unexpected quarter. A young man had recently joined our company and was sharing the house with our salesman, prior to being sent to Naraingunge where he was taking up a position of purchasing jute for the mills.

He was a likeable young man and, having met him on several occasions, we invited him to dinner one evening. Derek had been a wool broker in Australia, but not enjoying the life there he returned to England and was fortunate to land a responsible position in our company. He had always, he told us, had a longing to see India.

For some strange reason Mitzy, who had always disliked strangers, took to Derek and not only allowed him to pat her but had nestled up close to him. It was at this point that Derek mentioned how he had always admired the breed of dachshunds and would have liked to possess one. Our problem was solved.

Derek was delighted to accept Mitzy, the only snag being that he was due to leave for Naraingunge within the next few days and there were certain formalities which had to be observed before Mitzy could be sent on to him in what is now Bangladesh, but at that time was still Pakistan. It was arranged that Mitzy would travel by plane and would be met at Dacca airport.

Everything went according to plan. A special box with a barred front was made in the mill and Mitzy's bedding and her small belongings placed inside. We travelled with her to the airport. Mitzy was placed in the box and carried on to the plane. The last I saw of my Mitzy was her eyes, staring through the bars, deeply sad and yet trusting, as if I, of course, could never allow any harm to come to her. That is how I see her still.

As the journey was short Derek had promised that he would phone as soon as she arrived, but when no message arrived we phoned ourselves. Derek's assistant answered the call and assured us that Mitzy had arrived safely.

As in Pakistan the sale of bacon or ham is prohibited, I, as a mark of appreciation, sent off a parcel to Derek, but still received no acknowledgement nor yet a little word concerning Mitzy.

All that, however, was pushed into the background when a telegram arrived from my brother with the news that Mother had taken a stroke and was seriously ill. We immediately tried to phone Edinburgh, but through the interruption of some loud-mouthed babu, heard nothing. A few days later a second telegram arrived. Mother had died on 6 March. Death had removed her a mere few weeks before our arrival home.

For the next few weeks we were kept busy packing and making arrangements for our final departure in the middle of April. Any unease I felt over Derek's prolonged silence was quelled by the thought that he must have been kept very busy in his responsible position.

It was only weeks after our arrival in Edinburgh, that the whole truth came out, through Michael being back in Calcutta after we left and discussing what had happened with our friends.

Derek had never been a wool broker in Australia but instead was a shoe salesman in London possessed of a glib tongue with which he had succeeded in fooling us and many others. In Naraingunge he had access to large sums of money. One morning after collecting all the money he could lay his hands on, he simply boarded an SAS plane and fled to Copenhagen. There, unfortunately for him, he left a forwarding address and was promptly arrested and placed in prison, where he attempted to commit suicide by ramming his head against the wall but only succeeded in losing the sight of one eye. Such was the account in the papers, but nothing is known as to what happened to him later.

But what about Mitzy, you might ask? According to Derek's bearer, who treated her kindly and who happened to be a friend of a bearer in Kinnison, Derek paid not the slightest attention to her. Mitzy wandered outside, forlorn and lost, until one day a pack of wild dogs attacked and killed her.

With the day of our departure drawing closer a farewell reception, arranged by the staff of Kinnison was held in the Honey Pot. Speeches were made with a suitable response from Ron, at the end of which he was presented with a silver salver.

To our delight the *Bulimba* arrived in time for Michael to spend with us the last week in India.

One morning a deputation of workers called at the house inviting Ron to attend a reception in their quarters. As Ron prepared to leave

Shamsher Ali approached him. 'Sahib,' he said, 'you must wear a collar and tie – this is going to be a big day for them.' Big it was. A milling crowd – thousands strong – was waiting outside the gates to meet him. A *shamiana* (marquee) had been erected complete with chairs and decorated with flowers. Followed by this mass of humanity Ron was escorted to it.

Michael, who had joined his father, had a ciné camera with him and was able to record the whole episode for family posterity.

Representatives of various groups came forward to place garlands over Ron's head until he was literally swamped under them. Speeches were made followed by the babus presenting a copy of Rabindranath Tagore's *Towards Universal Man*. Ron in turn, speaking in Hindustani, expressed his thanks and also the love that he had always held for the people of India.

Perhaps over all the speeches the simple words of an old man conveyed all that could be said: 'Sahib, you have always known us, always understood us – we trusted you.'

The following morning we walked down the stairs of our house for the last time. Outside the servants were waiting. We shook hands with them all from the sweeper to Shamsher Ali Khan, our friend of more than twenty years.

The car moved slowly over the little bridge of the island and through the compound. It seemed somewhat strange to be leaving a place, full of memories, with the certain knowledge that we would never return.

Prior to leaving for the airport Michael was driven to his ship where we said goodbye to him. It was sad to realise that on his next visit we would not be there to welcome him. Fortunately many of our friends kindly extended their hospitality to him, each time the *Bulimba* docked in Calcutta.

A small group of friends joined us at the airport, including Ghopa, Hari, Mukta and Sandy. The faces of the others are long since forgotten. There was the usual small-talk, a joke or two and final goodbyes.

The last thing I remember of India, as the aircraft roared along the runway, was the sight of some white-clad figures waving farewell. Seconds later we were up into the blue.

After an uneventful flight of some twenty hours we landed in London, where we bought a second-hand car, spent the night there and drove on to Edinburgh the following day.

We were fortunate to possess our own house, but the future was uncertain. The days of wealthy nabobs enjoying their retiral were over. Most people home from India took up positions to augment their incomes. Meanwhile we settled down to enjoy our home life and were joined by our elder son George, who had decided to leave London.

One morning during the summer the postman delivered a letter from Northern Ireland. Brian Hall, of Mackie's in Belfast, was inviting Ron to spend a weekend with him in Belfast. Ron duly went there where he was taken round the works to see the latest machinery, had dinner with Brian and having spent the night with him and his mother returned home the following day.

A month went by and a second letter arrived from Northern Ireland. The Ministry of Finance in Thailand had written to Brian, asking him to recommend someone to run their modern jute mill situated near Bangkok. The terms offered were more than generous along with the house, car, driver, two servants and other perks. A few weeks later Ron was on his way to Thailand and I, having tied some loose ends and sold the car, was aboard an aircraft flying to join him. There were halts in Rome, Cairo and in Dum-Dum where a few months earlier I had been saying goodbye to my friends in India. No one except those travelling to Calcutta was allowed to leave. After sitting in the blazing heat for some time the flight resumed, this time on its last lap.

I remember looking down on to the evil marsh of the Sundarbans, soon to be left behind and on to Burma. The great jungle of Burma seemed sinister. Somewhere below was lying my cousin Roy and his broken plane. It was not surprising no trace of him was ever found.

We had been flying for almost four hours when suddenly I saw a bright green land and on drawing closer the silver ribbon of a river, houses, emerald rice fields and strange buildings touched with gold. The aircraft came down without a shudder. I was in the magic land of Thailand.

EPILOGUE
THAILAND AND SCOTLAND

Ron was awaiting me at Don Muang airport where after a cursory examination of my luggage I was allowed to go through. Outside in the bright sunlight, standing beside the Volkswagen was Semyem, the driver, a pleasant young man with whom on being introduced I shook hands. After a short drive we arrived at the mill situated in the Klongluang district quite near a small village of Rangsit and about forty kilometres from Bangkok.

The whole layout of the complex was completely modern. There were about 1400 workers out of which 1200 were young women working in two shifts. Male and female workers were housed in dormitories situated a bit away from the mill. Three of the dormitories were able to house all the female workers. Male dormitories were divided into two types for married and unmarried workers respectively. The mill provided free meals a day for the female workers only. Male workers were compensated by getting higher wages than their female counterparts.

There was a clinic staffed by a doctor and a qualified nurse called Chan. There was also a club which provided such facilities as a cafeteria, barber shop, hairdressing salon as well as a general store. This was necessary on account of the mill being located too far away from a shopping centre.

The girls were a cheerful lot who worked hard and were constantly sweeping the floors and dusting their machinery, a thing unheard of in India. All wore slacks, blouses and masks to prevent the inhaling of jute dust – also unheard of in India.

Although respecting Ron as their manager they also looked upon him as a father figure and usually referred to him as 'Pa' – a different approach from India.

Our house as well as the two for the assistant managers, with small gardens in front, stood apart from the mill. Built in the Thai style they

213

were modern consisting of lounge-cum-dining room, kitchen and two air-conditioned bedrooms upstairs. It was not in the luxurious style of the house on the Island, but well furnished and adequate.

In the house along from us lived one of the assistant managers known as Teddy and beyond him the other assistant manager named Punlop who was married to an Irish girl, Margaret, who he had met when training with Mackie's in Belfast. Margaret held a lucrative position in the office of BOAC at Don Muang airport.

One side of the land area was adjacent to Paholyothin Road which was the main highway coming from the north and the opposite side was flanked by a canal called Klongluang.

Such then was the set-up which could be described as a small village on its own.

Originally Ron was informed that our accommodation was allotted on a temporary basis as there were plans on the way for a manager's house and already the foundations were laid, but due to unforseen circumstances which occurred later they never got off the ground.

We were, however, quite happy and comfortable where we were as after all everything, as in India, was only on a temporary basis.

I was always fascinated by a delightful little house which stood quite close to ours and which I first imagined was a bird-table especially as there was often food laid out. It turned out to be a spirit house similar to many others seen in gardens all over Thailand. I often wished we could have had something similar in our garden at home as some, beautifully executed, were most attractive.

On my arrival I was met by my two girls, Somana and Soni. Both, placing the palms of their hands together, bowed and said 'Sawutdee Madame' (Greetings Madame) – I was no longer a memsahib!

We got along very well together and in no time at all the girls became quite at home with me and like members of a family would help themselves to anything they fancied in the fridge such as fruit or refreshing drinks. I did not mind this in the slightest and in fact quite liked it.

Somana, perhaps more clever and sophisticated than Soni, did the cooking and went shopping with me every week to the market in Bangkok. Soni cleaned and attended to the laundry. She was more of a country-style girl and in some ways I preferred her to Somana, who I suspected always had an eye to the main chance.

I settled down in my new surroundings even if I still found it quite amazing that after a mere four-hour flight I had arrived in a country so different from India, as to believe almost that I had landed in some distant corner of the earth or even on some strange planet.

With a few exceptions the Thais are not tall people. The women, although lacking the classical Indian beauty, have something of their own and being fun-loving are very attractive. The children, especially little girls with their dark up-tilted eyes, are lovely.

The phoo-yings (girls) are very outgoing. One sees them riding motor-cycles, driving tractors, running their places of business and holding important positions in banks or big concerns.

There is, however, in Bangkok a great deal of sexual freedom. Massage parlours flourish and perhaps it is not for nothing that I have heard Bangkok described as a bachelor's paradise.

Soon after my arrival Mr Ponsevat, a member of the Legislative Assembly and a close friend of Marshal Sarit, then Prime Minister of Thailand, invited Ron and me to a dinner party to be held in honour of a member of the Thai Embassy in London who was on leave in Bangkok with his attractive wife, an ex-beauty queen of Thailand. Mr Ponsevat was a man of great wealth, who possessed a fleet of cars and a beautiful house built round a kidney-shaped swimming pool.

A large number of guests had arrived and stood talking together in groups, with drinks in hand, in the usual manner of such gatherings. At this point, Margaret, who had also been invited, advised me to go back outside the main door where stood a row of shoes and place my own beside them. I had not noticed that all the ladies were standing barefoot and the gentlemen in their socks from some of which could be seen the odd toe peeping out.

Dinner was served on two round tables – the ladies seated at one and the gentlemen at the other. The dinner was Chinese, with everyone supplied with chop-sticks. Margaret, sitting beside me, was doing away nicely, but in spite of all her instructions on how to hold the chop-sticks nothing ever reached my mouth. Glancing across I saw my husband ordering the servant to fetch a spoon and fork, resulting in his enjoying his dinner and not leaving the table hungry as I did.

The highlight of the evening was a film taken in London by the member of the Embassy. His attractive wife was sitting next to me. I was expecting to see some interesting and perhaps unusual views of London and was therefore quite astonished to be presented with a film of a strip-tease female performing a variety of postures. 'How do you like the pictures?' asked the beauty queen and added proudly, 'My husband took them – he is very good with the camera.' As we were leaving Margaret spoke to Ponsevat's young son. 'How did you enjoy the film, Boon?'

'I've seen a lot better,' was the blasé reply of a twelve-year-old. I hasten to add, however, not all parties were like that; this was rather an exception to those I attended later.

On another occasion I was invited to the house for tea by Noo, who was Ponsevat's daughter and educated in England. Her husband Somnam was in charge of buying the jute from the Chinese brokers. The young couple lived with Ponsevat. The servants when offering drinks or tea always bent very low so as to ensure that they were below the head of the person sitting. Our own girls did the same. I was puzzled, until I discovered that the head is considered to be sacred. No Thai likes to have the head touched or patted.

Prior to my arrival King Bhumipol, a much-loved democratic sovereign, was celebrating his special birthday. It was the Year of the Rabbit and a great procession was to pass along Rajadamnern Avenue, where our head office was situated. When Ron suggested he could watch the procession from the office windows, Somnam threw his hands up in horror – no one was ever allowed to look down on the head of the King.

On some occasions we used to meet Noo and Somnam for dinner before going on to see a film. One evening during a discussion about films I asked Somnam if he had seen the famous film *The King and I*. My question obviously displeased him. 'That film', he said, 'tried to portray us as a backward people while the opposite was the case – it insulted Thailand and is not allowed to be shown here.'

The Thais are a very proud people and indeed are obsessed with the fear of losing face, a fear that can often result in violence and sadness.

There was a case in the mill where one of the young workers had been telling her friends that her boyfriend was coming to her parents' house with a view to arrange a marriage. The young man did not turn up so she took some weedkiller and died.

In the past I had often heard Bangkok described in glowing terms, but it was only when I myself set eyes on the wide clean streets, flanked by handsome Government buildings, palaces, temples, klongs and the whole splendid layout, I realised that here was a metropolis of no mean stature and was in fact one of the loveliest cities I had seen. Delightful also were some unexpected little lanes where could be found an old Thai-style house, a garden and the inevitable basket of orchids hanging against the walls.

The Thais are passionately fond of flowers especially orchids which are a common sight even outside the humblest house. There was a wonderful flower centre in Bangkok, a place I liked to visit, which offered a great variety of exotic flowers and pot-plants. In another large open space every weekend a flotilla of small boats arrived up the adjacent klong. In no time booths were erected and everything under the sun came up for sale, from priceless orchids to birds and monkeys. By

Sunday night all the stalls were dismantled leaving no trace of the lively market.

Through the week Ron was kept busy, but during the weekend we usually set off for Bangkok, or Krungtep, as it was called by the Thais.

There was always some place of interest to explore, from where we would go on to watch a film and finish up with dinner in one of the popular hotels. Nowadays I hear, thanks to a great increase of tourists, many hotels have opened up, but twenty years ago such hotels as the Erawan, the Rama and the Oriental were much favoured. The Oriental Hotel, the oldest in Bangkok, was known as the one started by Anna Leonowens's son. Anna was the governess in the famous musical and, later, film based on Margaret Landon's book *Anna and the King of Siam*. As well as hotels there are many fine restaurants serving European, Chinese, Korean and even Mexican food. We used to try them all but usually fell back on the Erawan where the setting and food were excellent.

One day, however, we decided to spend a weekend in Bangsen, one of the resorts in the Gulf of Thailand. It was a journey of about two hours which took us through the town and on to the countryside of scattered villages and at one part driving alongside a beautiful klong on the opposite bank of which, nestling amidst the palms were wooden houses on stilts, fishermen casting their nets, children swimming and diving – a peaceful scene disturbed only by small motorboats, dashing up and down over these quiet waters.

Ron had never described Bangsen to me, wishing, as he said later, to surprise me. Surprised indeed I was when after driving through coconut groves and swaying palms I suddenly beheld a sweeping curve of golden sands, a sapphire sea, people lazing in the sun and someone water-skiing in the distance. It might have been the Bahamas or some such other exotic haunt that I had read about but never seen.

The hotel was comfortable and the adjoining garden, set out with marble statues and urns, unusually attractive.

High above, standing on a hill, was Marshal Sarit's sumptuous residence, overlooking the bay. The Prime Minister was not present and rumour had it he was not in the best of health.

We spent the day swimming in these tropical waters or resting in the shade of a palm.

In the evening after dinner we went back to sit close to the sea. It was a peaceful moonlit night with not a soul to be seen except for a young couple, who kept running in and out of the water, playfully splashing each other, throwing up showers sparkling in the moonlight. After sitting at peace for some time, idly watching the young lovers, we returned to the hotel. I retreated to the bedroom leaving Ron on the balcony which overlooked a miniature golf course in the garden.

The night became stiflingly hot, thwarting all attempts to settle down, not helped by the sound of loud voices and bursts of laughter coming from the garden where some people were playing miniature golf. I was just on the point of expressing my displeasure, when Ron came in and invited me to join him on the balcony. 'Come,' he said, 'and hear what these people are saying.' I did so and was astonished to discover that the voices belonged to a group of Russians, but before I could discover where they came from and why they were here – all left the garden.

The following morning Ron and I went swimming and there found the same people bathing quite close to us. Seeing a pleasant-looking man I gathered my courage to approach him. He was most polite and friendly. We stood talking in the water for the best part of half an hour, during which time he discovered all that there was to know about me and I nothing about him, except that they were all members of the Soviet Embassy, spending a weekend in Bangsen where they had rented a house.

I was still swimming about when a motorboat passed near by with the Russian men, women and children on board. I waved to them in a friendly fashion, but received in turn a cold hard stare. No doubt they were certain I was a spy deliberately sent to Bangsen to watch them.

That same afternoon we returned home via Bangkok.

In 1965 we went back to Bangsen. A great change had taken place during that time. Masses of tourists were milling around. The beach was overcrowded, noisy, loud music blasting from some source, vendors pushing their trolleys. Gone was the peace of our previous visit. We turned the car and went on to Pattaya, some miles further on – a place as yet unspoiled by humanity.

Shortly after we set off on another journey we had promised ourselves when we arrived in Thailand. The destination was the war cemetery at Kanchanaburi approximately 150 kilometres from our house. We left in the early morning and after driving through Bangkok and Dhonburi carried on to Nakhorn Pathom. The road to Nakhorn Pathom, although flat, is pleasant, flanked by paddy-fields like pale green seas lightly ruffled by a playful breeze.

On approaching Nakhorn Pathom one of the rarest and most beautiful sights revealed itself. The massive Chedi, towering above the trees, glitters like gold in the morning sun. It is almost 380 feet high and is considered to be the largest Chedi and the most holy of Buddhist structures. The enormous dome is covered by highly glazed bronze-coloured tiles, brought from China. An outer pavilion encircles a building with the Chedi itself in the centre which is supposed to have been built in AD 500.

We spent some time wandering about, halting to study the stone figures of ancient Chinese warriors, old carvings representing animals, the various images of Buddhas.

Leaving Nakhorn Pathom the journey continued to Kanchanaburi and a little beyond it to the Allied Cemetery. Inside the arched entrance on a bronze plaque are etched the following words: 'I will make you a name and a praise among all people of the earth, when I turn back your captivity, before your eyes saith the Lord.' The cemetery is beautifully kept, but what strikes one immediately is the deep silence and an overwhelming sadness. There is hardly a sound to be heard and even the Thai girls in their large Thai hats move quietly, tending the flowers between the graves.

Some 7000 men are buried there including 140 unknown in a common grave. Row upon row of neatly flowered headstones testify to their premature end.

Ron and I left each other to walk alone with our thoughts. I stopped to read some of the epitaphs. One of the most moving was to a gunner aged twenty-two who had died just before the surrender: 'At the going down of the sun and in the morning we will remember you – Mum, Dad and Toots'. I was a little puzzled by the grave of a young sailor who had died at the tender age of eighteen, only weeks before the end of the war. He had been a prisoner for almost three years. 'How can that be?' I asked the caretaker, who spoke English. 'He was a young cadet on a ship when taken prisoner,' he replied. There was also Phoebe Mercer who had died aged twenty-six. I am quite old now and some names elude me, but the name of Phoebe Mercer still remains with me. Who was she? Where did she come from – the only girl amongst thousands of men? 'She was a nurse', the caretaker told me, 'who died just weeks before the surrender.'

Many people come to pay homage to the graves including Queen Juliana of The Netherlands who, on a visit to Bangkok, expressed a wish to visit the cemetery. On arriving at the graves of her Dutch soldiers the Queen, sinking to her knees, wept and prayed before them.

During our stay in Thailand I returned on several occasions to the cemetery at times with friends from Calcutta and once with our son Michael who had flown from India to spend a short leave with us. There was always the same deep silence with visitors talking in quiet voices, but on that day with Michael, the peace was broken by loud high-pitched voices and shrill laughter. This jarring noise came from two Japanese businessmen. We wondered what was it that they found amusing on this sacred ground.

There is a book in the entrance where visitors sign their names and pass comments. I had already done so but was curious to know what the Japanese had written. After they left, still laughing, I went over to the book and read the following words: 'Business is dead today.' Infuriated by such base insensitivity, I wrote below; 'The leopard will never change his spots.'

A dirt road past the cemetery leads to the famous bridge on the river Kwai (pronounced Kwey) described in the novel by Pierre Boulle and later the inspiration for the film.

Most of us know that the bridge was not made from wood but is a multipiered girder span with the Death Railway running across it and disappearing into the jungle. We also know that in reality it was quite impossible for anyone to run away and return to the site. The Japanese knew that full well. According to my brother-in-law who was there, it was possible at times to go to Kanchanaburi to buy medicine from the Chinese shopkeepers who accepted IOUs in payment which were later honoured by the British Government.

The prisoners had travelled from Singapore to a place called Ban-Pong from where they walked sixty kilometres to Kanchanaburi. The Death Railway, when completed in December 1943, extended 420 kilometres between Ban-Pong in Thailand and Thanbyuzayat in Burma. The construction claimed a life for every four sleepers or twenty-five per kilometre. Of these over 12,000 were Allied prisoners of war – Australian, Dutch and mostly British. The remainder of about 100,000 were Malays, Burmese, Tamils, Sumatrans, Javanese and others conscripted from the far-flung corners of the Japanese South East Asia Co-Prosperity Sphere.

Little is known about where the other victims are buried, but along from the Kanchanaburi cemetery stands an ugly monument to their memory, erected by the Japanese, neglected and overgrown by grass and weeds.

Perhaps the saddest feature of the Death Railway and the bridge, where men – starved, beaten and tortured – laboured in the blazing sun, is the futility of it all as the bridge was scarcely used and the railway only on certain sections. The rest has long since been reclaimed by the jungle.

On the Kanchanaburi bank was a small booth, selling beer, soft drinks and cigarettes; nearby a wooden table. After a picnic lunch there we hired a motor boat and were soon speeding down the Kwai and on to the opposite bank where was situated the Chunkai cemetery.

Along the banks children were splashing, a raft house perched on bamboo poles came sailing towards us, the people on it laughing and waving as they passed. In the distance could be seen the sombre hills of the jungle – no one could have escaped from them – I remember thinking. Below the foaming waters barely discernible were the remains of a broken bamboo bridge, probably used at one time for carrying supplies to the other side. Rough steps on the high bank at Chunkai took us up to a path leading to the cemetery. On the left of this path was still standing the wooden bungalow, once the abode of the Japanese commander. The cemetery, where lay some 4060 war prisoners, was beautifully kept, but there also the quiet atmosphere was tinged with sadness.

We could not linger long as time was short. Already on arriving at Kanchanaburi we found the short tropical twilight was closing in. Soon we were on our way home, halting *en route* for a meal in Bangkok.

In conclusion I may add that all I have described was taken from notes written by me almost twenty-five years ago.

The little hut where we used to buy beer and soft drinks I hear is now no more, but replaced by a flourishing hotel.

In December the whole of Thailand was shaken by the sudden death of the Prime Minister, Marshal Sarit Thanarat. There was immediate speculation as to what effect his death might have on the country. Marshal Sarit, the strong man of Thailand, was highly respected by the people including the King who lent his Royal urn to hold the Marshal's body until the cremation, which took place in March 1964. Meanwhile all appeared to be normal and business went on as usual.

Christmas came and went. It was nothing like the Christmas in India with the basket of oranges disguising the odd bottle of whisky and a gift or two.

The Thais ignore Christmas but attach some importance to the New Year. A celebration took place in the compound with all the phoo-yings and phoo-chies (men and women) joining in. We had gone along to join the fun and as the old year died Ron stood up and sang 'Auld Lang Syne', followed by a repeat, in Thai, by Mr Ponsevat. Margaret and I embraced and kissed each other but when Mrs Ponsevat joined us and I stepped forward to greet her in the same way, she suddenly recoiled. Later I was told that Thai women were not given to kissing each other.

I was beginning to realise that if we didn't understand the Indian we understood the Thai even less.

In time we learned that although the Thais are polite and friendly,

221

they do not actually care for the *farang* (European). That perhaps is not surprising as by clever manipulation they succeeded in keeping out the Europeans – British, French and Dutch – from dominating their country, which was more than their neighbours did. Like the Chinese they have an overweening conceit of themselves. I am reminded how on one occasion I left a prized scarf in the cinema. Ron went back immediately and reported the loss to the doorman who happened to be a Sikh, and, speaking with Ron in Hindustani, remarked, 'Sahib, by now the scarf will have vanished.' He suggested, however, that Ron should get in touch with one of his important Thai friends who would speak to the management. On appealing to Somnam the answer we received was that no Thai would ever steal such a thing. I also recollect when I was at home, how, listening to a talk on the radio from a tutor who had taught the Thai Crown Prince when he was in England, he described him as a pleasant young boy, but impossible to teach, as he imagined he already knew all the answers and resented being told otherwise.

The Thais have reason to be proud. Thailand is a wealthy land, one which has never known a famine, where the klongs, rivers and sea abound with fish, where grows an abundance of wonderful fruit and there are two harvests of rice each year. Not bothered by any caste system they eat almost everything – meat, chicken, pork along with a great variety of herbs, flowers, pods, leaves and the stalks of lemon grass which I have seen Somana gathering on the banks of the small klong at the back of our house.

The Thais do not use salt as we do. They prefer instead a sauce known as Nam-plah prepared from a large quantity of tiny fish all boiled up and then strained and put up in bottles. It had a pleasant sharp flavour and we soon got into the way of using it also.

Once every week Somana and I with Semyem used to set off for Bangkok to do our shopping. The first call was to a small shopping centre known as Gaysorn where I always bought our fruit. The sweet pink-fleshed pomelos and papayas were vastly superior to those we used to have in India, but the mangoes on the other hand were not so good and for some reason were usually eaten quite green.

Nearby was a small supermarket where I purchased some of our stores. From there we would go on to the big market to buy fish. Although there was a great variety of fish the only kind we enjoyed was known as Plah-kapong similar to that of bhekti in India. The great selection of prawns, lobsters and shellfish of every kind and size was such as I had never seen before. All kinds of strange things could be bought in this market. Fascinating to watch was a young Chinese girl, dressed up in a snow-white blouse, her hair beautifully styled, sitting amongst the chickens, carefully with the tips of her slender fingers and painted nails scraping away at the chicken intestines, cutting them up into short lengths in readiness to be crispy fried and served at the table – very tasty!

A well-known firm in Bangkok supplied our drinking water. It was known as 'Nam Polaris' (Polar Star water) and was used for many purposes in cooking and for the mixing with 'Klim' milk powder.

Our girls, like most Thais, did not go in for bread or butter, but it was amazing how quickly they took to it and the quantity they went through.

Another outing I enjoyed was when Margaret, on her free day, and I used to go to Bangkok together. There we would spend a happy time looking around all the shops and particularly those selling dress materials in pure silk and lovely colouring, a speciality of Thailand. On occasion when a dress length was chosen, this was followed by a visit to a dressmaker. Bangkok boasted numerous dressmakers who turned out excellent work and charged modest prices similar to the darzis in India.

I liked Margaret. She was a kind gentle girl, but had little happiness with Punlop, who, possessing a strange temperament and full of his own importance, led her a difficult life.

As the weeks went by, it was noticed that Mr Ponsevat was no longer visiting the mill, nor was his son-in-law, Somnam. Another young man, named Pachum, appeared on the scene who was now, instead of Somnam, buying the jute from the Chinese brokers. Pachum, a friendly individual, called at the house and brought me a sweet called Tako in small containers made up from banana leaves. The sweet, a delicious cream, is prepared from sweetened coconut milk and decorated with lotus seeds.

He was the brother of Thanpuying Vichitra, the widow of Marshal Sarit. According to the Buddhist religion a man can have as many wives as he desires. In this case Vichitra was the late Marshal's second wife and being his favourite inherited all his estate including the Bangkok jute mills.

Mr Ponsevat's departure was followed by those who considered themselves loyal to him, including Teddy, one of the assistant managers, and our driver Semyem with his wife and children.

The first replacement for Semyem was an elderly Thai who assured us that he was an expert driver and had a wide experience in driving members of the European diplomatic corps.

The following day I set off with our new driver to Bangkok. Not being a driver I rarely paid attention to how the car was being driven, but on this occasion became a bit perturbed when I observed that our 'expert' deemed it necessary for the white line dividing the road to remain at all times in line with the centre of the bonnet and after a few narrow escapes from head-on collisions arrived back in the mill totally shaken. Two days later on our way to a cocktail party in Bangkok, Ron, experiencing for himself the insane careering in the middle of the road, on reaching our destination, trembling with rage and frustration, told our 'expert' never to show his face again and after the party drove the car home himself.

Our new driver, Prasert, a reliable and honest young man, was a worthy successor to Semyem.

One of the many attractions outside Bangkok was a place called Khoa Yai reputed to be the brain-child of the late Marshal Sarit who had succeeded in cutting a road through the dense jungle to the top of a high mountain.

We left with Prasert one Sunday morning and after an hour's drive arrived at the entrance with the name Khoa Yai above it. As soon as we entered we were met by the strange buzzing sound of the jungle punctuated by the sharp calling of some unseen bird or animal. The jungle is never silent.

On either side was a solid green wall of gigantic trees, palms, creepers and heavy undergrowth. In some parts there were large gaping spaces in the protective fencing caused, according to Prasert, by marauding elephants. All Thais have a healthy respect for elephants and regard them as dangerous animals.

The road continued winding higher and higher until to our surprise we saw two young men sitting on the grassy verge and near them a car which had gone off the road and was lying at an acute angle, prevented by a trunk of a tree rolling down into the gorge below. It transpired that one of the young men had been engaged in taking a film of the surroundings and the driver, distracted for a moment, went off the road. Both had succeeded in climbing out of the car, but sitting inside were their aged parents – too frightened to move.

As suggested by Prasert, Ron and he with the two young men left the road, and stood on the downside of the car holding it, as best they could, to stop any sudden movement. I positioned myself between them opposite the open door to assist the old people and they clambered out and down using me as a ladder. We were all very relieved to get back up on to the road.

As the family had friends due to come down from the top, who would assist them to return home, we left them sitting there and continued on our way halting to admire the majestic view of the great expanse of the jungle, spread out below us, as far as the eye could see, divided by deep valleys and sparkling streams.

On reaching the summit we found a large clearing with a restaurant and several chalets which were rented out to people interested in studying wild life in the jungle. There was also an American Army base, but for what purpose we had no idea. After an indifferent lunch in the restaurant we strolled around for a bit prior to leaving for home.

On our way back we were astonished to discover the family sitting beside the car, now back on the road. They were all very cheerful. The old man, laughing happily, explained that a truckful of GIs had come along and as he said, 'These nice American boys just picked up the car and threw it back on the road.' An hour later we were back in our house having enjoyed our exciting trip to Khoa Yai – the first of many.

In the early autumn we received a letter from Michael with the welcome news that having received four weeks' leave from his ship he was flying over from Calcutta to join us.

On the appointed day we arrived at Don Muang airport, packed with a milling crowd as usual, as the Thais like nothing better than meeting or seeing people off. It was a great joy to see again the familiar figure coming through the Customs barrier and a wonderful break to have him with us for the next four weeks during which time we showed him quite a bit of Thailand. A day was spent in Kanchanaburi, Chungkai, Nakhon Pathom and in Bangkok, the King's Palace and all the places of interest. There was the unique occasion when on approaching the Temple of the Emerald Buddha, all cars were ordered to draw to one side. Crowds had collected on the pavements and in a few moments we were rewarded by the sight of a fleet of cars with the yellow Rolls-Royce carrying King Bhumipol in their midst who was driving past on his way to the Temple of the Emerald Buddha for the ceremony of changing the robes of the Buddha to suit the season. This ceremony takes place three times a year.

The best, but alas only too short, holiday was in Pattaya where we booked a cottage for a long week-end. Pattaya lies some distance beyond Bangsen. We travelled along the familiar road and eventually arrived at the cottage, situated in a bay surrounded by palms and close to the sea, a truly delightful place, of two bedrooms, living room and furnished with all cooking utensils and a small stove.

In those days Pattaya was wonderful and although popular, not spoiled by overcrowding, with a long curving beach of golden sands, flanked by palms and in the background a row of small cottages, a restaurant or two, a few little booths selling conch shells and local curios. Nearby, however, was a hotel being built, due to be finished in time for the coming New Year and to be named the Nipa Lodge. Before Michael's arrival Ron and I had visited Pattaya several times. We loved the place. It was there that Ron learned to water-ski and I mastered the ski-board. Motorboats were always available and the charge for the hour was quite reasonable. Only those who go in for water-skiing know what a delight it is to be skimming over the water behind a fast motorboat. One flamboyant character used to ski with his small dachshund sitting on his shoulder and another female exhibitionist had a monkey clinging to her neck. These acrobatics were beyond me but I enjoyed flying behind them even if I was the granny of them all.

We spent our time with Michael swimming and skiing and in the evening attending a lively restaurant where it was possible to have a meal while watching all the GIs dancing with their girlfriends.

One memorable day we decided to visit one of the offshore islands. Ron took over the wheel and everything was going well until we reached rough water where the small launch began to roll to an alarming degree and the young Thai boatman, quite unperturbed, took over. Soon we reached the island and in a sheltered bay beached the launch. The island was deserted except for one old man living in a small thatched hut complete with a tiny veranda overgrown by a magenta-coloured Bougainvillaea. In the background were palms, wild banana trees, flowering bushes, the whole seemed like something out of Robert Louis Stevenson.

We spent a lazy day swimming in the warm waters, basking in the sun, enjoying a picnic and Michael with Ron skiing out into the bay. In the late afternoon we left the island and were soon safely back on the main land.

By Sunday evening our holiday was over. Sadly we said goodbye to Pattaya and took the road for home.

Our next trip was to visit the Summer Palace in Bang Pa-In, a lovely haunting place I never tired of seeing. We left during the morning and after a short run arrived in the grounds of the Palace. We found the Palace rather dark and gloomy. Inside, hanging on the wall are numerous pictures depicting old battles between Burma and Thailand. What must have been a novelty at one time was a heavy Victorian bath encased in wood, but beyond that memory has not retained anything else of note.

What was beautiful was the garden, the colourful pavilion, so often featured in travel brochures, the graceful bridge, statues, tall urns with cascading blossoms of Bougainvillaea in white, pink and magenta all cunningly grafted on to one root, lawns, pleasant walks beside tall trees and the great variety of rare flowers.

The Chao Phya flows past the Palace gardens. In ancient days, the resplendent Royal barges carrying the King and Queen and their retinue would be seen sailing to the peaceful haven of Bang Pa-In.

It is easy to let one's imagination wander and visualise those Royal ladies strolling amidst the lovely surroundings, but in the year of 1881 a sudden tragedy overtook the Royal family. The Queen with her three children and some members of the household went sailing on the river when suddenly the boat overturned throwing all the occupants out. The Queen and her children drowned, helplessly watched by her servants, standing on the banks within reach who would have gladly saved the family but dared not touch them as any contact with a Royal person was punishable by death.

In the garden stands a monument to the Queen and her three children. On each side of the four sides are beautifully executed sculptures of each head – the Queen, a little girl, the baby, with the wreath of flowers on her head, and the young boy. It is the poignant lifelike expression on the face of the boy that seems to stand out. Below is the following inscription:

> To the Beloved Memory of Her Late and Lamented Majesty SUNAN-DAKUMARIRATN Who Wont to Spend Her Most Pleasant and Happiest Hours In This Garden Amidst Those Loving Ones and Dearest to her. This Memorial is Erected by CHULALUNKURN REX, Her Bereaved Husband, Whose Suffering From So Cruel An Endurance, Through Those Trying Hours, Made Death Seem So Near Yet So Preferable.
>
> 1881

In spite of the strangely sounding words one feels the deep grief expressed by the King. Chulalunkurn was a very progressive man who, following this tragedy , abolished the rule forbidding anyone on pain of death to touch a Royal personage.

In silence we left that sad corner of the garden and walked around for a short while. With the exception of a few visitors the grounds were deserted. A few pictures were taken – still in my possession – treasured reminders of a day spent in Bang Pa-In.

A few days later our happy interlude with Michael was over. We were back in Don Muang waiting to hear the call for Michael's departure.

After the plane departed we returned to the house and for some time the days seemed very long.

Thailand is hot – never as hot as west Bengal and never as cool. Old residents tell us that they do have a cold season, but we have not experienced it.

The air-conditioning in the bedroom made it a cool retreat where during the heat of the day I used to spend a lot of time writing and reading. We were fortunate in having an excellent library in Suriwongse Road, Bangkok, which had a great variety of books and magazines from Europe and America.

At times gazing idly through the window, I used to watch what went on in a small farm on the opposite side of the klong from our house. On one occasion there was a party taking place, accompanied by loud music never ceasing night or day for several days on end. It transpired the family were celebrating the departure of their son to serve his stint as a Buddhist monk. This is compulsory for every man including the King. Garbed in saffron robe, his head shaved he sets out daily from the monastery with only a begging bowl in hand. The time of serving can vary from a few weeks to several months or longer.

A month later there was another lengthy celebration in the farm with more music and noise. The young man, having completed his time, had returned to the fold.

From the time of the cremation of Marshal Sarit in March, rumours began to spread about him and his widow, Vichitra, having unlawfully appropriated, during the period in office, large sums of money.

In November, however, everything was revealed when in the *Bangkok World*, spread across the front page, was the startling announcment: Government Seizes Sarit's Funds Unrighteously Embezzled. The Prime Minister Thanom Kittikachorn, with the approval of the Cabinet, had issued orders seizing assets of the late Prime Minister Sarit Thanarat's estate and that of his widow, Thanpuying Vichitra, to reimburse the State for funds embezzled by Marshal Sarit. The seizure amounted to almost ten million pounds and to that were added shares in more than thirty concerns scattered over Thailand ranging from match factory, silk factory, insurance, shipping, construction companies and many others including the Bangkok Jute Company.

Two days later when Ron and I were sitting at peace in the evening, a fleet of police cars with sirens wailing drove into the compound. A search took place in the office, where all papers, books and safes were examined.

Margaret Punlop in a state of hysteria came running to our house. 'What is going on? What will happen to us?' she cried. Nothing untoward happened. The friendly Mr Pachum vanished from the scene and his place was taken over by Squadron-Leader Yu Thongves as Managing Director. Life continued.

Between Christmas and New Year our friends, John and Edith Lyon, arrived from India to stay with us for a short holiday. We decided to go to Pattaya and greet the New Year in the Nipa Lodge Hotel completed just in time for the festive season. This luxurious U-shaped structure, built around a swimming pool, with terraces and every convenience inside, was the first hotel to be built in Pattaya.

During the rest of our time in Thailand we used to visit the hotel regularly and got to know the members of the staff. The excellent chef, an Italian, was a friendly, humorous man who liked to chat with us. He kept two tiny monkeys in an enclosure out of which they periodically escaped and rampaged all over the place to the amusement of the guests. The manager had a miniature dachshund named Fritzy who was obsessed with these monkeys and would sit for hours on end under their perch never taking his eyes of them and as our Italian friend used to say, 'He thinka da monkeys, he dreama da monkeys!'

We spent many a happy day in Pattaya, but now, even as I write these lines, a friend who has just returned from a holiday in Thailand tells me that the Pattaya of twenty-five years ago has long since vanished. A string of new hotels has been built there. Massage parlours and brothels abound. The beaches are packed, the sea is polluted. Launches ply to and from the islands no longer deserted.

Together with the Lyons we brought in the New Year of 1965, went swimming in the sea and lazed in the sun and after three pleasant days returned to the mill. Kanchanaburi and the Summer Palace in Bang Pa-In were revisited and some sightseeing done in Bangkok.

After Edith and John left for Calcutta, Aikman Doig arrived on business in Thailand and spent a few days with us. We had an enjoyable time together reminiscing over the events we once shared in India. There were others who came to see us from India. Not knowing many people in Bangkok we were always delighted to meet old friends.

One day we received an invitation to a party from the British Trade Commissioner. There during the evening I was introduced to a Mrs Gerson, a pleasant lady, who was Russian and came from Odessa. Mr and Mrs Gerson had spent many years in Bangkok and were well known in business circles. I was delighted to make her acquaintance. We sat together enjoying a conversation in our own tongue. It seemed a strange coincidence that two people – one from the Arctic north and the other from the deep south of Russia – should meet of all places in Thailand. Another coincidence was that Mrs Gerson's two nieces were married to two brothers living in Edinburgh.

I was very pleased to be invited by Mrs Gerson to have lunch with her during the following week. She lived in a pleasant house with a lovely garden in Soi Chaisamarn off Sukumvit Road. I spent many a happy hour there as we got to know each other and kept in touch even after we retired to Scotland.

In the early spring two unexpected arrivals joined our menage. One of the young guards, Ton-Sook, having had an affair with Soni decided to marry her and settle down in the adjoining quarters. A few weeks later Soni produced a delightful baby boy named Pong, who I have to admit brought a pleasant diversion to our everyday life even if some of the household chores were now neglected. Little Pong was a very attractive child with bright uptilted eyes who rarely cried and readily laughed as he grew older.

In March a letter arrived from Michael with the news that having done his stint of four years at sea he had decided to give it up and try to find some work at home.

This was followed by a startling announcement from George who had got himself engaged and was now all set to be married in July.

As we were due to go on leave at the end of June we decided after a lengthy discussion that I would travel ahead by sea with some of our belongings and on arriving arrange our house and attend to some important matters.

There was also an arrangement with Michael to pick up the Citroën car Ron had ordered to be delivered in Britain.

Having had favourable reports about the East Asiatic Company I booked a berth on one of their ships sailing from Bangkok in May. On the day of my departure we arrived at Klong Toi where a launch took us out to the ship lying offshore. There, standing above, leaning on the rail was the First Officer, watching passively as Ron, with no help forthcoming, was himself forced to order the stevedores to carry up my trunk and baggage, which would never have been allowed on a British ship but no one here seemed to bother about anything.

A young stewardess directed me to a spacious and well-equipped cabin. After seeing me settled down Ron returned to Bangkok and the ship sailed in the late evening.

I soon got to know the other four passengers – a Mr and Mrs Farmer from the United States, Mrs Elsa Neilsen from Copenhagen and a young doctor whose name I cannot remember. We all got along very well and as often happens on long voyages learned a lot about each other.

It didn't take me very long, however, to realise that there was a lack of rapport between the members of the crew. It was in fact not a happy ship and didn't live up to my expectations although in fairness I have to add that Elsa Neilsen, who travelled constantly on the EAC ships to the Far East, assured me that this ship was an exception to the rule. Elsa and I shared the table with the Captain, on his last voyage prior to retirement. He was a pleasant enough man, but ineffective.

Nevertheless in spite of certain drawbacks there were compensations. Never having travelled before down the Malaysian coast I found it fascinating and all the ports of call most interesting.

At Singapore a family of a man, his wife and three children joined the ship. No sooner did they come aboard than the children took over, rampaging about the place, playing hide and seek, screaming at the pitch of their voices and generally making a nuisance of themselves. Priding myself on being tolerant I did not object, but was not exactly overjoyed when one morning I found my cabin flooded, with the cover off my typewriter and shoes completely ruined. It transpired that the little darlings had turned on a shower while playing and allowed it to run all night and seep through to my cabin.

While in Singapore, where we remained for three days, I went on a shopping spree. It so happened that in France my cousin Jenya's son, Maska, was getting married about the same time as our George. I bought two handsome dinner sets as wedding gifts and other presents for my friends and relatives.

From Singapore we sailed on through the Malacca Straits to Port Swettenham – a bus run took us to Kuala Lumpur, then on to Penang and a trip on the funicular railway to the top of the hill. From Penang across the awe-inspiring expanse of the Indian Ocean to Aden, the Suez Canal, Port Said and up to Beirut where the ship halted for a week.

It was a golden opportunity to see a bit of Lebanon. We hired a car to take us to the ancient Cedars of Lebanon. The driver-guide was a pleasant young man who kept pointing out places of interest as we travelled through the small towns and on to the mountains. He was a good driver skilfully negotiating difficult bends, skirting frightening gorges. Of the Cedars reputed to have been used to build the Temple of Solomon only a few remain, zealously guarded by fencing. Nearby is a stall selling small articles – ash trays, bowls, etc. – carved out of broken branches of the original Cedars and eagerly bought by tourists even if the description is open to doubt.

There was also a chalet where we enjoyed a speciality of the house prepared from lamb or goat and heavily spiced, followed by a selection of fresh fruit. On the walls were hanging life-sized portraits of the Shah of Persia and his wife, who used to visit those parts for winter sports.

Another day I set off on my own to try and find the place which sold water jugs of unique design particular to Lebanon. As I kept looking around a pleasant gentleman approached me and asked if he could help. On hearing what I was after he gave me full directions as to where I would find what I required.

I had to walk for quite a bit and continue through a busy market place beyond which in a little lane I found a kindly old potter turning out these jugs. I bought a pair and turned back. Outside the market I met two women who stopped to speak to me. Although past their youth they were very good-looking, dressed in long flowered dresses and soft-flowing veils kept in place by headbands. They asked me if I was British and when I nodded pointed to themselves and said, 'We – Syrian.' After a stilted conversation and expressions of mutual admiration I continued on my way. I enjoyed my solitary stroll around Beirut never dreaming how impossible it would be to repeat this walkabout twenty-five years later.

Our last evening in Beirut, the Farmers, Elsa and I decided to have a night out together. We chose a garden restaurant in the heart of Beirut and there under a starlit sky in beautiful surroundings enjoyed an excellent dinner and spent a happy evening together.

The next port of call was Le Havre, where I left the ship to go on to Paris. As the ship's final destination was Southampton arrangements were made for my crate to be kept there in storage to await my arrival – a matter of two to three days.

Elsa, with whom I had become very friendly, saw me off at the station. I never saw her again although we corresponded with each other for some years to come.

I arrived at Jenya's house in Paris all-in, still dragging the case with the dinner set. The young couple were delighted and immediately began to unpack the dishes, none of which to my relief was broken.

The bride, Elizabeth, whom I met, the daughter of a wealthy Parisian family, was a small, attractive girl with a friendly open manner and who we later discovered was highly intelligent.

The wedding was due to take place in August but already the usual joyful preparations had begun. Tamara arrived from Genoa with her Siamese cat Chi-chi. People were coming and going and presents being delivered.

Yet with this happy mood there was also grave concern over Jenya's health, who, in spite of being far from well, was putting up a brave front.

It so happened that some months earlier workmen arrived outside the gate of the house and began to dig a deep trench, causing great inconvenience to anyone going out or in. One day they placed an old door across as Jenya was going out and said, 'Voila, Madame – we have made a bridge for you!' Jenya trustingly stepped on the door, but the wood being rotten collapsed under her weight. She fell into the trench and sustained serious injuries crushing the bones of her feet. This dreadful accident set off an illness far more serious.

I stayed for two days, but had to go on as George's wedding was due to take place in July.

On returning to Le Havre and crossing over to Southampton, I went, as arranged, to pick up the crate only to discover that it had vanished and no one knew anything about it. It would be too tedious to describe all the inquiries and letters that followed. Sufficient to say it arrived four weeks later. The crate had been on an extensive tour. It actually did arrive in Southampton but for some strange reason was returned to Le Havre where it was placed on a coastal steamer and eventually reached Edinburgh.

Of the dinner set only half survived and there were other breakages and items missing. Although compensation in full was received from EAC nothing was just quite the same.

Meanwhile, after I had arrived in Southampton I went on to London where I was met by Michael in the Citroën. The glad news that he had been offered a post with the Esso Oil Company more than made up for my disappointment over the crate.

We spent the night in London and the following morning set off for Edinburgh and reached our house in the afternoon.

To my great relief a fortnight later and a mere week before our son's wedding Ron arrived from Bangkok.

On that auspicious day with hope and some anxiety we embraced our son and wished him well as he set off for the church accompanied by his brother.

Our daughter-in-law, Gay, a joyful, happy girl made a lovely bride. It was a pretty wedding with bridesmaids and a little flower girl.

From our own side came our nearest relations and the Indian contingent – Joan and George, cousin Mae and Jim, Edie and Aikman. There were also Jean and John Hebenton – from our early days in Lawrence – who had known the twins from the day they were born.

After the young couple had departed on their honeymoon and the reception was over we continued the celebrations in the early evening by throwing a cold buffet for the bride's parents and close relations and our own special friends.

The lull that followed the wedding allowed us to enjoy the remaining months of Ron's leave.

Prior to my departure from Bangkok Mrs Gerson requested me to take a small parcel to her sister Mrs Kris who was residing with one of her daughters in Edinburgh. We called there with the parcel and during our conversation with Mrs Kris and her daughter, Rena, her second daughter Sheva arrived and in this way we got to know the family and have kept in touch ever since and even as I write these lines I have to thank Sheva who was able to jolt my memory with some of the intricate names of places in Bangkok and pass on some extra information.

In August we received the welcome news from Jenya, who was planning to visit us with Maska and Elizabeth. We were delighted to be able to repay some of the hospitality we had received so often in the past. It was arranged that they would fly to England and be met by us in London. We left in the Citroën at daybreak and with a stop for breakfast arrived in time to meet them, as planned, and immediately took the long road to the north. Eventually after halting for lunch and dinner we reached our house shortly before midnight.

None of them had ever been to Britain far less Scotland and Jenya was especially excited when we approached the border and she saw the notice saying: 'You are now in Scotland.'

The weather was kind during their stay. We saw Blair Athol Castle, Scone Palace, Loch Tay, Loch Earn, the heather-clad hills. For Elizabeth the Highland cattle held a great fascination – she was determined to be photographed standing beside them.

Scotland was at her best the night we took them to the Military Tattoo at Edinburgh Castle. It had been raining heavily all morning but turned out to be a beautiful starry night. The sudden emergence of the Highlanders, marching to the music of the pipes through the Castle gates to the floodlit esplanade, had a tremendous impact, especially on Jenya, who often referred to it later as a splendid spectacle never to be forgotten.

There were several family gatherings, but what she and I really liked best was to sit quietly together in a corner and talk about people and places and the Russia that only we knew.

At the end of these memorable weeks we were on the road again this time to the south.

Leaving Edinburgh at crack of dawn we were unfortunate enough to strike London during the evening rush hour, but with Elizabeth, in her slightly fractured English, reading directions to Ron from the map, we arrived unscathed at Lympne, a small airport near Hythe on the South-East coast, having just made it in time for the take-off.

Spending the night in Hythe we embarked on a leisurely tour of southern England, all new territory to us, and visited Eastbourne, the New Forest, Dartmoor Forest, Clovelly and other places we had heard about but had never seen before. At the end of a week we were back in Edinburgh.

By late October Ron was in Thailand. I stayed on through the winter keeping the house open for Michael who was forging ahead in the north and arriving home for weekends.

In May after spending a few days with George and Gay, living in Banff, to welcome my first grandchild, a round-faced, dark-eyed sturdy lass, christened Tanya, I packed my bag and set off once more for Thailand stopping as usual for a day or two in Paris.

During her stay with us, my cousin's health had suddenly improved and we fondly imagined she was on the road to recovery, but now the drawn lines of suffering and sunken eyes told a different story. She and Petya were staying in their town flat in Billancourt. We spent these two short days sitting together in the little garden. Spring had arrived and the solitary white acacia was in full bloom spreading its sweet scent in the warm fresh air. As I was leaving Jenya walked with me down the path to the gate and held me close when saying goodbye. Both knew we would never meet again.

At the airport where I had booked my seat for Bangkok I received an unpleasant shock when informed that there was no trace of any such booking but eventually admitted that there had been, but owing to some misunderstanding it had been given to someone else. They suggested, however, that there was a vacant seat in the tourist class. I have found in the past that elderly ladies are often treated with casual indifference, in this case, however, they met their match. I agreed to their proposal but as my ticket was first class demanded the difference on the spot. They then suggested I should go to Rome where I would get a transfer to a first class passage. The argument might have continued indefinitely, if it wasn't for my casual reference to the Ministry of Finance in Bangkok. These little words worked like magic. Apologies followed – the important businessman was turfed out and I received my lawful place.

There were no more unpleasant incidents. After a dull flight enlivened somewhat by a conversation with a Chinaman, who for some strange reason kept asking me, 'Why are they stuffing us with so much food?' – I duly landed in Don Muang and was met by Ron.

On arrival at our house I was met with the smiling faces of Somana and Soni, holding little Pong. Pong was now a toddler, wearing a gold chain round his chubby neck. His mummy had done even better, for she was displaying a broad belt in two shades of solid gold! Her husband, Ton-Sook, was the guard who weighed in the jute arriving from Bangkok and perhaps this activity was related to the gold belt and chain.

Back in Rangsit the old routine took over with Somana and I paying my weekly visit to the market or Bangrak as it was known. It was a joy to be offered again the luscious selection of tropical fruit – the papayas, pomelos, bananas, litchis, but in June something very special and rare appears on the scene known as durian. As it is a speciality of Thailand and some parts of Malaysia it deserves a word or two about it. The durian is a giant pear-shaped fruit, larger than any melon with a thick greenish-brown, rough skin. It has two features – one is a most unpleasant smell on the outside, the other a delicious-tasting creamy mass inside. You bring it home, hold your nose, cut it open and scoop out the pulpy creamy part with the unique and delicate taste. It has been said that everyone who comes to Thailand must eat a durian once in their life. No one, however, is allowed to bring a durian aboard a plane nor is it welcome in trains or buses. The world is divided into durian lovers and durian haters. Ron could not bear it near him. I loved it, as did Somana, Soni and little Pong.

Our driver, Prasert, once took us to Chanburi where we saw a great mound of durians for sale and nearby the orchards, guarded by armed men and dogs. The durian plays an important part in the operations of the big-time fruit merchants. During our sojourn they were usually sold at sixty baht, or £1 each, but now probably the price will be tenfold more. It is reputed to contain vitamins A, B, and D, but it is not recommended for people with high blood pressure and if you should scoop out the creamy pulp and place it in a silver dish and leave it for one night you would find it blackish in the morning.

I ate as many as I could during the season with no ill effects and nowadays regret that I can never taste a durian again.

The year of 1966 was the Year of the Horse. In Thailand, as in China – and the Thais are originally Chinese – the years are named after twelve different animals, including such unpleasant creatures as the rat and snake. At the end of twelve years the cycle begins all over again. The most eventful birthday is when a man or woman reaches their sixtieth year. Our Managing Director, Squadron-Leader Yu Thongves, was born in the Year of the Horse. Great preparations were afloat for such an important birthday and person. A large dinner party was launched by the Chinese brokers in honour of Yu Thongves to be held in the grounds of his house. Some hundred guests were invited, including us, and all were expected to bring gifts. In passing I may add that Ron was also born in the Year of the Horse and had arrived at his important birthday, but being a mere farang did not expect any gifts and was therefore not disappointed.

On the appointed day the guests duly arrived at Yu Thongves's house. In the garden tables were set for dinner and groups of people were milling around. Madame Thongves was standing on the top step of the veranda and, with a brief and sharp scrutiny of each offering (a bottle of whisky was no great shakes) and not a vestige of a smile or any little word of welcome, was placing each gift on a table behind her, already piled high with a great variety of donations.

We sat down at one of the tables beside a Thai couple who although friendly could not converse in English, but no sooner did we settle down than a swarm of vicious mosquitoes descended to devour us. As it was quite impossible to sit and endure such agony, Ron approached Yu Thongves and asked him to excuse us. Our host, a kindly little man, did so and we gladly left the arena for the comfort and a pleasant meal in the Erawan Hotel. We arrived there just in time as suddenly the heavens opened up and torrential rain poured down, accompanied by thunder and lightning.

The party turned out to be a disaster. The guests had raced to find shelter wherever they could, but there was no room in the house to hold them all. The dinner never took place. So much for the Year of the Horse.

Meanwhile a tragic and frightening incident took place in Bangkok which shook the resident foreigners. It concerned the Polish Trade Commissioner, a well-known and popular figure in European and Thai circles.

One evening after attending the French Ambassador's reception the Pole with his wife and daughter on arriving home found the gates locked as usual but with no attendant to open them. He got out of the car and with that a rider on a motorcycle flashed by and opened fire. The Pole died instantly under a hail of bullets in front of his wife and daughter. They found their dog lying dead behind the gates. The servants had fled, leaving the house standing empty.

The murderers were never found. Rumour had it that the Commissioner had started an import business which clashed with the interests of a wealthy Chinese importer who had decided to have his opponent removed. This was a warning and a reminder to any farang as to what could happen if he crossed the path of some powerful operator.

Life was cheap in Bangkok where bribery and corruption flourished.

Our days and weeks continued following the same pattern. In Thailand there was always something new to see, another place to visit such as the ruins of the old capital, Ayutthaya, where it was easy to imagine what a magnificent city it must have been before it fell to the Burmese never to rise again to its former splendour. Bangkok itself offered a variety of spectacles. The Thai ballet in the Oriental Hotel was a special attraction. The graceful, flowing movements of the dance, and the ability of the dancers to bend their delicate hands back until the fingertips almost touched the wrists, held a fascination for me. Was this acquired or were they born with it I wondered. Both Somana and Soni assured me that from infancy their hands were gently massaged by their mothers to enable them to do this and to prove their point both girls bent their hands back with perfect ease.

The Oriental Hotel was the only one situated close to the river. At times, after watching the ballet or having dinner we liked to sit on the little jetty jutting out over the water. It was pleasant to sit at peace and watch the twinkling lights of the ships and country boats plying up and down the Chao Phya – a pleasure unfortunately we had to cut short and never repeat after a giant rat ran over my feet!

Life was good and might have continued to be so if it had not been for some unpleasant elements appearing on the scene. The Managing Director, Squadron-Leader Yu Thongves, a congenial man, had no knowledge at all of running a mill. His predecessors, Mr Ponsevat and Somnam, were hard-headed businessmen who would never have allowed anything but the best-quality jute to enter the gates, and Mr Ponsevat would not have tolerated any nonsense from the staff.

During Ron's leave at home his assistant manager, Punlop, took over, but on Ron's return found it demeaning to go back to his former position. Obsessed with his own importance and self-esteem, to follow a recognised procedure in any business was a loss of face to Punlop. He did everything he could to elevate himself, by having his office done up with many additions including a little Buddha placed on his desk and with an air of importance strutted around, courting popularity by inviting the young assistants to his house, to Margaret's annoyance, who, arriving home after a hard day's work, would find a party raging with Punlop and his friends drinking up all the brandy and whisky which she bought with her own earnings at the airport.

This ridiculous posturing Ron chose to ignore, but did say that when the end of the term came round in 1967 it might be best to retire home for good.

In December a letter arrived from France. My cousin Jenya after months of agonising suffering had died. 'Do not grieve,' Petya wrote, 'she is at peace – beyond all pain.' I did grieve – she was the last link with my childhood and France could never be the same.

Some days went by and we were into the year 1967. On New Year's Day we were invited by a Chinese friend, called Ho, to attend a party in his house. Ho had been introduced to Ron by another Chinaman

238

named Soong who had some connections with Dundee and had actually stayed with a friend we knew in Broughty Ferry.

We all became friendly, met in Bangkok, did a show, followed by dinner in a Chinese restaurant. The two wives were charming women and we had a lot of fun together and genuinely enjoyed each other's company. Ron, however, made one stipulation in spite of strong protests, that at all times he would share expenses.

It has to be admitted that at times we wondered, what was it that they saw in two elderly people much older than them. The parties continued until one day Soong did not turn up and made no further attempts to see us. The meetings with Ho, however, still continued.

One day Ho suggested that we should all, including his wife and three children, have a picnic in a country park beside a river – a delightful place, almost isolated.

We had our picnic after which the children, Ho's wife and Ron decided to go swimming while I, preferring to watch the fun, decided to sit in a small shelter near by. I was joined by Ho and for some time we sat chatting together about this and that until suddenly, out of the blue, he appealed to me to use my influence on Ron to make him more lenient when inspecting the jute arriving at the mill. 'It would make a difference to our lives,' he added, 'perhaps to Ron as well.' Completely taken aback, after a few moments of silence I replied, 'My husband believes in certain principles and neither I nor anyone else could ever make him deviate from them.' We never saw Ho again.

Ron continued making claims on behalf of the Ministry of Finance, if he thought the quality was not up to the mark. The Chinese brokers strongly objected and actually complained to the Ministry of Finance which was ludicrous and got them nowhere.

One morning Ron said to me, 'I have decided we will leave in April at the end of my current agreement.' Half joking, half in earnest, he added, 'I sometimes wonder if a large lorry might suddenly cross our path when we are on the road home one night.'

He informed Yu Thongves that he would not be asking for another contract.

During the last week of our sojourn in Thailand I went to Bangkok to do some final shopping and called on Mrs Gerson to say goodbye. We were never to meet again, although we kept in touch with letters and cards until her death some years later.

On the eve of our departure we attended a farewell dinner party arranged on our behalf in a private room in one of the restaurants in Bangkok. There were Yu Thongves and other representatives from the Ministry of Finance and Punlop with Margaret. Yu Thongves stood up and delivered a speech in which he expressed the gratitude of the Ministry for Ron's contribution to their prosperity plan. At the end Ron was presented with a large silver candelabrum with a suitable inscription which unfortunately proved very cumbersome for travelling on the aircraft. I also received a silver set in an attractive Thai design of a necklace, bracelet and earrings as well as a few lengths of lovely Thai silk.

The following day with Somana, Soni and little Pong we set off for the Don Muang airport, where we were met by Punlop and Margaret.

An amazing and unforgettable sight met our eyes – all the phoo-yings, hundreds of them, had arrived to see us off. They were crowded on the balcony above and all the places they could find. All waving and calling 'Pa – Pa – Pa.' These were the last voices I heard still echoing in my head as the aircraft began to gather speed on the runway. It was evening, there was no last glimpse of Thailand except for a few twinkling lights in the darkness.

The flight was uneventful. We spent a relaxed week in lovely Vienna and from there went on to Paris, where we collected our new Citroën car and carried on to Rats-Gris.

Elizabeth, who was the Principal of the College of Agriculture where Maska also lectured, did not arrive until the following day. Their child, the baby grandson Jenya never saw, was being taken care of by a young German nanny with an assertive manner and loud voice. Petya spent most of the time sitting beside the cradle. 'This is all I have now,' he said sadly. The old happy atmosphere was gone, replaced by something cold and alien.

We went with Maska to Jenya's grave. The cemetery overlooked the valley and the river which Jenya knew and loved so much. I laid my flowers and stood in silence for some moments.

We left the following day, went on to Dieppe where we crossed over to Newhaven. Breaking our journey to spend one night in a hotel we took the road for Scotland after breakfast. Soon we were driving through the border country and drawing nearer to Edinburgh.

It was a bright morning. On our left the fast-flowing Tweed was tumbling over boulders, sending up spray, sparkling in the sunlight. On the distant hills snow still lay in scattered patches. On our right were fields with sheep grazing. An old man went by with a dog trailing behind him and raised his arm in a friendly gesture.

'You know,' I said to Ron, watching a lamb gambolling around its mother, 'it's grand to be back in Scotland.'